CHARLES BRENTON FISK
Organ Builder

VOLUME I

CHARLES BRENTON FISK
Organ Builder

VOLUME ONE
ESSAYS IN HIS HONOR

EDITED BY FENNER DOUGLASS,
OWEN JANDER & BARBARA OWEN

The Westfield Center for Early Keyboard Studies
Easthampton Massachusetts
1 9 8 6

Designed by Carol J. Blinn at Warwick Press, Easthampton, Massachusetts
Printed by The Studley Press of Dalton, Massachusetts

© 1986 The Westfield Center for Early Keyboard Studies, Inc.
Manufactured in the United States of America

ISBN 0-9616755-0-0
VOLUME I   ISBN 0-9616755-1-9

TABLE OF CONTENTS

PREFACE

DURING THE WINTER of 1976, Charles Fisk came to North Germany on one of several trips he made to research the Wellesley organ. I was in my second year of study with Harald Vogel and was granted the privilege of driving Charlie to hear a few of the North German organs. A two-day trip during that visit shall always be my fondest memory of Charles Fisk. Charlie, Frank Taylor, Lynn Edwards, and I traveled to Denmark to hear the Compenius organ in Frederiksborg Castle; Charlie was interested in the winding system and the extraordinary reeds. I can remember demonstrating the instrument, at first somewhat timidly, but then with more courage as Charlie's gentle manner and intense curiosity reassured me that he was not only interested in the sounds the organ made, but also in the music, and in me as the performer connecting those sounds with the music. Ten years later my memory of the Compenius organ has grown fuzzy, but my memory of those days when I first got to know Charles Fisk and Frank Taylor is still strong and clear, and very dear.

Following Charlie's death in December 1983, the idea for a memorial publication was in the air. Many of the Trustees of The Westfield Center had enjoyed close personal and professional ties with Charlie Fisk and The Center is closely associated with his organs at Wellesley College and at the First Congregational Church, Westfield. This was a natural project for The Center to undertake and in March 1984 it resolved to do so.

This has been an enormous project and there are many people to thank: the Board of Trustees for having vision and faith, both in The Center and in this endeavor; Lynn Edwards for being a wellspring of encouragement, energy, and support; Barbara Owen for doing such an excellent job with Volume II; Fenner Douglass, Owen Jander, and Barbara Owen for serving on the editorial Board for Volume I; Virginia Lee Fisk for offering valuable advice and support and, together with all the people at the Fisk shop, especially Robert Cornell, for making available important archival information; Quentin Peacock for helping to enlist the support of institutions with Fisk organs; Deborah Robson for serving as editorial consultant; Eileen Hunt for helping to proofread; Linda Zorek for assisting with library research; Michael-Thomas Gilman for completing a first draft of the translation of Harald Vogel's article; and Carol Blinn of Warwick Press for designing the books with such extraordinary skill and care— and for enduring friendship throughout.

Particular thanks also go to the District of Columbia American Guild of Organists Foundation and to the 104 Subscribers listed in Volume I. Without their support this tribute would not have been possible.

EDWARD C. PEPE
Executive Director
The Westfield Center
for Early Keyboard Studies
Easthampton, 1986

DEDICATION

It is with pride and a sense of great accomplishment that The Westfield Center presents these two volumes in memory of Charles Brenton Fisk, beloved friend and cherished colleague.

The articles in Volume I are a loving tribute to a man never afraid to ask questions. The summary of Charlie's work prepared by Barbara Owen in Volume II enlivens our memories of Charlie's playfulness, unique perceptions, and colorful use of the language. I'm thankful for that.

Years ago, Charlie urged Ed and me to found The Westfield Center. His interest and support, his intense curiosity, and his unique ability to discover the secrets hidden in the pipes and windways of old organs have sustained and inspired The Center's beginnings. With great and enduring love we dedicate these volumes to his memory.

LYNN EDWARDS
President
The Westfield Center
for Early Keyboard Studies

LIST OF SUBSCRIBERS

Mr. and Mrs. Robert Sivertsen
St. Paul, Minnesota

House of Hope Presbyterian Church
St. Paul, Minnesota

Herbert Nanney
Stanford, California

Music Library, Wellesley College
Wellesley, Massachusetts

Owen Jander
Wellesley, Massachusetts

Jacques Littlefield
Portola Valley, California

Roy F. Kehl
Evanston, Illinois

John C. Holtz, Jr.
Farmington, Connecticut

The First Church of Christ in New Haven, Inc.
New Haven, Connecticut

Jerry R. Witt
La Jolla, California

Mount Holyoke College
South Hadley, Massachusetts

The Parish of the Epiphany (Episcopal)
Winchester, Massachusetts

George Kent and the Choirs of Christ Church
Westerly, Rhode Island

Jane and Fenner Douglass
Wellfleet, Massachusetts

Robert D. C. Long
Charleston, West Virginia

Eleanor and James Ferguson
Chapel Hill, North Carolina

Shirley Lindberg Finley
Cincinnati, Ohio

Helen Badenhausen
Ipswich, Massachusetts

Linda Zorek
Boston, Massachusetts

Corinne Berg
Bainbridge Island, Washington

Marian Ruhl Metson and W. Graham Metson, Jr.
Newburyport, Massachusetts

Herman C. Greunke
Oberlin, Ohio

Stuart J. Bellows
Princeton, New Jersey

Carolyn T. Beard
Raleigh, North Carolina

Joan and Curtis Lippincott
Skillman, New Jersey

Linda and Steven Dieck
Gloucester, Massachusetts

Frances Conover Fitch and Gregory Bover
Gloucester, Massachusetts

Scot L. Huntington
Stonington, Connecticut

Anne Utter
Westerly, Rhode Island

Wilton Edmund Prescott
New York, New York

William F. Czelusniak
Southampton, Massachusetts

Stephen Paul Kowalyshyn
Newburyport, Massachusetts

Sebastian Matthew Gluck
New York, New York

Giles Buckner Cooke
Williamsburg, Virginia

Talbott Library, Westminster Choir College
Princeton, New Jersey

Hellmuth Wolff
Laval, Québec

Dr. George E. Becker
San Francisco, California

The Albert and Marie Steinert Foundation
New York, New York

Bradley F. Millard
Tacoma, Washington

Rex McKenzie Range
Mesquite, Texas

Duke University Music Department
Durham, North Carolina

Lillian F. Bellows
Princeton, New Jersey

David E. Roepke
Ashland, Ohio

Edward C. Pepe
Florence, Massachusetts

Boston Chapter, American Guild of Organists
Boston, Massachusetts

Henry Karl Baker
Braintree, Massachusetts

Palmer Memorial Episcopal Church
Houston, Texas

Frank S. Grosso
Rochester, New York

First Presbyterian Church
Mrs. James N. (Jane Ann) Blackerby and Mr. Samuel M. Hughes
New Bern, North Carolina

Walter B. Hewlett
Palo Alto, California

Mr. and Mrs. Wesley C. Dudley
Williamsburg, Virginia

John Daniel and Ellen S. Kiser
District of Columbia

Dirk A. Flentrop
Santpoort-Zuid, Holland

Richard E. Page
Andover, Massachusetts

L. Cameron Johnson
Storrs, Connecticut

David Griesinger
Cambridge, Massachusetts

Nannerl O. Keohane
Wellesley, Massachusetts

Ivan E. Danhof
Grand Prairie, Texas

Julia Gunn Kissel
Seattle, Washington

Kerala J. Snyder
New Haven, Connecticut

William Gardner Perrin
Boston, Massachusetts

Ronald L. Gould
Youngstown, Ohio

James H. Cannon
Edgartown, Massachusetts

Frederick Swann
Garden Grove, California

Emery and Joyce Painter Rice
Brookline, Massachusetts

St. Michael's Church
Marblehead, Massachusetts

Eugene Bonelli
Dallas, Texas

John T. Fesperman, Jr.
District of Columbia

Virginia Lee Fisk
Gloucester, Massachusetts

Yuko Hayashi
Brookline, Massachusetts

Dr. Robert T. Anderson
Dallas, Texas

Westfield State College
Westfield, Massachusetts

Lois and Quentin Regestein
Boston, Massachusetts

Memorial Church, Stanford University
Stanford, California

Leonard Raver
New York, New York

New England Conservatory of Music
Boston, Massachusetts

Downtown United Presbyterian Church
Rochester, New York

First Presbyterian Church
Charleston, West Virginia

A. David Moore
North Pomfret, Vermont

Memorial Church, Harvard University
Cambridge, Massachusetts

Moore Ruble Yudell
Santa Monica, California

Richard and Mary B. McMillan
White Bear Lake, Minnesota

James David Christie
Boston, Massachusetts

H. Guinn Lewis
Hattiesburg, Mississippi

Kirkegaard & Associates
Downers Grove, Illinois

Reverend Alfred von Schendel
Loretto, Pennsylvania

Douglas M. Woodard
Denver, Colorado

Joseph E. Blanton
Albany, Texas

In Memory of Patricia Ann (Patty) Enos
Central Christian Church
Huntington, Indiana

Richard H. Graff
San Francisco, California

Christ United Methodist Church
Greensboro, North Carolina

Clyde Holloway
Houston, Texas

Rice University
Houston, Texas

First Congregational Church
Westfield, Massachusetts

Yale University
New Haven, Connecticut

Lynn Edwards
Northampton, Massachusetts

First Congregational Church
Winchester, Massachusetts

In Memory of Walter Holtkamp
Charles Pierpont
Uvalde, Texas

Old West Organ Society
Boston, Massachusetts

Andover Organ Company
Methuen, Massachusetts

J. Michael Barone
St. Paul, Minnesota

Margaret Irwin-Brandon
Northampton, Massachusetts

Fritz Noack
Georgetown, Massachusetts

CHAPTER ONE

The Character and Function
of the Dutch Organ
in the Seventeenth and Eighteenth Centuries

KLAAS BOLT

Translated by Adrianus de Groot

FOR THE FIRST FIFTY to one hundred years after the Reformation began in the Netherlands, the organ was silenced during worship services. Calvinism excluded art music—for choir and organ alike—from the church. The organ was considered a form of mechanized choir, and was seen as a "papal" trapping, like the altar, statues of saints, and other objects. Also, strict Calvinists thought solo organ playing to be an offensively worldly affair, which served only bodily pleasures. Until far into the eighteenth century, many preachers vehemently opposed the organ's use during worship services.

This prohibition had, on the positive side, a significant influence on the blossoming of the art of organ playing outside the worship services (cf. Sweelinck's public performances on the organ)—a change whose fruits are still harvested in our extended concert practice—and on the development of congregational singing. Even today, congregations rarely sing as much or as well as they do in the Dutch Reformed (Calvinist) Church. In our day of increasingly passive music consumption and weak singing voices this accomplishment cannot be too highly valued. Furthermore, the music found in the Dutch hymnal still used today forms one of the greatest musical treasures of any country or time. It consists of the Geneva Psalm melodies of the sixteenth century along with hymns of diverse origins and styles.

Psalm singing in fully occupied churches must have had enormous power and intensity. Tempi were much slower than those we are accustomed to today: most likely, people sang each syllable with one breath and with full power. A syllable was held as long as possible, until one ran out of breath. Then one's lungs would once again be filled for the singing of the next syllable, and so on. At this slow tempo, any sense of the melody was lost, and for this reason a *voorzanger* (literally, "before–singer") was appointed to loudly give the next note during the "breathing" pause (and to simultaneously silence competitors, wiseacres, and false singers). Despite these efforts, the sheer volume and energy of the singing often resulted in chaos, particularly in less cultivated areas (such as fishing villages).

An increasing number of complaints about this disorder led to the reintroduction of the organ, to give support to the *voorzanger* as he introduced the next note during each breathing pause. For this very practical reason the organ was readmitted to the church service between 1630 (in Leiden and Hooglandse Kerk, for example) and 1680 (in Amsterdam, the last of the "Holland"[1] cities to catch on). This cooperation between organist and *voorzanger* lasted well into the nineteenth century, when congregations had apparently become sufficiently "cultivated" that the organ alone could control congregational singing.

The organ changed to meet its new requirements. In order to be effective in supporting congregational singing, the organ had to both emphasize the melody and fill the church with adequate volume. As a result, the doubling of treble pipes already common in the *Prestant* 8' was applied to other stops. Also, mixtures were enlarged and more trumpets were added. The *Cornet*—the most important supporting stop for congregational singing—was added to the specifications of many organs; in most cases, the ranks of this labial stop were mounted directly behind the façade pipes, preferably in the *Rugpositief*.

Next to a strong melody line, the bass was the most important support for congregational singing. Therefore an independent pedal division, with a *Trompet* 16' (*Basuin*) as the most important pedal stop for congregational singing, was added to many organs. The free pedal was of "northern" origin and was imported by German builders. Some examples of independent pedal divisions added at this time are:

—1640 at Zutphen, Grote Kerk, by Hans Hendrick Baders, 5 stops
—1642 at Rotterdam, Laurenskerk, by Hans Goltfusz, 5 stops
—1645 at Zeerijp, Jacobikerk, by Theodorus Faber, 3 stops
—about 1650, at Noordwolde, Reformed Church, unknown builder, 5 stops
—before 1662, at Groningen, Aa-Kerk, by Jacobus van Hagerbeer, 8 stops
—about 1625, at 's Hertogenbosch, Cathedral of St. John, the large organ may have had a pedal of 3 stops, including a "*Groot Trompet of Bombart 16vt*" ("a large trumpet or bombarde 16' ")[2]

1. The western part of The Netherlands, currently the provinces of Noord-Holland, Zuid-Holland, and Utrecht, was formerly referred to as "Holland." The relatively independent school of organ building found here is what is called "Hollandic" (or "Dutch" if you wish), in contrast to the schools of organ building in those regions of the country that were under foreign influence. For example, the organs in the northern provinces of Groningen and Friesland are distinctly related to the North German School of organ building. In the south, organs are more French/Belgian/Flemish-oriented.

2. It is remarkable, however, that even as late as the eighteenth century some large organs were still

From its very beginnings, psalm accompaniment was based on continuo practice. Indeed, without the development of the figured-bass practice during the seventeenth century, psalm accompaniment would have been unthinkable. The melody was played loudly in the right hand, a strong bass was provided for support, and the left hand filled in the middle register with chords. This figured-bass practice developed in the Baroque period out of the monodic style of Italy. But even melodies from much earlier times—such as those of the sixteenth – century Genevan Psalter—were treated in this way. The careful four–part harmonizations which are still found in most accompanimental hymnals originated during the late nineteenth century, and best fit the melodies of that period.

In the history of art, periods of dramatic change alternate with periods of quiet assimilation. Accents shift from a detailed variety of forms to greater homogeneity, and to more monumental unity. Such a clear and radical transition occurred in northern Europe around 1630, at the same time that organs were beginning to be called upon to accompany congregational singing. Mannerism, the last stage of the Renaissance, gave way to the Baroque, and with this transition came changes in musical attitudes which made the accompaniment of congregational singing by the organ musically acceptable.

The transition from Mannerism to the Baroque affected the organs themselves, both visually and tonally. Since the outer appearance of an organ was considered as important as its sound—and the visual element was recognized in its power to enhance the auditory experience—organ cases and façades of the day were designed and constructed by great artists and architects. Mannerist architecture favored diverse forms and rich details; it called for unexpected and capricious successions of joints and sections, while nearly every plane was subdivided and filled with decoration. Dutch architects of the period included Lieven de Key (known for the tower of the Nieuwe Kerk in Haarlem of 1613) and Hendrick de Keyser (whose Westerkerk in Amsterdam dates from 1620).

The organs built during the Renaissance period (roughly 1530 to 1630) were distinguished tonally by richness and variety of color. (The most important

built without an independent pedal. For example, in 1700, Jan Duyschot built an organ for the Nieuwe Kerk in the Hague with three manuals, but with only a pull-down pedal to the Great. The Great, with its 16′ labial and reed stops, functioned here also as a bass manual—a practice left over from two previous centuries of Dutch organ building.

1–1. Nieuwe Kerk, Haarlem—tower designed by Lieven de Key in 1613. The tower is a good example of the Mannerist style; the church building of 1649, with its monumental and simple forms, exemplifies the classicism of the Dutch Baroque style.

CREDIT: After a drawing dated 1650 by Pieter Jansz. Saenredam (1597-1665). Original in the Gemeente Archief of Haarlem.

composer representing the late Renaissance style—Mannerism—was Jan
Pieterszoon Sweelinck, 1562-1621.) They were built for solo use, and possessed
both light action and diversified specifications. The *Hoofdwerk*[3] was essentially
the old *Blokwerk*, now provided with separate sliders for the *Prestant, Octaaf,
Mixtuur,* and *Scherp*. But in addition, several stops of new invention were
placed in the upper part of the main case on a separate chest: flute stops, reeds
and the *ruisende* (German *rauschende*, literally "rustling") *Cimbel*. This group
of stops, initially connected with the *Hoofdwerk*, later developed into the
independent *Bovenwerk*. The *Hoofdwerk* formed the *"volle Werk"* and could
not usually be coupled to the other manual(s). The *Rugpositief* was a miniature
of the *Hoofdwerk* and *Bovenwerk*; it possessed principals and flutes, and often
reeds as well. Sometimes the stops were divided over an upper and lower windchest. The pedal "division" of these organs were pull–downs to the Great, but
they often possessed an independent *Trompet* 8′ for *cantus firmus* use. The
best–known builder from this period was Hendrick Niehoff, whose organ in the
Oude Kerk in Amsterdam was built in collaboration with Hans van Co(v)elen
in 1539 and later played by Sweelinck.[4] (In 1724 it was replaced by a new
organ, built by Christian Vater.)

Originating in Italy and responsible for reshaping many artistic attitudes
throughout Europe, Baroque ideas reached northern Europe around 1630, as
we have noted. Outside Italy, however, Baroque concepts were never fully

3. Translator's note: In this translation I have maintained the Dutch terms.
 Hoofdwerk = Great
 Rugpositief (also *Rugwerk*) = commonly known here by the German term *Rückpositiv*, meaning
 that division sitting on the gallery/balcony edge (behind the organist)
 Bovenwerk = upper/over division, above the Great and usually visible in the façade of the organ
 Pedaal = Pedal, sometimes only referring to the pedal keyboard in the case of a pedal pull–down
 from the Great

4. Cf. Cor H. Edskes, "The Organs of the Oude Kerk in Amsterdam at the time of Sweelinck," in:
Alan Curtis, *Sweelinck's Keyboard Music* (Leiden/Oxford University Press, 1969).

The old organ in Amsterdam's Oude Kerk had the following specification at the time of Sweelinck:

Rugpositief:		Hoofdwerk:		Bovenwerk:		Pedaal:	
Prestant	8′	Prestant	16′	Prestant	8′	Trompet	8′
Quintadeen	8′	Octaaf	8′	Holpijp	8′	Nachthoorn	2′
Octaaf	4′	Mixtuur		Openfluit	4′		
Holpijp	4′	Scherp		Nasard	3′		
Sifflet				Gemshoorn	2′		
Mixtuur				Sifflet			
Scherp				Tertscimbel			
Kromhoorn	8′			Trompet	8′		
Baarpijp	8′			Zink	8′		
Schalmey	4′			(treble)			

Couplers: Pedaal + Hoofdwerk
Rugwerk + Bovenwerk

1–2. Large organ of the St. Laurenskerk, Alkmaar.

CREDIT: Ink drawing by Pieter Saenredam signed and dated May 27-28, 1661. Original in the Centraal Museum, Utrecht.

realized. In the Protestant countries they were only partially accepted, because of different cultural expectations, and because the new style evoked emotional responses the Protestants associated with Catholicism and Rome. As the Renaissance and Mannerist influences died out in Protestant North Germany and Holland, there was a renewed interest in the "classical" architecture of the sixteenth century, which in turn was, of course, strongly influenced by the classical (Greek) orders and proportions. (Interestingly enough, the early Italian Baroque musicians had also been influenced by classical thought.) We can, therefore, speak of a "classical Baroque" style in the North which sought to be distinguished by monumentality, yet with a certain soberness derived from a clear form and unified structure.

The greatest Dutch architect of this period—the middle of the seventeenth century—was Jacob van Campen,[5] who designed several monumental organ cases—including those at Leiden (Pieterskerk, 1639), Alkmaar (Laurenskerk, 1641), and Amsterdam (Nieuwe Kerk, 1645). These organ façades resemble the classically inspired buildings of the period. They show well–balanced, refined proportions, and recall an atmosphere of Dutch stateliness and distinction.

It was this very shift toward monumentality, simplicity, and unity which allowed the organ accompaniment of congregational singing to be accepted from a musical point of view, for congregational singing itself is monumental and simple.[6] A good example of the new, classically inspired, Baroque style in organ *music* is offered by the Psalm variations and fantasies of the *Tabulatuur-boek* (1659) of the Amsterdam organist Anthoni van Noordt (c. 1620-c. 1675). Unlike the music of Sweelinck, van Noordt's work was issued during its own time—a rare occurence in Holland at that time.

It is interesting to observe in specific organs the form taken by the general trends discussed above. As we mentioned, organ building was in a transitional state during the half–century between 1630 and 1680, and organs were not everywhere adapted to the accompaniment of congregational singing. The "classical Baroque" organs of Leiden, Amsterdam, and Alkmaar, mentioned

5. Born in Haarlem, van Campen created such monumental buildings as the Amsterdam Town Hall from 1648 (now the Royal Palace on the Dam) and the Nieuwe Kerk in Haarlem from 1645.

6. When the Prince of the Netherlands, Frederik Hendrik, paid a visit in 1640 to the city of Groningen, his secretary, the poet, composer, and lover of church and organ music, Constantijn Huygens, wrote: "This morning His Royal Highness, surrounded by the distinguished people of the city, went to the service in the Grote (= Martini) Kerk and heard with much satisfaction the beautiful organ, which is used there to accompany congregational singing, which is done with so much solemnity and majesty that it is a miracle—to such a degree that everyone was edified by it!"

earlier, whose façades were designed by the architect Jacob van Campen and represent the new ideal of architectural massiveness, were built by van Hager-beer and offer good examples of the organs from this period of change.

The development of the Alkmaar organ, originally built in 1641–45, illustrates an important passage in the history of Dutch organ building. The original 16′ *Hoofdwerk* was extended with a contra–octave starting from FF, so the case reached 24′ proportions. A number of stops came into use after c. 1630 and were also incorporated into the Alkmaar organ, including tierce stops, in the form both of single–ranked stops and of a treble Sesquialtera to strengthen and fill out the *plenum*.[7] Another addition was the Vox *Humana* (reed), actually a somewhat more "civilized" successor to the *Regaal*.

The Renaissance tradition was still evident in Alkmaar, however, in the form of many flute stops (including a *Sifflet* 1′) and four 1½′ Quint stops (the Quint 2⅔′ was still uncommon). The pedal division was not yet assigned a bass function, but had, in addition to those stops pulled down from the Great, a *Trompet* 8′, *Prestant* 8′, and *Octaaf* 4′. The Great still possessed the characteristics of the *Blokwerk*, but was now divided into separate stops. It was not yet possible to couple this manual to other manuals.

During this period in Holland, the rich variety of Renaissance reed stops was progressively reduced until only the trumpet stops and the Vox *Humana* remained, even in those organs not yet used for the accompaniment of congregational singing. The organ in Alkmaar had four trumpets and one Vox *Humana*.

In about 1675, the Alkmaar organ began to be used to accompany congregational singing. In 1684, the organ was altered for this purpose by the builder Johannes Duyschot. The manuals of the *Bovenwerk* and the *Hoofdwerk* were switched, so the *Hoofdwerk* keyboard was now in the middle position and the *Bovenwerk* keyboard in the upper position. From this location, the *Hoofdwerk* could easily be coupled to the *Rugpositief*. Since there was no room for an independent pedal, the bass function of the *Hoofdwerk* was enforced by changing the *Trompet* 8′ to a *Trompet* 16′ extending only to f′. These changes resulted in greater wind demands and the bellows had to be replaced. On the *Bovenwerk*, the combination of Vox *Humana*,[8] *Baarpijp*, *Quintadeen*, and Tremulant—a favorite combination in Holland—was provided. Strangely enough, Duyschot did not add a *Cornet*.

∿

7. This was a development which paralleled changes initiated in France by Mersenne.

8. In combination with the *Baarpijp*, *Quintadeen*, and Tremulant, the Vox *Humana* became extremely popular in the western provinces. Listeners would place bets on whether there was singing coming from the organ loft or whether the Vox *Humana* was being played. Many organs were enlarged with "Vox *Humana*" divisions.

One of the first totally new organs to be built in Amsterdam after the introduction of organ accompaniment of congregational singing there (1680) was that constructed by Roelof Barentsz. Duyschot for the Westerkerk. This organ possessed two *Cornet* stops, one on the *Hoofdwerk* and one on the *Rugpositief.* The pedal division contained 16', 8', 6', and 4' stops, and reeds 16' and 8'. In all, it had three trumpet stops—on the *Rugpositief, Hoofdwerk,* and *Pedaal.* In 1727, Christian Müller added a *Bovenwerk,* including the above–mentioned quartet of *Vox Humana, Baarpijp, Quintadeen,* and *Tremulant.*

The organ for the Ronde Lutherse Kerk in Amsterdam, built by Cornelis Hoornbeeck in 1719, was patterned after the Westerkerk organ by Duyschot. In 1721, only two years after it was built, Christian Müller added a *"Vox Humana"* *Bovenwerk* of eight stops to this organ. (During a church fire in 1822, the organ was unfortunately lost. It was replaced by the still extant—and recently restored—Bätz organ of 1825–30.)

It is remarkable that most of the organs built during this period were not equal to the upcoming task of accompanying the massive volume of congregational Psalm singing. It was not only organs of earlier times, but also organs built during the interim period, and organs built later in Holland by German builders in the North German style, that had to be improved, enlarged, or even replaced to meet the new requirements.

A good example of this kind of failure in design is the organ built in the Oude Kerk of Amsterdam in 1724 by Christian Vater, a pupil of Arp Schnitger. The new organ had to be altered and enlarged as early as 1738 by Johann Caspar Müller of the Hague (a relative of Christian). The windpressure was increased; the reeds were strengthened; the scalings of the flues were widened by shifting them upwards toward the treble; the doublings were spread over more stops (even the highest octave of the *Woudfluit* 2' on the *Rugpositief* was doubled!); the mixtures were enlarged; new stops were added; and the *Cornet* was enlarged to nine ranks, including a 5⅓'.

Some German builders who settled in Holland nonetheless learned quickly and well how to adapt their skills to Dutch taste. Among these were Christian Müller, Rudolf Garrels, and the Bätz generation. The development of the Dutch organ into a "vocal" instrument capable of effectively accompanying congregational singing reached its peak in the work of Christian Müller (1690–1763), as seen in his city organs as well as in his village instruments.

Christian Müller became well-known after he built the organ in 1727 for the Grote Kerk in Leeuwarden. This was a large three–manual instrument with thirty–eight stops over *Hoofdwerk, Rugwerk, Echowerk (Bovenwerk),* and *Pedaal.* Its specification included five trumpet stops and a *Bazuin* 16', *Vox Humana* and *Dulciaan* as secondary reeds, and a *Cornet* in the *Rugpositief.*

In 1734 Müller completely rebuilt the 8' organ in the Waalse Kerk in

Amsterdam, originally built in 1680, into a 16' instrument with independent pedal. The *Rugpositief* was changed from 4' to 8'. The existing *Rugpositief* case was not enlarged, however. Instead, new carvings were used to cover the new and longer pipes. The organ had twenty–six stops, of which five were reeds: the *Hoofdwerk* had *Trompets* 16' and 8', as well as a *Vox Humana* 8', and the *Pedaal* had a *Fagot* 16' and a *Trompet* 8'. There was not enough space in the *Pedaal* for a *Bazuin* 16' (thus the *Fagot* in the *Pedaal* and the *Trompet* 16' on the *Hoofdwerk*) nor for a *Cornet* and reed in the still–small *Rugpositief* case. Müller therefore provided that division with a *Scherp* in the treble.

Doubled ranks in the treble, common in Müller's organs, are found in the principals and the *Quint* 3'. The Amsterdam organ curiously lacks a Flute 4', a stop not richly provided by Müller in the first place (and, when included, often only on an *Echowerk* as a *Gemshoorn* 4' as in Leeuwarden, or as a "secundant" for solo reeds on a flute–*Bovenwerk*, as in Beverwijk).

The monumental, and now world–famous, organ Müller built in the Grote or St. Bavo Kerk in Haarlem (1735–38) was conceived as a congregational organ and as a representative city organ. It has sixty–two stops, divided over *Hoofdwerk*, *Rugpositief*, *Bovenwerk*, and *Pedaal*.[9]

For accompanying congregational singing, it has a widely scaled and power-fully voiced *Cornet* in the *Rugpositief* (directly behind the façade pipes), doubled trebles in the principals and mixtures, a large number of trumpets, and a heavy pedal division with *Principaal* 32', reeds 32' and 16', and Quint basses at 12' and 6' pitches.

For public performances, the organ was given a rich variety of solo stops and registration possibilities. Hence, the reeds are not limited to the trumpets and *Vox Humana*, but include a *Fagot* 16', *Hobo* 8', *Dulciaan* 8', *Regaal* 8', and *Cinck* 2'.

It is interesting to note, in contrast to the specification of the monumental organ in Haarlem, the design for a small village organ, built by Müller in 1727 for the Reformed Church in Menaldum (prov. Friesland), near Leeuwarden. (Unfortunately this organ was replaced in 1860.) Aside from the *Cornet*, which was an important melody stop, and the *Praestant*, the *Rugpositief* is full of flutes. The *Trompet* 8' on the *Hoofdwerk* was divided to reinforce the *cantus firmus* in the treble. The specification was:

1727, Christian Müller
Reformed Church, Menaldum (province Friesland)

Manuaal:		Rugwerk:	
Praestant	8'	Praestant	4'

9. Cf. Klaas Bolt, *De Historie en Samenstelling van het Haarlemse Müller-Orgel* (Amsterdam: Arti*Novo, 1985).

1–3. St. Bavo Kerk, Haarlem. Organ built by Christian Müller in
1735-38.

CREDIT: Design for the new organ, ascribed to Hendrik de Werff, not signed,
not dated (ca. 1735). Colored ink drawing on parchment, 970x630 mm.
Original in the Gemeente Archief of Haarlem.

1–4. Dutch Reformed Church, Beverwijk. Organ by Christian Müller, 1756.

CREDIT: Photo courtesy of Flentrop Orgelbouw.

Quintadeen	8'	Holpyp	8'
Octaaf	4'	Gemshoorn	4'
Quint	3'	Fluit	2'
Super Octaaf	2'	Cornet	
Tertiaan		(treble)	
Trompet	8'		
(divided)		Manual coupler	
Mixtuur		Tremulant	

The following accompaniment of Psalm 6 is found in a 1741 Psalm book of a village schoolmaster and organist named Lootsma, who lived near Menaldum. On the organ in Menaldum, this accompaniment could have been played with this registration:

Melody (right hand): *Hoofdwerk*: 8', 8', 4', 3', 2', *(Tertiaan, Mixtuur)*, *Trompet* (treble), coupled to *Rugpositief* with *Cornet* (treble)

Accompaniment (left hand): *Hoofdwerk*: 8', 8', 4', 3', 2', *(Tertiaan, Mixtuur)*

Bass: played in *Pedaal*: pull–down to *Hoofdwerk*, to be played only in the lowest octave to give a quasi–16'

The organ built by Müller in 1756 for the Reformed Church in Beverwijk, a town near Haarlem, may be one of the best examples of an instrument suited to the accompaniment of congregational singing. It was restored in 1981–83 by the Flentrop firm. Its specification is as follows:

1756, Christian Müller
Reformed Church, Beverwijk

Hoofdwerk:		
Prestant	8'	1756, double treble choir 1983
Roerfluit	8'	1756
Octaaf	4'	1756
Quint	3'	double treble choirs, mostly 1983

Super Octaaf	2′	1756, double treble choir 1983
Sexquialter III		1756, one 1⅗′ double choir 1983
Mixtuur IV-VI		1756
Trompet	8′	1756/1983

Bovenwerk:

Prestant (treble)	16′	1756, in façade, a′-c‴ double choirs
Holfluit	8′	1756
Quintadena	8′	1756
Gemshoorn	4′	1937
Nachthoorn	2′	1756
Cornet IV (treble)		1756 (composition: 4′, 3′, 2′, 1⅗′)
Schalmeij	8′	1983
Vox Humana	8′	1756/1983

Pedaal:

Bourdon	16′	1756 (oak)
Prestant	8′	1756
Octaaf	4′	1756
Woudfluit	2′	1756
Fagot	16′	1756/1983
Trompet	8′	1756/1983

Manual compass: C-c‴
Pedal compass: C-c′
Manual coupler divided in bass and treble
Pedal coupler to the Hoofdwerk
Tremulant to entire organ
Pitch: c. ½ tone below a′ = 440Hz
Temperament: after Kirnberger (1983)

It is not clear why a *Rugpositief* was not chosen, since there was ample space. Perhaps financial constraints precluded it (the organ was a gift). Or perhaps a *Vox Humana* was a top priority. In order to make this stop sound as much like the human voice as possible, it has to sound from a distance. It is thus best placed not in a *Rugpositief*, but in a *Bovenwerk*.

In Beverwijk, the *Cornet*—which Müller normally preferred in the *Rugpositief*—was placed on the *Bovenwerk*, right behind the *Prestant* 16′ treble in the façade. This 16′ treble stop played an important role in the accompaniment of singing, together with the treble of the *Hoofdwerk Mixtuur* (which was based on 16' pitch). Congregational singing is concentrated in the tenor, and the added 16' pitch and resultant fifths (of the *Mixtuur*) made it possible to accentuate the tenor, even though the melody was played in the soprano. In the Beverwijk organ, the divided coupler also made it possible to add the *Schalmeij* (a narrow trumpet) of the *Bovenwerk* to the melody played on the *Hoofdwerk*.

The following Psalm accompaniment, from 1731 and the hand of Gerhard Frederick Witvogel, organist on the Hoornbeeck/Müller organ of the Ronde Lutherse Kerk in Amsterdam, can be played in Beverwijk with this sample registration:

Melody (right hand): *Hoofdwerk:* 8', 8', 4', 3', 2', *Sexquialter,*
    Mixtuur, Trompet + treble coupler to *Bovenwerk* with *Cornet,*
    Schalmeij 8', and *Prestant* 16' (treble)
Accompaniment (left hand): *Hoofdwerk:* 8', 8', 4', 3', 2', *Sexquialter,*
    Mixtuur, Trompet
Bass: *Pedaal:* 16', 8', 4', 16', 8' + coupler to *Hoofdwerk*

My *"basso continuo"* solution:

Two additional examples of Psalm accompaniments further illustrate the development of accompaniment styles during the eighteenth century. The melody is familiar as "*O Mensch bewein dein Sünde gross*" (both Psalm 68 and Psalm 36 use this melody). The first example is from the hand of Conrad

Friedrich Hurlebusch, organist of the Oude Kerk in Amsterdam, and dates
from 1766. In his setting we witness a tastefully ornamented melody: our next
example will show later developments.

The second example, from the hand of Jacob Potholt (1720–82), Hurlebusch's
successor, dates from 1777. Here we find a short introduction and the appearance of interludes between the lines, a practice which lasted until the second
half of the nineteenth century. The ornaments, unlike those of Hurlebusch,
have been reduced to rigid, stereotypical upbeats, and indicate the transition
from the Rococo or Gallant style (with its grace and liveliness) to the Classical
style (with more evenly paced lines and ornamentation).

Duties of the Organist

The tasks required of organists during this period in Holland were well defined
in the instructions, written down in 1756, for the organist of the new instrument in Beverwijk. On Sundays and other special days, the organist accompanied the singing of the Psalms; before and after the service *(predicatie)* he
played the organ for fifteen minutes. In addition, he played every Monday and
Saturday from 11:30 a.m. to 12:30 p.m. and was required "to demonstrate the
organ's sound most favorably to the public." His tasks also included the
winding and regulation of the clock, and the tuning of the reeds every fortnight.

Since calcants were required in order to play the organ, it was not easy to use the instrument other than during the times mentioned above. Hence, when the organ was played it was a special event and served three purposes: it was a public "entertainment," provided a form of maintenance for the instrument, and offered the organist some "practice" time. (Organists everywhere during this period practiced on other instruments—particularly the clavichord—at home.)

Organ performance consisted mostly of improvisations, preferably on Psalm tunes. The tasks of the organist can further be deduced from an account of the skills required of organists who auditioned for a position in Beverwijk in 1756. "The audition consisted of playing a hymn of praise to Zechariah [that is, the melody of "An Wasserflüssen Babylon"], first as a chorale, then followed by two verses in variation form. Each organist was allowed to play according to his own pleasure and show the organ to its best advantage. The time alloted each was half an hour . . ."

During an audition for an important city organ position,[10] the following abilities had to be demonstrated:

1. improvisation of the accompaniment of a Hymn or Psalm

2. improvisation of a chorale variation and of chorale preludes in differing forms, and the improvisation of a fugue, sometimes with a countersubject

3. the playing of modulations

4. the playing and realization of figured bass

5. the playing of a free improvisation, whereby careful attention would be paid to the use of the organ, i.e. the art of registration

6. the improvisation of trumpet music, flute concerti, duets, and, toward the end of the eighteenth century, imitations of nature, such as birdsong and thunderstorms, and of war battles, etc., and

7. knowledge of the construction of the organ, and skills in its maintenance.

Requirements of this sort existed not only in Holland, but also in Germany (compare the similar requirements, conveyed to us by Mattheson, for the audition for the position of Cathedral organist in Hamburg in 1727).

The playing of existing compositions—considered an inferior form of music making—was strongly forbidden; everything had to be one's own "invention."

10. Cf. Jan Zwart: *Van een deftig Orgel* (the Garrels organ of 1732 in Maassluis), 1937.

The playing of organ literature only began to gain ground in Holland during the second half of the nineteenth century. In Haarlem this practice was furthered by the Bavo organist Johannes Gijsbertus Bastiaans (1812–75). He had studied with Mendelssohn and introduced Bach's organ works (along with those of other composers) in Haarlem around 1860.

Postscript

In the nineteenth century, the popularity of the interlude, generally of a quiet nature, called into being still another type of organ. The stoplist of the *Hoofdwerk* remained basically unchanged (although its sound and scalings were romanticized—in other words, directed more toward stateliness and less towards eighteenth–century playfulness). However, the second manual, which by preference had been a *Bovenwerk*, became an echo division and was used to play the interludes.

Since the 1970s, the revival of the seventeenth– and eighteenth–century "congregational singing" organ and thorough research of its interrelated aspects has resulted in instruments that are more effective for accompanying Psalm singing than the so–called neo–Baroque organs of the post–World War II era. Nineteenth–century organs were also more capable of fulfilling this task than neo–Baroque organs are and luckily there is an increasing appreciation of nineteenth–century concepts of Psalm accompaniment.

There is no clear unanimity in The Netherlands on what type of organ is the best, but most builders agree that the old organs themselves are still our best teachers. They provide clues for the way future building will—and/or should—progress.

CHAPTER TWO

Toward the Restoration of Grace in Early French Organ Ornamentation

FENNER DOUGLASS

PAUL GOLDBERGER, architecture critic for the *New York Times*, speaks of "preserving the original function as well as detail" for buildings being restored nowadays: ". . . the notion of a sleekly modern shop or apartment housed within an old shell is no longer either new or striking."

> The last few years have seen a welcome surge of . . . pure restoration. Along with the established tradition of landmark preservation, it represents a genuine commitment to the country's architectural heritage. There are still plenty of good buildings lost, and plenty more that are renovated and altered out of all resemblance to their original condition. But there is also a greater willingness than ever before to get to the essence of a work of architecture and to try to bring out once again the qualities it had when it was new.[1]

Goldberger goes on to emphasize that some old buildings are not worth saving, since they are not "icons of our culture."

All of these comments could apply as well to historic organs, many of which have only in very recent years been recognized as "icons of our culture." There is now a greater willingness than ever before to preserve the remaining antiques because they are the only link between notated music of the past and various attempts at interpreting it.

Unfortunately, most ancient organs have been so relentlessly modernized that it is impossible today to recognize or even to piece together their original musical function. For centuries the temptation to restore by enlargement or interior reshuffling has resulted in "sleekly modern" instruments housed within old shells—that is, behind elegantly redecorated antique façades. Meanwhile, characteristics of touch, sonority, and articulation of organs played by a Bach, a Böhm, or a Handel have been needlessly and permanently obscured.

In France an official policy called "reconstitution" has actually guided the majority of government-sponsored restorations over the past fifty years or so,

1. Quoted from Paul Goldberger: "Restoration," *New York Times Magazine*, Oct. 7, 1984.

while the general public has been led to believe that its tax money was being spent for the preservation of their national treasures. One by one, classified instruments have lost the qualities they had when they were new. If the Commission had simply abandoned the organs of Nicolas LeBègue, François Couperin, or Nicolas DeGrigny, we would know much more today about how those composers wanted their music to sound and how to make practical sense from their rather intricate shorthand system of notation.

There are a few well-preserved French organs of the seventeenth and eighteenth centuries, and they have unique value for the interpretation of the so-called French baroque organ music. Instruments being built today cannot be quite suitable for reviving the French repertory unless such antiques are used as models. One antique organ, played with the grace and delicacy the music invites, can teach us more than a dozen treatises on registration, on ornaments, or even on fine points of organ building. The theoretical comments out of their proper contexts remain at best a dangerous asset.

I do not propose to add here to the volume of source materials already available to the performer interested in authenticity when playing on modern instruments. Rather, my aim is to alert the player to the need to interpret the music, if not at the antiques themselves, at instruments which resemble the early masterpieces as closely as possible. This means instruments which embody the original function as well as the external detail. I will draw attention to the question of touch, which was not much discussed in early theoretical comments on the organ, though it lies at the root of all the organ's responses to the will of the player. While relationships of pipes and wind have been given deserved notice in recent years, there has not been sufficient emphasis on the merits of ancient key actions—in particular, the French key actions. For it was only through the keys that the players and composers could transmit the choicest expressions of their soul and wit. We have restricted ourselves too narrowly, relying on stop-names rather than the varying articulations of organ pipes; on ornament tables rather than the study of their function; on tedious *inégalité* rather than the need to limit its use; on early fingerings rather than the physical attributes of the instruments for which they were devised; on improvised embellishments as an exhibition of stylishness rather than as the irresistible byproduct of a musical style long forgotten. Unless the importance of touch and key action in these musical questions is better understood, the hunger for authenticity in performance will lead continually to despair of it ever being attained.

To reiterate, for those who have heard and played the few remaining French organs of the eighteenth century, or the seventeenth—the earlier the better— there must still linger in the ear's memory a strong and vital sense of their unique sonorities, and an awareness of the role the instruments must have played in the development of a very distinct musical style. There were rules for notating embellishments, for choosing stops to suit particular musical textures or certain portions of the Mass, or for explaining the conditions that encouraged players to liberate themselves from the exact notation of rhythmic durations in the score. The French set these rules down because uniformity was imposed from Paris over the provinces;[2] but they were also concerned that foreigners might misunderstand their music.[3] For over a hundred years these customs prevailed, surviving changes of musical fashion, but this kind of stability was only possible because the instrument remained basically unchanged in its technical design and general layout.

Fortunately, at the very end of the period, an excellent organ builder, Dom Bedos de Celles, a Benedictine monk, was commissioned to contribute to *Descriptions des arts et métiers*, published by the *Académie Royale des Sciences*. The result was *L'Art du facteur d'orgues* (1766–70), in which just about everything a master builder could impart was set down in words and scale drawings. Such is the richness of technical detail supplied by Dom Bedos that one wonders why there is any question today about how the music of LeBègue, DeGrigny, or Couperin should sound. Yet, when the French classical music is heard on modern instruments, the results are usually very disappointing.

We are hampered by the vast stylistic gap created by the nineteenth century, and by too little awareness of changes in musical fashion during the generations before Dom Bedos. Using the perspective of the two centuries since 1770, we should, on the contrary, be even better able than Dom Bedos to examine and to understand those changes. It was not Dom Bedos' inclination, nor anyone else's in the late eighteenth century, to pay heed to the music or the advice from the remote past. This was so even for music composed for instruments that had not changed much through the years. In a footnote to the fourth chapter of his Volume III, Dom Bedos makes reference to changes of taste in his own century:

> Towards the beginning of this century, an organist named LeBègue published some organ pieces. Appended to his collection were the stop combinations suitable to the way in which organs were built and to the quality of sound they produced. Tastes have changed since that time. Because of different uses of stops and ways of treating them, certain alterations in those earlier combinations have been necessitated. Given here are those generally in use, at least by the majority of the best organists today.

2. Nicolas LeBègue stresssed in the preface to his *Premier Livre d'orgue* (1676): "These pieces (if I am not mistaken) will also be of some use to organists who cannot come great distances to hear the numerous and diverse types of stops which have recently been in use here."

3. Jacques Boyvin said in his *Premier Livre d'orgue* (1689): "The general manner is known. . . . However, as my book could fall into the hands of foreign musicians, it will be useful to them to find here some instruction about registration."

Dom Bedos, still building organs that would suit LeBègue's music quite well, dismissed LeBègue with a footnote. Over the span of a century (i.e., back to 1676, rather than to "the beginning of this [eighteenth] century"), the fashion in organ music had moved away from the delicate figurations of the seventeenth century, patterned after the unique touch characteristics of certain combinations of stops. LeBègue was dead. Nor would a Nicolas DeGrigny re-emerge to compose fugues in five voices that would fascinate a Johann Sebastian Bach. Rather, one would take note of Michel Corrette's "*recette pour contrefaire l'orage et le tonnerre,*" an early prescription for making organ storms and thunder. Curious that Dom Bedos in this time maintained the ancient techniques of building that had inspired a great creative output during the *grand siècle*, while the players of his day were setting the stage for the flamboyant Lefébure-Wély of the 1840s and '50s. It took a Lefébure-Wély to squeeze out the last drop of appeal for that kind of music with his depictions of storms and shipwrecks at sea. As the wretched sailors knelt to sing "Out of the Depths I cry to Thee," the gas lights would go out while the audience shivered with fright.

In June 1770, when Dom Bedos' fourth volume was finished, Dr. Charles Burney recorded his impressions of the organ playing in two Parisian churches. About Claude Balbastre, Burney said: "he played between each verse several minuets, fugues, imitations . . . even to hunting pieces and jigs, without surprizing or offending the congregation. . . ." At the church of St. Gervais, "though M. Couperin [Armand-Louis] has the true organ touch, smooth and connected, he often tried, and not unsuccessfully, mere harpsichord passages, smartly articulated, and the notes detached and separated."[4] To Dr. Burney, French music was "notoriously hateful to all the people in Europe but themselves. . . ." At the time, the most popular Parisian organist was Daquin (d. 1772), who was praised by Marchand and Rameau for having "maintained for the organ the majesty and grace that suit it." But the same Daquin was reported in the *Tableau de Paris* to have performed as follows: "More sublime than ever, Daquin thundered in the *Judex crederis*, imparting to the hearts of the listeners impressions so vivid and profound that everyone turned pale and shuddered."[5]

The French organ music we try to bring back to life today was forgotten by Balbastre and Daquin, and never heard by Dr. Burney. It was the music Bach admired—D'Anglebert, Raison, DeGrigny, and perhaps others as well. It invites more graceful and majestic performance than the music Dom Bedos was accustomed to hearing. We do not take sufficient note of this fact when we read Dom Bedos on registration and interpretation. He had no more notion of

4. Charles Burney, *The Present State of Music in France and Italy*, 1773, Vol. I, p. 24.

5. Quoted by André Pirro in "L'Art des Organistes," *Encyclopédie de la Musique*, p. 1349.

how DeGrigny should be played than did the nineteenth-century organ builder Cavaillé-Coll. But the technical approaches in the builder's craft were slow to change, and on these essential matters Dom Bedos is most helpful to us today.

If we begin by deciphering ornament tables, no matter how authentic they may be, we have just barely started the search for a fluent playing style. Yet prior to the mid-eighteenth century very little instruction was put down in writing— a comment here and there, or a description of finger position that would apply to the organ and harpsichord alike, and so on. We lack a real heritage of organ methods comparable to Couperin's *L'Art de toucher le clavecin* (1727) or the numerous practical treatises for singers, flutists, or viol players. For organists, the technique of performance must be essentially reconstructed before a graceful style of ornamentation can be developed.

Between about 1650 and 1750, the French style of writing for the organ came to resemble that for the harpsichord. Thus remarkable differences arose between French and Italian, or between French and German, music. In France, much emphasis was placed on the composers' predilection to think in terms of certain timbres as appropriate to particular musical textures, and upon the inclusion of ornaments in more or less copious detail. The appropriate execution of the ornaments was occasionally described in the composer's words. The fact that François Couperin complained about harpsichordists who added ornaments to his published music gives some idea of the care and precision with which the ornaments had been applied to it in the first place.

Couperin's harpsichord manual stressed posture, hand position, fingering, and the qualities of the key action. He did not speak about fine points of harpsichord touch, speed of attack or release, or the like. It would have been extremely difficult then, as it is today, to describe manners of expressive performance on the harpsichord, and even more so on the more complicated organ keyboard. It seems that written comments of Couperin and his contemporaries who composed for the organ pointedly avoided examining refinements in the key action and requirements for expression. Some things were not brought up, such as finger pressure, speed of pallet opening, percentage of key dip necessary to produce full speech of pipes or rapid repetitions, or various amounts of pressure required for different keyboards or for ranges of the same keyboard. Yet these are crucial points if the player is to draw the most expressive responses from the organ.

More lucid comment is available about performing techniques for instruments held with the hands or legs. Unlike keyboard instruments, flutes and stringed instruments were so intimately associated with their players that the players expected to respond to the instruments as much as the instruments did to them. Therefore, method books on flute or string playing were apt to discuss in minute detail the shades of energetic response or articulation necessary for particular musical results. Bow strokes, or *coups d'archet*, on the viol should be *exprimés, nourris, soutenus,* or *jettés,* as occasion demanded. For French viol music such fine points were essential, because technique of articulation and mastery of musical expression were synonymous.

The articulateness of the French organ's musical message was probably not all that different from the articulateness required of the viols. We learn from John Hsu's Handbook of *French Baroque Viol Technique* (1981) that viol players sought to achieve an attack similar to the plucking of a harpsichord string. This approach to technique lasted from about the 1630s, when it was first described by Mersenne, to the mid-eighteenth century, when Hubert LeBlanc (1740) outlined the six different ways of varying bow strokes as practiced by the famed Marin Marais (1656–1728). LeBlanc said:

> [The French viol bow strokes] are *simples*, with the bow striking the string as the jack plucks the harpsichord string, and not *complexes* like those of the Italians, where, by use of smooth and well-connected up-bows and down-bows whose changes are imperceptible, there is produced an endless chain of notes that appear as a continuous flow. [Hsu's translation.]

Marais, the most famous French gambist of the period, used bow strokes intended to sound like plucking, or *pincé*, of the lute or guitar. Such is the detail found in the French manuals on viol playing that a modern player can reconstruct the old technique, given an antique instrument or a faithful replica.

French organ music of the same period, like music for viols, also resembles harpsichord or lute music. If the delicate expressions of the harpsichord's plucked strings inspired the players of other stringed instruments to imitate the harpsichord with their bow techniques, then finger action for the French organist might well also have been described as *simple*, rather than *complexe* (like the Italians). Thus the organist would strive to produce an agreeable plucking effect, or *pincé*, as the organ's wind caused the pipes to speak. The simplicity of the mechanical connections between the organ's keys and pallets should make it possible for the player's fingers to act with the same acute sensibility as they would on the harpsichord's keys. This would apply especially for harpsichord-like textures, while still leaving the player free to de-emphasize the *pincé* for connected, legato effects, like those encountered in the sustained textures that have always been associated with the organ.

For the organ builder of the seventeenth century, the word *pincé*, or pluck, did not refer to the ornament by the same name (𝄿), but rather to the resistance experienced by the player at the very top of the key dip. The key action was designed and balanced so that the player's finger could comfortably cause the pallet at the other end of the action to pull free, causing air under pressure in the pallet box to enter the key channel below the pipe feet. The "pluck" in organs with mechanical action is comparable to the pluck of the harpsichord string. This is significant in determining the articulateness of organ music, because the organ "pluck" varies with the speeds of attack and release in pipe speech as dictated by the player's fingers. One can see that efficiency, control, and delicacy in the design of the key action were of the essence to seventeenth-century organ builders.

For about one hundred and fifty years prior to the Revolution, French manual key action was the lightest and most responsive being built. It was "suspended" (mécanique suspendu), as opposed to "balanced." To understand the difference between the two, refer to Figures 2-1 and 2-2. A balanced key is levered at the middle point. A suspended key is hinged from a fulcrum at the back end and hangs from a tracker forward of its center point. The key actually hangs from the tracker, which holds it up by the tension of the pallet spring. The suspended action not only provides the maximum mechanical advantage for the fingers, but it makes possible a simpler design between key and pallet than is ordinarily the case with balanced action. A well-designed and adjusted suspended action eliminates the spongy feel typical of the balanced action, caused in part by the additional motion required in the balanced key. Because the suspended key is actually held up in readiness by the tension of the pallet spring, the entire mechanical connection of trackers, stickers, or backfalls also stands at attention, poised for action. The player not only feels the absence of slack in the suspended key, but his fingers seem continuously to be lifted up in such a way that extravagant expenditure of energy or wasted finger pressure is actually discouraged by the instrument. It is not always necessary, or even desirable, to depress the keys fully to the key bed—rather, only enough to cause the corresponding pipe(s) to speak clearly with their correct pitches. While for long pipes the pallets require full opening, the very short ones, that is, a foot or less in length, speak perfectly with the lightest touch. The expressive possibilities in the realm of touch are enormous, provided the player learns to spend a minimum of energy. LeBègue referred to the need for relaxation and economy of motion when he said, "Those who have trouble executing certain ornaments, where they are found too difficult to play, are advised to pass them by, for it is essential that the hands remain relaxed."[6] Tense or heavy fingers, even when playing on the most elegant organ actions ever invented, can only fail to bring grace and charm to the ornamented textures of early French music. How could LeBègue have imagined with what clumsy efforts organists of the future would struggle with his ornaments, and how fruitless their labor would be on the highly complex key actions of two hundred years later?

6. LeBègue, Premier Livre d'orgue, 1676.

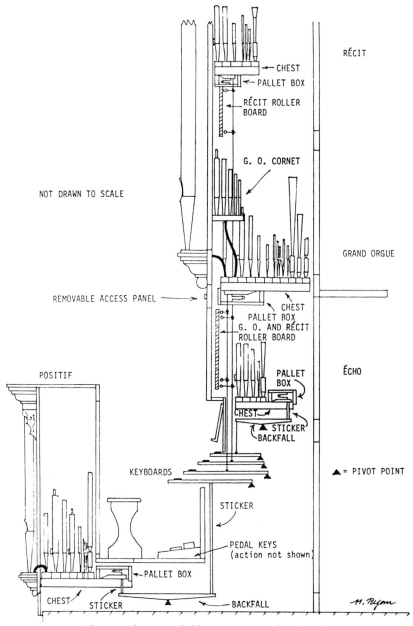

2–1. Side view of a suspended key action (French Classical style).

CREDIT: Drawing by Norman Ryan.

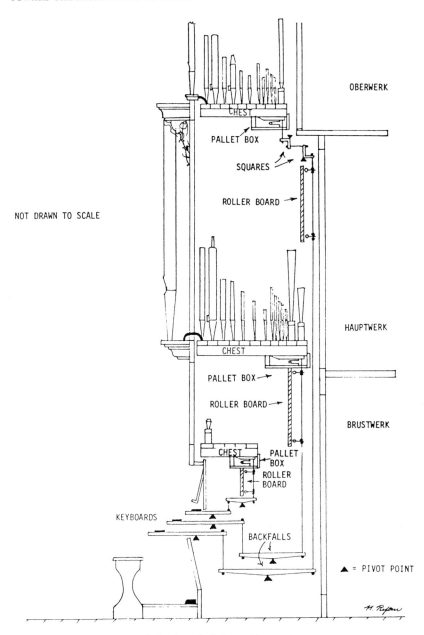

OBERWERK

CHEST

PALLET BOX

SQUARES

ROLLER BOARD

NOT DRAWN TO SCALE

HAUPTWERK

CHEST

PALLET BOX

ROLLER BOARD

BRUSTWERK

CHEST

PALLET BOX

ROLLER BOARD

KEYBOARDS

BACKFALLS

▲ = PIVOT POINT

2–2. Side view of a balanced key action.

CREDIT: Drawing by Norman Ryan.

The lightness and articulateness we try to describe are characteristic of all suspended actions, if they are well-designed for an instrument of suitable disposition and layout. What is most interesting for performers of the French music under discussion is that French organ builders, or the musicians who advised them, insisted on maintaining simplicity and directness in the key action, even at the expense of other considerations less urgent to them. At a time when highly ornamented, harpsichord-like musical textures were the vogue, it seemed that no Frenchman was interested in disrupting the equilibrium that made it possible to play their music comfortably. To bring that music back to life today, should we not seek to re-create the wonderful touch that gives it spontaneity and verve?

French-designed key actions were kept as uncomplicated as possible, and this meant the avoidance of turns or awkward horizontal movements. Toward that end, the pallet box for the *Grand Orgue* was placed in the front of the windchest, so that trackers could lead from it directly down to a rollerboard, and then straight down again to connect from the forward half of suspended keys. Manuals were always set into the case *(en fenêtre)* to make this possible. The German actions, on the other hand, were directed from pallets at the back of the windchest (located under the reed pipes) for optimum speech through rollerboards, trackers, squares, and/or backfalls. Thus, for the sake of the promptest possible reaction from the *Hauptwerk* reeds, the Germans were willing to put up with a more complicated key action—a notable awkwardness which affected the player's touch.

When it came to the *Positif-de-dos (Rückpositiv)*, the French went to extremes to cut down on friction and lost motion. The pallet-box was inverted, so that the pallets could be lifted by very short stickers attached to the ends of long backfalls. Longer stickers then led from the backfalls to the under side of the *Positif* manual keys. Dom Bedos showed this standard design in his famous Plate 52 (Figure 2-3). But, in order for this most convenient system to operate without a rollerboard, the pipes on the windchest were arranged chromatically, and the backfalls fanned out in the order of the keys themselves. A few bass pipes were placed on the treble end of the chest, with a small rollerboard to transfer the action for those keys. Note that this concession was made only for the keys least likely to require delicate touch.

Of course, other influences were at work on the key action—friction, wind pressure, volume of wind as controlled by measurements of the key channels and pallets, voicing techniques, key dip vs. pallet opening, and the stoplist itself. Large organs brought increased difficulty in design. French builders in this period gave highest priority to lightness and responsiveness in key actions, and they were generally content to work within limits imposed by a fine mechanical action. This meant a stable approach to tonal design and layout. It

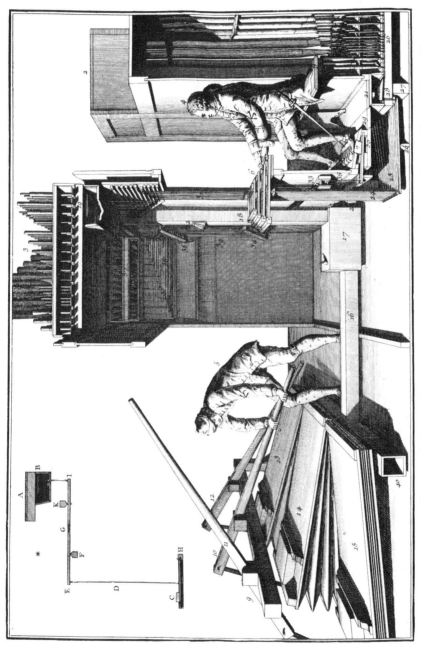

2–3. Plate 52 from Dom Bedos, *L'Art du facteur d'orgues*. CREDIT: Plate 52 from Dom Bedos, *L'Art du facteur d'orgues*, Paris, 1766–70.

was not until the nineteenth century that the time-proven principles were abandoned.

Because of their locations and their tonal dispositions, the various manual sections of the instruments allowed differing degrees of responsiveness to the player's will. The *Récit*, a half keyboard, had only small pipes, as only the top two octaves of the keyboard actually functioned. The *Echo* was also not supplied with pipes for the bass octave. The pallets corresponding to these two special-purpose keyboards could be quite small and the actions relatively uncomplicated. For the *Récit*, with its chest above the *Grand Orgue*, two small rollerboards were needed, while the *Echo* operated with superb efficiency, using a tracker, a backfall, and a little sticker.

On the other hand, the *Grand Orgue*, by far the largest division, required two chests and longer rollers. Even though the action remained quite simple, substantial volume of wind was called for to give full speech to its open 16' and 8' registers, and this imposed deeper key actions and larger pallets. In order to gain full speech from the lowest pipes of the *Montre* 16', the organist played to the bottom of the key dip, the depth of which was determined by the appetites of the wind-guzzling pipes. Thus, when playing on lighter sounds calling for delicacy and tactile ease the player found the *Grand Orgue* less easy to control than the *Récit* or the *Echo*.

The *Positif-de-dos*, because it occupied a separate case placed forward of the rest of the instrument, assumed certain musical tasks of leadership. It had the acoustical advantage, with potential for the most effective articulation. Therefore, to enunciate complex melodic textures and to maintain snappiness in the full sound, the key action was made as direct as possible. To fulfill this musical role, the pallet box was inverted, most of the key channels were arranged chromatically, and backfalls were substituted for a rollerboard. The lowest manual keyboard was always reserved for the *Positif* because it was close by, and the action could be virtually free of complications. Thus the *Positif* became the ideal vehicle for complicated melodic articulations. Only the French savored the touch potential of the *Tierce en taille* or *Cromhorne en taille*.

Of the four manual keyboards, each controlling pipes in the customary location, the *Echo* and *Récit* were the snappiest in their musical response. The *Echo*, relegated to the most remote space available, but still close to the keyboards, spoke with exaggerated attack, and this especially clear articulation could reach the ears of distant listeners. The *Récit*, on the other hand, was given the best location in the main case, high and directly behind the front pipes. It invited the player to embellish with startling declamations and decorative flourishes. For *Dialogues* and pieces with *Cornet* melodies, the *Récit* keyboard was more than a convenience for registration; it had the best touch for such ornamental musical textures.[7] Small wonder that today's players, struggling with spongy tracker actions or the irritating invariability of electro-pneumatic action, flounder in their attempt to discover the "secret" of performing early French ornaments.

The maximum touch-potential of the *Positif-de-dos* was somewhat hampered by its location behind the player. Yet no one quarreled with its forward placement. It was worth the trouble of designing an action that really worked. Similarly, in order to create the marvelous sonority of the 16' *plenum*, certain concessions were required in the *Grand Orgue* action. But what of the stiffer key resistance when these two main divisions were coupled? Not only did coupling make ornaments harder to play, it diffused much of their acuity, because there were two sound sources separated by a considerable distance from each other. Were the *Grand Plein Jeu* and the *Grand Jeu*—the most majestic sonorities in the ancient French organ—supposed to be ornamented to the same extent as the *Petit Plein Jeu*, the *Tierce en taille*, or the *Cornet séparé?*

Touch requirements for coupled manuals were clearly different, as for each key the player was opening two pallets, rather than one. Ornaments were less beautifully articulated. Doubtless the composers were instinctively more aware of these limitations than modern players can be. For instance, when Boyvin wrote a *Grand Prélude à 5 parties, à 2 choeurs*, he recognized the futility of ornamenting a 5-part texture to be played with coupled manuals; yet, for the sections on the *Positif*, flourishes and trills abounded (see Figure 2-4). One should, therefore, not consider it good performance practice to add any ornaments whatsoever to this, or similar works. The same reasoning goes for the *Fond d'orgue* (requiring the manual coupler), a sonority that cries out for sustained, unornamented touch.

But what of the flute dialogues? We find rather complicated ornamental textures, say, in DeGrigny, or even better, in Clérambault's fluffy *Flûtes* from the second suite. The French were disposed to color and sonority, and the sound of coupled flutes was just too appealing to disregard. Luckily, the trebles of flute stops are more beautiful than the basses, and the tiny pipes (stopped 8's are only a foot long at middle C) speak comfortably with very little wind. The pieces for flutes are written with those important facts in mind, and only notes in the soprano range are ornamented, affecting pipes of about six inches or less. The player, aware of the composer's sensitivity to the agreeable range, lightens his touch so that, even with manuals coupled, ornaments can be executed at the very plucking point. Indeed, it may be difficult to hear the difference between the natural chiff of flutes at high pitch and a lightly articulated *pincé*,

7. One could further suggest that convenience in registration may have been no more than an afterthought. Since the sound of the *Cornet séparé* was not distinguishable from the *Grand Cornet*, the reason for adding the *Cornet séparé* may have been simply to provide a key action with very small pallets better suited to the recently adopted virtuoso singing style in the soprano range.

2–4. Boyvin: *Grande Prélude à 5 parties, à 2 choeurs.*

scored by the composer to emphasize a melodic or harmonic stress point.

Returning, finally, to the question of the appropriateness of complicated ornamentation in the *Plein Jeu*, more thought should be given to whether or not a coupler was intended. There is no reason to assume, for instance, that DeGrigny's *Kyrie en taille à* 5, which is clearly scored for the *Plein Jeu* with *cantus firmus* on the *Trompette* in the pedal, should be played on the *Grand Plein Jeu* with coupled manuals. This and similar works have rather complex written-out ornaments and four- or five-part textures calling for wide manual stretches. They might well have been played on the *Positif* or on the uncoupled *Grand Orgue*. Not only would the fingers be better able to play the ornaments beautifully, but quite surely the *cantus firmus* would be heard more clearly. We have no evidence that at Reims the pedal *Trompette* was strong enough to penetrate the coupled *Grand Plein Jeu*. Indeed, judging by the flowery claims of the provincial organ builder Jean de Joyeuse, sufficiently strong pedal *Trompettes* were hard to find. Why else, one wonders, would he have boasted in his contract for the Cathedral of St. Jean, Perpignan in 1688 (to mention only one such claim by de Joyeuse) that "a large-scale pedal *Trompette* will be made . . . very dazzling so as to be heard distinctly when the *plain jeux* is played, even when the 2 manual keyboards are coupled."[8] Perhaps at Reims, in 1700, the pedal *Trompette* was not sufficiently strong to be heard clearly through a coupled *Grand Plein Jeu*. Thus, with the evidence found in De-Grigny's textures and many other examples, we may appropriately suggest that players make more frequent use of the *Petit Plein Jeu du Positif*, especially where the composers have decorated their scores with ornaments. It is noteworthy that among the composers who left instructions for registration, the following mentioned no coupler when describing the *Plein Jeu:* Raison, LeBègue, Nivers, Jullien, and Chaumont. The coupler was included only by Boyvin, G. Corrette, and M. Corrette. This subject deserves more study in the future.

Organist-composers such as LeBègue and DeGrigny understood better than we can today the expressive ranges of the French key actions and the richness of the tonal pallette available to them. The results were so successful that their music can have excitement and verve even when played on inappropriate instruments. But we should not forget that this literature was virtually abandoned and neglected, despite Pirro and Guilmant, for almost 150 years, and revived in a period when articulateness in the key action had not yet been rediscovered. Unless the original function of the early instruments can be preserved as an essential feature of the music itself, there will be less and less possibility in the future that the particular qualities of that complex and beautiful repertoire might be realized.

8. Quoted in N. Dufourcq, *Jean de Joyeuse*, 1958, p. 62.

The renowned LeBègue, organist for the King and consultant to the King's organ builder, put it quite bluntly when he told his public that if they lacked the right stops they should find other pieces to play. Had he thought about it, would LeBègue have gone on to advise those who did not have appropriate key actions to leave out the ornaments?

CHAPTER THREE

Smaller Organs:
Evolving American Attitudes Since 1933

JOHN FESPERMAN

Small Organs and Chamber Organs

THIS DISCUSSION IS CONCERNED with organs of modest size, designed for use in
American churches or similar public spaces, and intended to permit the
playing of as large a segment of the repertoire as possible, and for the support of
congregational singing. This includes organs having one or two keyboards and
pedal, and not more than twenty independent stops.

Chamber organs are excluded, since they are by definition intended for use
in domestic spaces and are meant for the playing of a rather specialized
repertoire, including ensemble music. Chamber or "domestic" organs are
usually distinguished by their mild voicing and limited dispositions, as well as
by the absence of a second manual and pedalboard; a few are designed to be
movable, as well. While some positive organs may also in fact be chamber
organs, the term *positive* properly applies to other than domestic instruments.

Dispositions of sixteen small organs have been arranged chronologically and
placed before the concluding section of the text. They provide a sampling of the
insights and influences bearing on the work of present-day American builders,
beginning with the "Portative" by Walter Holtkamp in 1935.

Size and Sound

Modest size need not imply modest sound or a miniaturized big organ, shorn
of subtlety and color; neither does it justify the sometimes deceptive unification
employed by earlier electric action builders. Traditional organ registers which
blend to form a chorus are just as interesting and more versatile, when well
scaled and voiced, than the "fancy solo stops" which Holtkamp began to
criticize in the 1930s. The organs cited here, some of far less than twenty stops,
give sounding evidence that small instruments can possess versatility and
power, as well as charm.

The success of such small instruments also indicates that economic considerations need not demolish artistic ones in determining the effectiveness of a new
instrument. This is no argument against large organs, of course: one has yet to
meet the builder who does not relish the chance to build an instrument of
monumental proportions for an appropriate space.

Despite limitations of funds or space, an experienced builder will design the
organ to suit the room in which it is heard and to play the music required of it.
"The organ has the right size for the chapel. I dislike to make it larger, even if I
could get twice as much money for it."[1] This declaration by D. A. Flentrop,
referring to a possible design for Fairchild Chapel at Oberlin, epitomizes an
attitude held by responsible organ builders.

Whatever the preference, more than half a builder's work is likely to consist
of small organs. A tally of the work of two established American builders and of
two European ones who exported to the United States yields the following
comparisons for roughly two decades before 1980:[2] of 88 organs exported to this
country by D. A. Flentrop (1954–76), 76 had 20 or fewer stops; from Rudolph
von Beckerath came 51 organs (1956–77) of which 33 had 20 or fewer stops; of
40 organs by Charles Fisk (1958–79), 25 had 20 or fewer stops; of 79 by Fritz
Noack (1962–78), 67 had 20 or fewer stops. While some of these were chamber
or studio instruments, most of these small organs were for churches.

Holtkamp as Advocate

Before the revival of traditional organ building in the United States, most
electric action builders spent their best energies on large organs. Existing
examples suggest that many small instruments were relegated to routine production methods, and one-manual organs seem to have been regarded as little
better than makeshift. A depressing example (despite its elegant case) is the
organ made by Ernest Skinner in 1929 for the Chapel of the College of
Preachers at Washington Cathedral. It has a disposition of three 8' flue registers,
extended to seven over its single keyboard and pedal. Its characterless voicing
renders it incapable of playing any significant repertoire, and its mouse-like
sound stifles congregational singing.

But there was one adamant and articulate exception: Walter Holtkamp. His
pronouncement of 1933 provided a starting point, not only for a new respect
for small organs, but for integrity in organ design in the United States: "The
watchword should be smaller organs, of finer quality, in advantageous positions. They are more of a pleasure to build and certainly more of a pleasure to
listen to."[3] Henceforth, this then relatively unknown builder, with his small

1. D. A. Flentrop to Fenner Douglass, November 21, 1956.

2. According to Opus Lists in Pape, *The Tracker Organ Revival in America* (Berlin: Pape Verlag).

3. Walter Holtkamp, writing in *The American Lutheran* for March 1933.

shop in Cleveland, became the spokesman for a view of organ building as a rigorous art. The time spent in his shop by Charles Fisk (1953–55), and by other would-be builders, is indicative of his influence on the American scene, which was to continue well beyond his death in 1962.

Realizing the most versatile result from minimal resources requires a clear idea of what is essential. Walter Holtkamp, Jr., observes that the motto :*Multum in Parvo*," as used by his father, ". . . extended well beyond the Portatives and was part of his general philosophy. . . . He not only believed '*Multum in Parvo*,' he lived it."[4] A Holtkamp contract dated November 1, 1937 proposed an organ of three manuals and pedal with only sixteen stops for St. James' Church, Cleveland. Of this situation, Walter Blodgett, then organist at St. James', wrote, "I remember at St. James', money was not a concern. Yet we decided to build as small as possible yet having the proper character for each division."[5]

Mechanical action builders seeking to revive traditional practices shared two of the aims recognized earlier by Walter Holtkamp and Donald Harrison: to reinstate traditional principles of design in a technological age beguiled by mass production, and to find a distinctly American enunciation of these principles, without destroying them. In the design of small organs these principles emerge in their most distilled and readily identifiable form.

Holtkamp and Harrison were prevented from fully realizing their aims because they relied on electric action and because some of their designs were too eclectic for unity to be maintained. Walter Holtkamp was especially apprehensive of too much influence from abroad: "We Americans must get back to first principles, forget our fancy solo stops and develop an American organ to suit our own conditions. Europe can be used as a storehouse for information. Europe can help in our organ education just as she helps in the education of our doctors, architects, painters, etc., but she cannot be our model."[6] It remained for the present generation of builders and players to absorb more of what Europe had to teach—not only that factors other than a "classic" disposition are required to make a traditional organ, but also that size is unrelated to quality.

Donald Harrison at the Aeolian-Skinner Company, while best known for his large instruments, also took small organ design seriously (see organ disposition No. III, below). But Holtkamp's insistence on "smaller organs, of finer quality . . ." was unique; it continued to concern him, even as he created important

4. W. H. Holtkamp, Jr., to J. Fesperman, November 8, 1984.

5. Cited in John Allen Ferguson, *Walter Holtkamp, American Organ Builder* (Kent: Kent State University Press, 1979), p. 38.

6. Walter Holtkamp in an address to the Cleveland Chapter, American Guild of Organists, 1932. Cited in Ferguson, p. 86.

large organs, beginning with the Cleveland Museum instrument of 1946. While both Holtkamp and Harrison were acquainted with European work, they did not proceed to adopt mechanical action, nor did they foresee the overwhelming influence which old and new European organs were to have on American players in the future.

European Influences

Soon after World War II, Fulbright scholars and other Americans had opportunities to travel and study in Europe. They were impressed not only with what they saw of surviving old organs, but also with new instruments by builders working in traditional ways. Their urging, along with the favorable exchange rates, made importation of European organs an attractive and afford-able idea. Many of these imported organs went to music schools, and the students who used them were exposed to a high quality of workmanship, as well as to the versatility inherent in instruments designed according to traditional principles. And, most of these organs were of modest size.

While the 1958 Flentrop organ in Harvard's Busch-Reisinger Museum was not the earliest significant imported organ, it had a vast influence, both because of its location in a prestigious university and because of its use for broadcasts and especially recordings by E. Power Biggs. Not all imported instruments could be called small, of course. The Busch-Reisinger organ had 27 stops and the 1957 Beckerath organ for Stetson University had 37. However, most of the imported organs were not large by American standards; the 1957 Flentrop instrument of 16 stops, for the old Chapel at Salem College in North Carolina, is more typical in size (see No. V). Whatever their size, these imported organs enabled players to assimilate the advantages of mechanical actions and of pipes voiced on slider chests on somewhat lower wind pressures.

Because of the first imported organs by such builders as D. A. Flentrop, Rudolph von Beckerath, and Josef von Glatter-Götz of the Rieger firm, north European ideas of design exerted a strong influence on both American players and builders. But the builders forming the cutting edge of the classical revival in this country soon sought a more comprehensive approach: *eclectic* is the wrong word to describe this—*American* is more apt. Their growing interest in English, French, and nineteenth-century American organs is reflected in the dispositions cited here. Often the names given to registers take on an Anglo-American cast, as attitudes to overall design outgrew the influence of only one style. Not all builders leaned in this direction simultaneously, of course, and many excellent American instruments rely on north European instruments as prototypes (see Nos. XII and XIV).

The north European style was least well served by the electric action builders, since traditional voicing was not congenial to electro–pneumatic windchests, and there was often a zealously rigid adherence to *Werkprinzip* dispositions, while other important ground rules (the use of cases, for instance) were
ignored.

Comparing Dispositions

Discussing dispositions without listening to organs often conveys more of the
speaker's preconceptions than the builder's intent. It is essential to understand
that different scalings and voicing techniques produce different sonic results, as
do dissimilar acoustical environments. Nomenclature can also be misleading,
although the builder normally intends a specific relationship between the
name given to a stop and the pipes themselves. For instance, *Prestant* properly
means the open Principal pipes seen in the façade of an organ; *Spindle Flute*
refers to tapered open pipes, whose shape roughly suggests a spindle; *Trumpet*
denotes a reed stop with flared, full-length pipes, and so forth.

When a printed disposition is the only information for envisioning an organ,
the limited information given by stop names can be amplified by noting three
factors: (1) the relationship between the number of higher and lower pitches
throughout the organ, (2) the proportion of open to stopped registers, and (3)
the pitch of the open stop on which the main chorus of the organ is based.
When a given work is performed on an instrument with 8′ and 4′ Principals in
the main chorus, the effect will be quite different from a performance of the
same work on an instrument of the same number of stops, but with only
stopped flute registers at these pitches. Such differences can be seen if not heard
by comparing dispositions Nos. VI and XI (single keyboard) and VII and XV
(two keyboards).

Of the dispositions which follow, Nos. I–IV have electro–pneumatic actions
and are unencased. Nos. V–XVI have mechanical stop key actions and cases,
unless otherwise noted. Comments given with the dispositions recount special
circumstances or other information related to the designs.

I

1935, Walter Holtkamp
"Portative," now in the Smithsonian Institution, Washington, D.C.

Manual:
   Copula   8′
   Principal   4′
   Mixture   III (in a swell)

Casework designed by Richard Rychtarik.

Probably seven of these self-contained organs were made during 1935 and 1936. They represent Holtkamp's attempt to revive mechanical action several decades before other builders in the United States did so. Although modestly priced,[7] these little organs failed to command the attention they deserved. Joseph Sittler has quoted Walter Holtkamp: "This urge to natural, functional expression and the almost complete lopping off of encrustations has marked our work more and more. The Portative is a typical example of this direct design— even in spite of 'no market.' The prevailing market was for the unit organ with two manuals and pedal *but* with fewer pipes than the Portative."[8]

7. The price was $756, according to a letter from Walter Holtkamp to Christ Church, Shaker Heights, Ohio, dated October 10, 1935.

8. Sittler, "A Biographical Sketch of Walter Holtkamp's Evolving Tonal Philosophy." (Holtkamp Archives.)

II

1937, Walter Holtkamp
Emmanuel Lutheran Church, Rochester, New York

Great:
    Principal   8'
    Nachthorn   4'

Swell:
    Quintaton   8'
    Prestant   4'
    Mixture   IV–III

Pedal:
    Soubasse   16'
    Choral Basse 4'

Couplers: Gt/Ped 8', Gt/Ped 5⅓', Gt/Ped 4', Sw/Ped 8', Sw/Sw 16',
              Sw/Gt 16', Sw/Gt 8', Gt/Gt 4'
Slider chests
Electro–pneumatic action

III

1938, Donald Harrison (Aeolian-Skinner Organ Co., Opus 978)
St. Thomas More Chapel, New Haven, Connecticut

Great:
    Principal   8'
    Nachthorn   4'

Swell:
    Bourdon   8'
    Prestant   4'
    Plein Jeu   III

Pedal:
    Bourdon   16'

Couplers: Sw/Gt 8', Sw/Gt 16', Gt/Gt 4', Sw/Sw 16', Gt/Ped 8',
              Gt/Ped 4', Sw/Ped 8'

Donald Harrison wrote to William King Covell (April 5, 1939), referring to a similar small instrument: "I built another one for St. Mark's Church, St. Louis, which even turned out better than the New Haven instrument, due to the fact that it was placed on a little west gallery with all the pipework exposed. The full organ sounds like a large instrument and is entirely satisfying. It has one extra stop, a Spitzflöte on the Great, and there is also an 8′ Flute in the Pedal, of course extended from the Bourdon . . ."[9]

Although he designed many large organs, Harrison's comments suggest not only an interest in small instruments, but a special concern for good placement.

IV

1955, Walter Holtkamp
Massachusetts Institute of Technology Chapel, Cambridge, Massachusetts

Great:
Copula	8′
Dulciana	8′
Principal	4′
Hohlflöte	2′
Mixture	III

Positiv:
Quintaton	8′
Rohrflöte	4′
Principal	2′
Cymbel	II

Pedal:
Quintadena	16′
Gedackt	8′
Choral Bass	4′

Couplers: Pos/Gt, Gt/Ped, Pos/Ped

9. Copy of letter courtesy of Joseph F. Dzeda.

V

This organ and No. VI were imported during the 1950s.

1957, D. A. Flentrop
Old Chapel, Salem College, Winston-Salem, North Carolina

Hoofdwerk:
Gedekt	8'
Prestant	4'
Fluit	4'
Octaaf	2'
Mixtuur	III
Sesquialter	II

Rugwerk:
Gedekt	8'
Roerfluit	4'
Prestant	2'
Quint	1⅓'
Cimbel	I–II
Kromhoorn	8'

Pedaal:
Bourdon	16'
Gedekt	8'
Woudfluit	4'
Ruispijp	III

Couplers: R/H, H/Ped, R/Ped

VI

This organ and No. V were imported during the 1950s.

1958, D. A. Flentrop
St. Andrew's Church, Montevallo, Alabama

Manual:

Holpijp	8'
Quintadeen	8'
Prestant	4'
Roerfluit	4'
Gemshoorn	2'
Cymbel	II

Coupler: Pedal permanently coupled to keyboard

VII

1959, Charles Fisk (Andover Organ Co.)
Redeemer Lutheran Church, Lawrence, Massachusetts

Great:

Stopt Diapason	8'
Principal	4'
Larigot	1⅓'
Mixture	III
Cymbal	II

Choir:

Spitz Flute	8'
Chimney Flute	4'
Fifteenth	2'

Pedal:

Bourdon	16'
(Flute	8')
(Flute	4')

Couplers: Ch/Gt, Gt/Ped, Ch/Ped

This was the first all-new mechanical action organ built by Charles Fisk, who was then President of the old Andover Organ Company.

VIII

1968, Charles Fisk
First Church of Christ, Scientist, Belmont, Massachusetts

Great:
Prestant	8'
Stopped Diapason	8'
Spire Flute	4'
Mixture	III

Swell:
Dulciana (from c)	8'
Chimney Flute	4'
Principal	2'
Sesquialtera	II
Tremulant	

Pedal:
Bourdon	16'
(Gedackt	8')
(Gedackt	4')

Couplers: Sw/Gt, Sw/Ped, Gt/Ped
Mechanical action
Slider chests
Electro–pneumatic stop action

IX

1969, Fritz Noack
Pohick Church, Truro Parish, Lorton, Virginia

Great:
Chimney Flute	8'
Principal	4'
Spitzfloete	4'
Gemshorn	2'
Mixture	IV
Sesquialtera	II

Choir:
Stopped Diapason	8'
Stopped Flute	4'
Fifteenth	2'
Nineteenth	1⅓'

Pedal:
Bourdon	16'
Diapason	8'
Trumpet	8'

Couplers: Ch/Gt, Ch/Ped, Gt/Ped

X

1971, Charles Fisk
Trinity Church, Collinsville, Connecticut

Manual:
Prestant	8'	
Stopped Diapason	8'	(bass/treble)
Spire Flute	4'	"
Fifteenth	2'	
Sesquialtera	II	"
Mixture	IV	
Bassoon/Hautboy	16'	"

Pedal:
Bourdon	16'	
Bassoon	16'	(transmission)
Hautboy	8'	"

Coupler: Man/Ped

XI

1974, Fritz Noack
St. Timothy's Church, Raleigh, North Carolina

Manual:
Principal	8'	
Gedackt	8'	
Octave	4'	
Chimney Flute	4'	
Spitzflöte	2'	
Cornet	V	(from c')
Mixture	IV	
Trumpet	8'	

Pedal:
Subbass	16'	
Principal	8'	(transmission)
Gedackt	8'	"
Octave	4'	"
Chimney Flute	4'	"
Spitzflöte	2'	"
Mixture	IV	"
Trumpet	8'	"

XII

1974, John Brombaugh
First United Methodist Church, Oberlin, Ohio

Great:
Quintadena	16'	
Praestant	8'	
Holpijp	8'	
Octave	4'	
Quinte	3'	
Octave	2'	
Cornet	V	(treble only)
Mixture	IV	
Trumpet	8'	

Echo (Brustwerk):
Gedackt	8'	
Spitzgedackt	4'	
Waldflöte	2'	
Cimbel	II	
Vox Humana	8'	
Tremulant		

Pedal:
Subbass	16'	
Octave	8'	
Octave	4'	
Trumpet	8'	(Great)

Couplers: Echo/Gt, Echo/Ped, Gt/Ped

XIII

1980, Taylor and Boody
Westminster Presbyterian Church, Charlottesville, Virginia

Great:
    Bourdon   16'
    Principal   8'
    Rohrflöte   8'
    Octave   4'
    Quinte $2\frac{2}{3}'$
    Superoctave   2'
    Gemshorn   2'   (prepared)
    Tertia $1\frac{3}{5}'$
    Mixture   IV

Positive (expressive):
    Gedackt   8'
    Rohrflöte   4'
    Octave   2'
    Quinte $1\frac{1}{3}'$
    Zimbel   II
    Regal   8'

Pedal:
    Subbass   16'
    Octave   8'
    Trumpet   8'

Couplers: Pos/Gt (shove), Gt/Ped, Pos/Ped
Tremulant to entire organ
Zimbelstern (prepared)

XIV

1984, Gene Bedient
St. Basil's Church, Tahlequah, Oklahoma

Manual:
Bourdon	16'	
Prestant	8'	(bass/treble)
Rohrflute	8'	"
Octave	4'	
Sesquialtera	II	(treble)
Mixture	III-V	
Trompete	8'	(bass/treble)

Pedal:
Subbass	16'
Trompet	8'

Coupler: Man/Ped

XV

1984, David Moore
Chapel of Mary, Stonehill College, North Easton, Massachusetts

---

Great:
Principal	8'
Bourdon	8'
Octave	4'
Twelfth	2⅔'
Fifteenth	2'
Seventeenth	1⅗'
Nineteenth	1⅓'

Positive:
Chimney Flute	8'
Spire Flute	4'

Pedal:
Bourdon	16'

Couplers: Pos/Gt, Pos/Ped, Gt/Ped

XVI

1984, George Bozeman
Dix Chapel, Trinity Church, New York City

Manual: (All stops divided except where noted)

Violin Diapason	8'	
Celeste	8'	
Chimney Flute	8'	
Principal	4'	
Spindle Flute	4'	
Nazard	2⅔'	(treble only)
Recorder	2'	
Tierce	1⅗'	(treble only)
Mixture	IV	
Cremona	8'	(bass only)
Trumpet	8'	(treble only)
Tremulant		

Pedal:

Bourdon	16'
(Bourdon	8')

Coupler: Man/Ped

This organ has electric stop action and sixteen general pistons, and is entirely enclosed, using a case from an instrument of c. 1911 with the keyboards located, beneath the side gallery, where the organ itself is placed. There is a device for shifting the keyboard division from c'-c♯' to b-c'.

Observations and Conclusions

The increasingly serious attention to instruments of modest size parallels the revival of traditional organ design and cannot be separated from it. The early twentieth-century American view of the organ as an imitation orchestra, denounced by both Walter Holtkamp and Donald Harrison, was discarded by musicians as well. The growing respect for smaller organs was based on a clearer understanding of the traditional repertoire and what resources were really needed to play it. Organ building and organ playing changed together, because builders and players saw the relationship between the integrity of the instrument and its music. Just as Holtkamp relied on such musicians as Melville Smith and Walter Blodgett in Cleveland during the 1930s and '40s and Harrison on Carl Weinrich and E. Power Biggs, so have their successors continued to influence each other.

Building on the insights gained during the Holtkamp years and on lessons learned from earlier organs, the American revival of traditional organ building began in the eastern U.S. with the small new and rebuilt mechanical action organs by Charles Fisk in the late 1950s and early '60s (for instance, No. VII). Because the Fisk shop was hospitable to and learned from other builders, several builders (Fritz Noack, John Brombaugh, and David Moore among them) spent time there before establishing their own shops. The time was right and new builders began to appear, not only in Fisk's New England area, but in other sections of the country as well. In Texas, 1956 saw the completion of a nineteen-stop organ by Otto Hoffman (using pipes supplied by D.A. Flentrop) for the Presbyterian Church in Albany; the following year, Joseph Blanton's influential book, *The Organ in Church Design*, was published by the Venture Press of Albany.

The newer shops usually began with orders for small instruments. But, a new value was placed on small organs. They were viewed as viable musical instruments, rather than truncated ones. This assumed a coherent understanding of the nature of the organ seen in the light of its repertoire. Holtkamp had spoken of "lopping off encrustations," and D. A. Flentrop aimed for "unity in design." This return to essentials is reflected in the dispositions cited here. What emerges is an American attitude toward small organ design, which preserves its integrity without being totally derivative of any one European style or falling into a formless eclecticism. Some main characteristics are as follows:

1. A *return to freer wind supplies and to slider chests with mechanical stop and key actions.*

While Holtkamp did not follow his small "Portatives" of the mid-1930s with more tracker instruments, he did continue to build slider chests in many organs, at least for the Great division. (The Portative now at the Smithsonian

Institution, which was probably the first one made, also has a pneumatic stop action.) Some small organs by later builders retained an electro–pneumatic stop action (see Nos. VIII, XVI) with mechanical key actions, but mechanical stop actions are the norm. Wedge bellows have begun to appear to provide a free wind supply without intervening reservoirs.

2. *An insistence that the organ be placed in a free-standing position within the space where it is heard, and a heightened regard for live acoustics.*

While respectable organ builders have always argued for good locations for their organs, Walter Holtkamp went further. He not only led a crusade for smaller organs; he was adamant that placing the organ in the most favorable location was not merely desirable but essential. This unequivocal requirement was taken up by later builders, who found themselves more able to decline to build an instrument in an unsatisfactory location.

The importance of a live acoustical environment was also better understood, especially as acoustical engineers learned how to provide for both speech and music instead of resorting only to sound-absorbent surfaces.

Organ chambers have all but disappeared, even when a Swell is included. "Smaller organs . . . in advantageous positions" were seen to possess presence and versatility, especially when compared with ". . . organs which growl and roar from the cavernous organ chambers."[10]

3. *An appreciation for the organ case.*

While electric action builders had not regarded encasement as important, even for small organs in free-standing positions (see Nos. I–IV), small instruments imported from the mid-1950s on were usually in traditional cases. The blending and focusing effect of these cases was not lost on American builders, who began to design organs with cases which had acoustical as well as architectural functions.

4. *A new regard for single keyboard organs as viable instruments (see Nos. X, XI, XIV, and XVI).*

5. *The disappearance of combination actions and octave couplers.*

While small electric action organs of the 1930s (see Nos. II and III) usually contained couplers at sub- and super-octave pitches, by the time of the M.I.T. Chapel organ, Holtkamp supplied only normal unison couplers (1955, see No. IV). Both redundant couplers and combination actions found no place in later small traditional organs, beginning with the first imported instruments in the 1950s. (For a remarkable exception, see No. XVI.)

6. *The movement to a* plein jeu *or chorus based on an* 8' *open stop.*

Beginning with the first imported organs, including the sixteen-stop Flentrop instrument for Salem College, the main chorus often did not include an 8' Principal (see No. V). In single keyboard instruments, such a basis for the

10. Walter Holtkamp in *Present Day Trends in Organ Building*, 1940.

chorus was even more unusual (see No. VI). Such designs proved surprisingly versatile, and they had the virtue of not requiring significant ceiling height for the organ case. They most often represent the north European concept of a small organ as a Positive, based on a 4' Principal.

The "positive" approach influenced some American tracker instruments, partly because much of the initial impetus for traditional design came from Holland and Germany (for instance, Nos. VII and IX). Later small organs, including single keyboard instruments are more often based on an 8' Principal (for instance, Nos. X and XI). The broader sound provided by the latter (see also Nos. XIV, XV, and XVI) removes them from the north European positive style and shows a combination of Dutch/German, French, English, and even Italian (see No. XV) influences. A more generous allotment of unison registers, as well as wider scaling and less aggressive voicing (where appropriate to the environment) has accompanied the change.

7. *The increasing use of unequal temperaments and adoption of compasses (usually) of C-g''' for manuals and C-f' for the pedal.*

Although not noted in the sample dispositions, these reduced ranges have become normal and the use of one of several other-than-equal temperaments is found more and more frequently.

Swell:

Bourdon	16'	97 pipes, a "unit"[6]
Violin Diapason	8'	"61 pipes," but must have had 73 pipes to provide the top octave for Great Octave
Stopped Diapason	8'	from Bourdon
Viole d'Orchestre	8'	by duplex action from Great
Vox Celeste [sic]	8'	from tenor C, 49 pipes
Dolce	8'	by duplex action from Great Dulciana
Orchestral Flute	4'	from Bourdon [like Flauto Traverso, a completely misleading name unless the type of pipes changed part way up the compass of the unit]
Twelfth	2⅔'	from Bourdon
Piccolo	3'	from Bourdon
Oboe	8'	61 pipes
Vox Humana	8'	61 pipes

Pedal:

Bourdon	16'	12 pipes, the rest from Great Doppel Flöte
Lieblich Bourdon	16'	from Swell Bourdon
Flute	8'	from Swell Bourdon

6. "Under the Sassafrass Tree," brochure of the Midmer-Losh Company, 1930. A "unit organ" is one in which the ranks of pipes do not have a "home manual" to which they belong but are grouped arbitrarily in swell boxes and made available electrically on all or several keyboards of the instrument and each at several pitches. Thus a few ranks of pipes serve for a great many stops. This is the principle of the theater organ, and it was developed early in the century by Robert Hope-Jones, who also advocated the elimination of mixtures and cultivated extremes of color and loudness in individual registers. Unification requires that there should be as many magnets as there are pipe valves. The term "unified" is applied loosely and by extension to individual registers of an organ that is not necessarily a true "unit organ" when these registers are made playable at a number of different pitches by the use of additional wiring and relay switches. Such stops must be mounted on a "unit chest" with a magnet for each valve. "Duplexing" is a much cheaper method of deriving more than one stop from a rank of pipes, but it is also much more limited in its possibilities. It requires double primary and double stop actions, but not a separate magnet for each pipe valve. Usually a stop is duplexed at the same pitch on a second manual or at the octave. The disadvantage of any kind of borrowing or extension is that each rank cannot be scaled, voiced, regulated, and located to fit a particular use but must be designed as a compromise for several. Another disadvantage occurs when off-unisons or mutations are derived from a unison rank; such stops will not be at the true pitch of the corresponding harmonic but will be tuned to a note of the tempered scale. The cost savings realized by obtaining stops through borrowing varied according to the builder's construction methods.

In its general conception, this was the quintessential American "eight-foot organ" of the period with not a single independent rank above that pitch. What distinguished this ordinary-looking scheme from others like it was its "careful duplexing," designed to extract the maximum flexibility from its ten ranks of pipes without the cost and complication of "unification" beyond the single rank of Bourdon pipes. (Richards had been credited with "the very first octave duplex" in a small organ for the Methodist Church in Pleasantville, New Jersey, built in 1910.) In the Elks' organ, the Great Octave was derived not from the Open Diapason, with which it had to combine, but from the Swell Diapason, which could be regulated independently for better blend and balance. Unless the whole organ was in one swell box, this duplexing also allowed a modicum of the "compound expression" so passionately advocated in Audsley's *The Organ of the Twentieth Century*, which Richards must have devoured when it appeared four years earlier. It was Audsley's idea that by distributing the pipes of one division between two swell boxes, in effect producing two independent subdivisions, one could obtain dynamic shading of one subdivision relative to the other. Richards later called this "the Audsley effect" and claimed that it played no part in his design of the Convention Hall organ.

When he rebuilt and enlarged his residence organ the following year, Richards nevertheless carried the idea of "compound expression" far beyond anything Audsley dreamed of, though the extraordinary layout was probably as much a solution to problems imposed by space and by the necessity of incorporating an existing instrument (a twenty-two stop Estey of about 1916) as it was an attempt to gain dynamic flexibility. The organ spoke from a very deep chamber into a double-cube room forty feet long by twenty feet wide and high.[7] A diagram in the description that Richards contributed to *The Diapason* for October 1922 (page 4) was essential to an understanding of the description (figure 4–1). "Expressive division II" spoke through one set of shutters *into the back* of "expressive division I" and through another set into the back of "expressive division III." With luck, and with the assistance of generous scaling and pressures, the tone found its way through the pipework of those divisions, out the front shutters, through the "unexpressive division," and into the room. By manipulating the four sets of shutters, the organist could mix the sounds of II with either I or III or both, coloring the front registrations with as much or as little of the rear ones as desired and shading the result (or balancing it with the "unexpressive division") with the front shutters. Behind these various shutters were seventeen ranks of flues and eight of reeds at 8' pitch (three of the "reeds" were apparently Haskell "reedless" types; Haskell worked for Estey, though it

---

7. It is illustrated in *TAO* 1945/176. A picture taken in the opposite direction showing his last organ is on page 90 of W. H. Barnes and E. Gammons, *Two Centuries of American Organ Building* (Melville, New York, 1970).

It is not possible to reconstruct the interaction of unification and duplexing in this scheme from the published data, but it clearly provided much opportunity for experiment along those lines and enabled Richards to write with some authority in his first contributions to *TAO*. The issue was a hot one in 1923. Two years earlier, R. P. Elliott, formerly associated with Hope-Jones, had written what he claimed to be the first description of the unit system to appear in any journal (1921/366), though of course unit organs for cinema theaters were already making the fortunes of many builders. The editor of *TAO* was stimulated to organize a two-year debate on the relative merits of unit and straight organs, and in 1923 Richards contributed two of the articles (342 and 602). The first (the fifth in the series) took a selective approach. Soft flutes, dulcianas, gemshorns, and, perhaps surprisingly, reeds might be unified advantageously, but not strings and, above all, not diapasons. One should not expect unification to take the place of mixtures, and although the derived mutations were not in tune with the mixture ranks, the discrepancy was not serious enough to prevent their being combined in the same scheme.[9] Richards almost never used any other tempered mutations than quints (the single exception I have noticed was a few tierces derived from a bourdon unit in his big, semi-theater-type Kimball for the ballroom in the Atlantic City Convention Hall— an instrument in which, however, all niceties of tuning would have been thrown to the winds when the solo-to-solo couplers at 6⅖', 5⅓', and 4⁴⁄₇' were on!). What he did use around that time were tierces and septièmes derived from flat *céleste* ranks; this was a normal practice of Midmer-Losh and may have originated with them (1923/602).

His second article advocated a middle ground between straight and unit organs which he had evidently termed "combination" but which the editor translated into "augmented." His argument took the form of an evaluation of three three-manual stoplists of approximately equal cost—a cost that was verified by the submission of each to three different builders for bids.

	RANKS	STOPS	AVERAGE OF THREE BIDS
Straight	28	26	$14,392
Augmented	23	39	14,046
Unit	11	40-50	15,400

In the "augmented" one, a unit bourdon and a unit dulciana, each at five pitches including 2⅔', supplemented a manual scheme otherwise straight except for a borrowed tuba clarion. Not only was this the cheapest, it was clearly the best in its author's view—a view seconded by "a very well-known organist."

9. Seibert Losh, builder of the High School and Convention Hall organs, was an advocate of derived mutations (1923/602).

Richards continued to unify selected ranks in organs that he considered essentially straight until around 1930, but by the summer of 1932 (after his first German tour), when challenged to write the specifications of an "ideal organ with no restrictions," he produced a no-frills design of forty-three stops with no borrowing or extension of any kind (1933/455).[10] He then, it is true, at the editor's request, fleshed out the scheme with color stops of many kinds, doubling the size in the process and this time introducing seventeen borrows in the pedal (1933/502), but within a year he had repudiated all but a trace of pedal borrowing as well.

The definitive rejection of unification and other kinds of borrowing appeared a year later (1934/560) in a retrospective article entitled "Looking Ahead." Scattered through it are remarks such as "I have tested the combination of the straight and unit and feel that the result is not satisfactory. . . . For me the experiment is ended," "Flexibility is an attractive trap," and, "I stand for the straight organ." So stoutly was this stance maintained that when it came time to print the stoplist of his last residence organ (1946/38), the eight pedal borrows were listed with the couplers so that the summary could read proudly, "B–0" ("Borrows Zero").

In February of the same year that Richards's first articles for *TAO* appeared, *The Diapason* announced the signing of the contract for his first really important organ, to be installed in the Atlantic City High School (February 1923; Richards had been chairman of the school committee before being elected to the state assembly). The next month more details appeared: "Among points of special interest is the complete diapason chorus on low pressure wind, voiced and modeled after the English practice as well as a chorus of high pressure diapasons in accordance with American practice." This is the first we hear of Richards in connection with the "diapason chorus"—what the enlightened 1980s call the "plenum." His experimentation with this most essential department of an organ would continue through the 1920s to its climax in the Convention Hall organ. *The Diapason* of January 1924 reported the opening of the High School instrument (the speed with which Midmer-Losh completed its gigantic undertakings was breathtaking), and in July *TAO* printed a long article on it by Richards himself.

The diapason experiment was "most interesting. Standing side by side, we have the high pressure, high cut, narrow mouth, leather lip Hope-Jones type

10. No frills, that is, except an "ancillary string organ." But the scheme hardly lacked solidity, with its thirty-eight ranks of principal choruses, two full-length 32's and tubas on 30″ of wind. The challenger was Buhrman. In 1934, Richards designed "a classic organ of three manuals" to cost about $15,000 (the same scheme would now cost at least twenty times as much), giving scales and mouth widths (1936/91). It was "given to Mr. Harrison to serve as the basis of much discussion between the two" (1937/48), and may well have influenced Harrison's design for the Church of the Advent, Boston (1936), with which it shares certain salient features including the absence of reeds on the Great and a separate Positive on the Choir.

SCHULZE MIXTURE — V — RANKS — 305 PIPES

3¾" Wind—2/7 Mouths—44 Scale Diapasons Free-Toned

COMPOSITIONS AND BREAKS

CC-G :	15	-19	-22	-26	-29
Tenor G-C :	8	-12	-15	-19	-22
Treble C-C4:	1	- 5	- 8	-12	-15

HIGH PRESSURE CHORUS:

REGISTER	WIND	SCALE	BASS	TREBLE	MOUTH
Diapason	16' 7½"	30	29 Zinc	32 Metal	1/5
Diapason One	8' 12 "	38	17 Zinc	44 Metal	1/5
Diapason Two	8' 7½"	40	17 Zinc	44 Metal	1/5
Octave	4' 3¾"	54	5 Zinc	56 Metal	2/9
Octave	4' 7½"	54		61 M. 7 S.M.	1/5
Fifteenth	2' 7½"	68		61 Metal	1/5
Grand Cornet	VII 7½"				1/5
	8'	42			
	5⅓'	49			
	4'	55			
	3⅕'	60			
	2⅔'	60			
	2²⁄₇'	67			
	2'	70			

As the specification shows, they produced two different choruses, one modeled on the work of Edmund Schulze, a German builder emigrated to England, whose famous five-rank mixture at Armley (near Leeds, Yorkshire), 1869, had all of its ranks to the same scales as the principals. The materials shown in the partial disposition printed above were fleshed out with flutes, a string, and "a newly-designed register developed for Senator Richards, called Wald Horn, intended to bridge the gap between the Gamba and the Diapasons. . . ." There were also "the usual High pressure chorus reeds, at various pitches, in use on both manuals and pedal." Only the Grand Cornet was under expression. All the ranks of this last register could be drawn separately and the whole thing made to speak an octave higher. Richards's design was criticized by Barnes (technical editor of TAO) for leaving too much outside the swell box; he was not impressed by Richards's insistence that enclosure would "take the shine off them" (p. 95). The scales were criticized by Arthur J. Thompson (1928/172),

who also did not like the octave transfer of the Cornet. Richards defended
himself (p. 227), saying essentially that Thompson did not know what he was
talking about and that since the Schulze mixture was "an exact reproduction of
the Mixture at Armley" it was beyond criticism.[13]

By 1927 Richards was not the only American to cultivate the diapason
chorus; the Skinner stoplist of Worcester's Wesley Methodist Church, printed
immediately after Richards's defense on p. 228, had complete choruses on both
Swell and Great, and an Estey in the same year had one on the Great; but
good-sized organs by Pilcher, Kilgen, and Möller had none, or if the names
were there the stops were borrowed.[14] Casavant in Canada had always provided
complete choruses—the large four-manual of this same year for Andover
Academy was a striking example—but the upper work was so apologetic as to
disappear behind the massive 8's. Lip-service was occasionally paid to the
plentiful choruses of the nineteenth-century American builders, but no one
seems to have tried to emulate them.

In April of 1928, Richards published an article on broadcasting the organ,
apparently in response to objections that satisfactory radio reproduction of the
instrument was not feasible. It was full of miscellaneous advice and ended by
citing the success with which the High School organ had been broadcast by
WPG (p. 123). The great news of that year came in October (1928/418 and
445): "$300,000 appropriated for Six-mnual [sic] Organ to be Designed by
Senator Richards." This, of course, was the Convention Hall behemoth. The
report contained many of Richards's arguments for the choice of an organ over
other music-producing engines or organizations. These added up to the in-
escapable fact that the room was simply too big for anything but a very loud
organ to make any impact, much less lead the singing of forty-one thousand
people. "The tentative design proposed by the undersigned is not intended to
produce just a very large organ, but merely to produce an organ adequate to
supply the musical needs of any convention under any ordinary conditions."

13. Much later, Richards wrote of the St. Mark's venture that he had "warned the music committee
previously that it would be much too loud. [It must therefore have been Audsley who suggested the
Schulze design.] Situated in the west-end organ, it almost blew the elderly ladies completely out
of their seats in the rear pews. I recently rescued this mixture and, after recasting its composition
into five breaks, used it as the top of a reed chorus in a 26-stop Swell Organ [in his residence]. I
revoiced the whole thing on more moderate lines, softened all the quints, and placed it in the rear
of the Swell chamber where it successfully forms a brilliant top to a chorus of Willis-type reeds."
His next try with a Schulze mixture was in the Convention Hall, where it was "quite at home,
although still far from being subdued" (1948/81). John Norman has recently pointed out that the
Armley Great, while now "quite shattering," "had no particular reputation before arriving at
Armley church [it had started life as a very large residence organ]; it is the interaction between the
Schulze style and this reverberant and lofty church which creates the magic" (The Organs of
Britain [Newton Abbott, Devon: David & Charles, 1984], page 300).

14. A Skinner very similar to Wesley Methodist was also installed in 1927 in Lake Erie College,
Painesville, Ohio. Perhaps these two organs reflected the arrival of Harrison at the factory.

discussion of why they were *not* there or even the suggestion that they had ever existed. It is conceivable, of course, that he wished to sell himself to the assembled organists as an architect who could be engaged without the risk of designing something that would repel or frighten them, but then would he have been interested in the job himself? He hardly needed the fee.[19]

In April 1931, the first of the long series of articles on German organs appeared. The first tour took place in the summer of 1930 and probably began with a visit to a number of organs in England—Richards does not make the sequence clear except to say that the account did not follow the order of the tour.[20] The German part of his account consisted of four articles on Bavaria, where he benefited from the guidance of Steinmeyer (1931/213, 277, 341, 405). After a report of a recital on the big Walcker in the cathedral of Ulm, the greater part of the first article was devoted to the larger of the two Riepp organs in Ottobeuren Abbey (c. 1760; about fifty stops on four manuals). The instrument was a revelation. Richards could not say enough of the power and brilliance that poured out of this organ on only 2¼″ of wind. The full organ was "simply a blaze of tone," obtained through mixtures and not reeds. "This method of gaining power through the mixtures is one of the impressive things which I learned from the examination of these old organs." Part of the secret was "pipes of rather large scale, with wide mouth and an extremely low cut-up . . . nearly all of pure tin." He found that these mixtures supplied not only power but also foundation through their synthetic resultants. The ensemble "shimmered like silver," but individual flutes and gedeckts also had "a lovely, singing quality all their own. . . . It would be difficult to find a finer solo effect than the Copel, Nazard and Tertz. . . ." Only the trumpets "were too thin and rough to suit our taste." The article ended with a paean of praise:

> The organ shines with the irridescent colors of mother-of-pearl. What an amazing difference when one hears a fine musician like Kobele [the abbey organist] interpret Bach on such an organ! The inner parts and the counter melodies stand out as vividly as the figures in the frescoes overhead. Contrapuntal music becomes alive with a new meaning. There is a vivacity and a sparkle undreamed of. Hooty Diapasons and modern Tibias have no opportunity to obscure the sharply-cut figures with a musical fog.

This from one who, only seven years before, could write, "Where only one Diapason is to be included, our experience seems to indicate that the Hope-Jones

19. The address was reprinted by Barnes in the first edition of his *Contemporary American Organ* (New York, 1930), page 152, but dropped from later ones.

20. *The Diapason* had slightly "scooped" *TAO* with a series of articles on a German tour by Howard D. McKinney beginning apparently in the November, 1930, issue, but they were far more general and the author was apparently unable to bring Richards's expertise to his observations.

type [high-pressure, high-cut, narrow-mouth, leather-lip] is to be preferred"
(1924/406).

The rest of the tour offered nothing to compare with this. At Weingarten
most of the immense complement of mixture work was silent owing to defects
in the action. At Neresheim (1792–96) the mixtures were again responsible for
a "telling ensemble," but the action had been electrified and the new console
was just being fitted. Richards noted that "one can already observe a departure
from the design of the older organs toward the 'eight-foot organ' of today"
because of the greater number of 8' stops and the reduced power of the
mixtures. The rest of the organs were all Steinmeyers, one at Norlingen, two at
Memmingen, and the enormous 208-stop five-manual in the cathedral at
Passau, at the time the largest organ in Europe. In his description of a
Steinmeyer at Memmingen, Richards showed that he still lumped all early
German instruments under one stylistic rubric: Steinmeyer had used "the same
voicing methods common to Silbermann and his predecessors, such as we
found at Ottobeuren and Weingarten." It is not clear that he had yet heard a
Silbermann, much less a Schnitger. The Passau organ was "certainly the finest
modern church organ in Germany," though the ensemble was "much more
like a good English organ than a traditional German ensemble," and from the
gallery, "even darker and more rugged than when heard in the church." Greatly
as he admired German flue ensembles, however, he was appalled by the
method of stop control, unimpressed by the quality of workmanship in mechanical matters, and displeased by the reeds.

The last two articles on this first tour were devoted to England (1931/473,
537). The first begins with a promise to return to Germany, as if Richards had
seen more there than he wrote about. He did not, however, return until the
second series of articles, in 1934. Richards had known Henry Willis III in
America in 1925 (*The Diapason*, January, 1964, 42), and it was Willis who
piloted him about England, concentrating on organs that he had built or
rebuilt. Richards remarked particularly on Christ Church Westminster Bridge,
whose Lewis organ (rebuilt by Willis) contained a diapason chorus in the
Schulze manner (with constant scales), said to have "influenced the tonal
design now affected by a well-known American builder" whom he declined to
identify, reminding the reader of his own pioneering chorus for St. Mark's,
Philadelphia, in 1926. The London example seemed "to gather the whole
organ together and give it a solidity, brilliance, and life which is not present
until it is added to the ensemble." On the other hand, he also admired the
"dreamy," "cantabile" qualities of some early English pipework in St. Anne's,
Soho, which carried him "back into the days of the Restoration—of Pepys,
Addison, Pope, and the classicism affected by the intelligenzie [sic] of the day."

The second English article dealt with some of the greatest organs in the country: Liverpool Cathedral (the largest organ in England), St. George's Hall, Liverpool, and, in London, Westminster Cathedral, St. Paul's, and the Alexandra Palace. It ended with a rapid tour of the north, including a visit to the Schulze organ at Armley and a final evening at Canterbury Cathedral. Writing of Armley as if he had never heard the instrument before, he described the diapason chorus:

> The Diapason on the Great . . . is bright and not so very big in itself, but it blends wonderfully with the whole chorus. The Mixture, made of light-winded, wide-mouthed, low-cut Diapason pipes, is responsible for the tremendous power of the organ. When this Mixture is added to the ensemble, no reeds are really requisite. It adds the brilliancy and power without the reed quality. The ensemble, while big, is crystal clear.

This was the very mixture of which Richards had made "an exact copy," but not a word of comparison. Could his own have come out the loser? The original has not, in any case, been universally admired; Clutton and Niland's *The British Organ* (London, 1963) calls it "devastating" (p. 98), and Harrison spoke of "the absolute confusion when one tried to play polyphonic music" with it (1937/48).

Richards praised all the great organs of Liverpool and London (where he had the advantage of Dupré to demonstrate the instruments in Westminster Cathedral and St. Paul's), but his most enthusiastic raves were reserved for the Father Willis organ of 1875 in the Alexandra Palace—an opinion still sustained by connoisseurs.

The three years between September 1931, when the final article of the first tour appeared, and September 1934, when the first of the new series was published, were important to the development of the American classic organ. Richards took his share of the credit in the foreword to the second series:

> The series of articles upon German organs that I contributed to *The American Organist* several years ago apparently aroused considerable interest. The many letters I received, seeking further light on the subject or containing constructive criticism and comparison with American organ standards, indicated that there was already a searching of hearts—and perhaps some doubt concerning the tonal integrity of the American organ. It became evident that those articles were to influence the trend of American design.

In October, *TAO* printed the stoplist of the 124-rank Aeolian-Skinner for Harvard's new Memorial Church. Here was a rare example of an American organ with complete diapason choruses to mixtures and batteries of chorus reeds at 16', 8', and 4' on each of four manuals with not a single manual borrow. Even more revolutionary was the pedal, which was founded on completely straight choruses of diapasons and reeds, though these were filled out by a number of borrows. In his most hilarious and trenchant article to appear in *TAO* (1933/145), Richards tore into the disastrous "Colonial Baroque" interior of the church, "as dead as a Boston codfish," in which "all of the high hopes, loving care, and extraordinary skill" of the builder had been "completely ruined by the most abominable bad taste and deliberate disregard of the natural laws of acoustics." The instrument, for which Richards was full of praise, sounded its best only *in* the chambers; out in the church, it sank into insignificance. "No organ could possibly overcome the premeditated annihilation of all musical sound such as has been achieved here." But nevertheless it supplied the opportunity for which Richards had been hoping "of late years" to demonstrate the superiority of the classic ensemble in organ design.

> That the result at Harvard is disappointing is the best argument in its favor. What would have happened had the ordinary "American" design been used? The effect would have been nothing but an indefinable roar without any musical quality whatever.

It was in this room that Charles Fisk would install his first four-manual instrument over the vigorous protest of a few of Harrison's admirers, including Richards.[21]

If 1927 was the year of the diapason chorus, 1933 was the year of the independent pedal. It was Richards who provided the original impetus for this advance, according to William King Covell (1934/269). At least five articles, pro and con, appeared in 1933, and there were more the following year. Three—naturally pro—were by Richards, who sought to prove that straight pedal divisions were, if not actually cheaper, only negligibly more expensive than augmented ones. His method—sending specs. out for bids—was precisely the same as he had used in 1923 to prove the opposite: that augmented organs were both better and cheaper than straight ones (1933/499, 547; 1934/43). Harrison (1933/549) chimed in with Richards's "excellent article" and described the sixteen-rank pedal of his organ for All Saints, Worcester, then being built, without, however, discussing costs. Barnes defended the old augmented pedal (1933/515 and 614) and the editor mediated.

Two other events of importance for the American classic organ took place in 1933. One was the appointment of Harrison as technical director of Aeolian-Skinner to replace Skinner himself. The company ran a two-page sketch of Harrison and his accomplishments, mentioning Princeton University (opened

21. It appears to have been William King Covell who chiefly enlisted Richards's support for the protest movement; the correspondence is in the Boston A.G.O. Library.

October 13, 1928) as first among the instruments to show his influence (438-9), and the same issue printed an address by Harrison to the National Association of Organists, consisting mostly of an unusually clear account of the change of taste in English organ building from the mid-nineteenth to the early twentieth centuries, but incorporating the tribute to Richards quoted above and rejecting any attempt to copy old organs. The other event of 1933 was the installation by Holtkamp of the first twentieth-century American *Rückpositiv* in the Cleveland Museum to help fit the existing Skinner organ for a complete Bach series (597). Arthur Quimby, the organist, and perhaps Melville Smith, his assistant, seem to have been the moving forces behind this innovation; but here again, Richards had anticipated them with his 1925 article on the Choir organ.[22] Also in 1933 a pair of articles on Silbermann organs by Oscar Schminke appeared (pp. 249 and 301). Not until the end of the second did one learn that behind the technical information stood Richards; the articles were based largely on Rupp and Flade, both of whose books he had come to know in Germany and had suggested to the author and to Buhrman.

The second series of articles on Germany began with a long foreword in which Richards tried to lay down the differences between the classic and romantic organ—a terminological distinction, by the way, which is so familiar to us that it is hard to realize how new it was in the early 1930s as applied to organs. Evoking Bach and Schumann, and a Greek temple versus the Alhambra, he defined the classic organ as one in which every stop was designed to play a part in the chorus, to augment and enrich the whole, while it conceded to the romantic organ "the individualistic voices—the so-called orchestral colors—the vague, atmospheric, indeterminate tones. . . . Like an Italian opera it disdains a harmony of the whole. Each voice sings by itself with little regard for its neighbors." The classic design was to be preferred because "the overwhelming proportion of organ music" was written for it, though into it should be integrated "those modern achievements in tone color that are suitable to give adequate expression to modern music."[23]

The materials for the new German articles were gathered in two trips to England, Holland, and Germany, the first in September and October of 1931 and the second in October and November of 1933, immediately following on Richards's stint as acting governor of New Jersey. The 1931 visit was made in company with Steinmeyer; the 1933 "adventure" included Henry Willis III and

22. In an address to their convention in Cleveland in 1932, Richards had advised the American Guild of Organists "to give up playing the organ works of Bach," for lack of the right instruments as well as for ignorance of a properly lively playing style (1935/17).

23. 1934/403. Subsequent articles were on pp. 453, 499, 547, and 1935/13, 55, 106, 145. For Richards, the "romantic organ" was the American organ of the period before and after the first World War—the orchestral, eight-foot organ—and not the great European instruments of the mid-nineteenth century by Willis, Ladegast, Walcker, and Cavaillé-Coll.

for a time, Arthur Poister, as well as Steinmeyer. The foreword included character sketches of his two builder-companions and a rather labored and inconclusive analysis of the impact of their opinions upon his own, one that reveals perhaps more clearly than anything else the somewhat defensive pride with which he viewed his own expertise vis-à-vis that of distinguished professionals. In Holland, though rushed, he was able to hear, and to varying degrees study, five old organs and one from the nineteenth century. The accounts are cursory, and none of the instruments seems to have made any very deep impression. Of the ones now famous, he saw only Gouda.

In Germany, it was a different story. He was able to hear and study the Totentanzorgel in Lübeck's Marienkirche and the smaller organ of the Jakobikirche, both ancient instruments incorporating the work of several builders, including Stellwagen. There were also five Schnitgers: Cappel, Lüdingsworth, Stade, Steinkirchen, and Hamburg; one instrument by an unknown builder in Altenbruch; six Silbermanns: Rötha (two), Freiberg, and Dresden (three); two putative Bach consoles at Arnstadt and Leipzig; and thirteen modern organs, of which he had praise only for the Steinmeyers and a Ladegast in the Nikolaikirche, Leipzig. He also heard several examples of old pipework in later instruments (for example, Arnstadt and Lüneburg) and evidently more Bavarian organs of which descriptions were promised but never printed (1935/149).

Whether from his companions, from reading, or from direct experience, Richards had learned much since his earlier German articles. Gone was the naïveté and confusion, and in their place were perceptions completely new to American writing on organs, sometimes anticipating by thirty years their assimilation into ordinary thought and practice. He now saw the differences between the styles of Schnitger, Silbermann, and, though he only intimated it (1935/149), the south German builders. His summing up of Schnitger is an example of his writing at its most eloquent:

> I would not advocate the reproduction of the Schnitger organ as the ideal organ. It lacks refinement. But it does have a lusty virility, a saltiness that smacks of the sea upon whose shores it was born. It has an integrity, a blunt honesty, a straightforwardness that inspires respect and understanding. It achieves power and clarity in rhythm with the musical compositions that it interprets. It is never hard but it is uncompromising. It does not leave one in doubt. It is capable of saying what the composer had to say but it has none of the romantic organ's ability to conceal his inspirational deficiencies in a musical mist (1934/457).

On the other hand,

> There is a sophistication about the Silbermann that betrays its Latin influence [earlier he had given an account of Casparini and his possible influence on the Silbermanns (1935/57–8)]. It is smoother, more subtle in its build-up. Unquestionably it is the last word in an organ built solely to express contrapuntal music" (1935/149).

Silbermann was the "basis upon which to reconstruct the classic organ." And this in spite of the fact that "the Schnitger organ and not the Silbermann organ was the Bach organ." But his favorite of all the German organs was the Totentanz organ. "Clear and incisive, but never screaming, this organ sings its way into your hearts because of its straightforward honesty, its devotion to an ideal, and its message for the future" (1934/502; the instrument fell to Allied bombs in 1942).

As one might imagine, he had much to say about the independent pedal divisions with full harmonic development in the North German instruments, and he often remarked on the lovely metal Gedeckts to be found in these organs. He also perceived, though he did not insist upon it, the differentiation of pitch between divisions—Great at 16', Positive or Oberwerk at 8', and Brustwerk at 4'—probably the first adumbration of the idea of the *Werkprinzip* in American thinking (1934/500, 548). He did not advocate placing the Positive behind the organist, perhaps to avoid appearing to mount the Holtkamp bandwagon, but he did argue strongly for bringing pipework out where it could be heard, half a year before Holtkamp would describe his pioneering organ for St. John's, Covington, Kentucky, with its fully exposed Great and Pedal (1935/269).[24] Richards began with a demand that a "crusade for the elimination of all kinds of organ chambers must be inaugurated at once" (1934/548), but then went far beyond Holtkamp or anyone else for the next twenty years in pleading that "the beautiful organ-cases of Lübeck should have their counterparts in America as a matter of regular routine." The most surprising of all his observations, however, was that "played in favorable keys, an organ does sound better if tuned in unequal temperament" (1935/107). He made an effort to inform himself on matters of tuning by studying early German writings on the subject (he does not say which) and decided, apparently for himself, that Silbermann's tuning was "a compromise between un-equal [by which he probably meant mean-tone] and equal temperament."[25]

24. Pioneering for the thirties, perhaps; in the nineties Jardine had made a handsomely arranged and totally exposed organ in the gallery of St. George's church, New York (cover and frontispiece of *TAO* for August, 1934); it was destroyed by Austin.

25. In 1943 N. Lindsay Norden would suggest that mean-tone tuning was necessary to the flavor of the old classic organs (1943/85).

In spite of these many acute and, for the mid-1930s, revolutionary perceptions, we must not imagine that Richards enjoyed an unobstructed view of the future of American organ design. To the end he resisted the idea that anything was to be gained by a return to slider chests and tracker action. When, following the publication in 1938 of an article by Walter Holtkamp advocating slider-chests (1938/136; 1939/13) TAO ran a series of "viewpoints" (1939/61, 94, 131, 157, 159, 205), Richards contributed one of his longest and most tightly reasoned articles, entitled "The Sliderchest's Many Serious Defects" (1939/119), in which he pointed out first that Holtkamp's chest was not, in any case, the traditional pallet-and-groove type and then adduced various phenomena of fluid mechanics to prove that the traditional kind had a deleterious effect on pipe speech. One of the speech defects it was liable to foster was what later became the cherished discovery of the 1950s and was lovingly cultivated not only by organ builders but eventually by their electronic competitors: "chiff."[26] His arguments against tracker action were those of any sensible American in the 1930s who simply had no experience with what a well-designed mechanical action in good condition could do for organ music under the fingers of a player trained to profit by its advantages. If he faltered in his perceptions it was by failing to see that the playing that occasionally so fired his enthusiasm in Germany—for example, Walter Kraft's on the Totentanz organ—was as much the product of the physical interaction between player and instrument as it was of pipe measurements and mixture composition. Melville Smith was one of the first exceptions to the "sensible American" viewpoint (1936/347), and Ochse cites the stir caused by Gilman Chase's observation in the June 1940 *Diapason* that playing might be more musical on tracker action.[27] Richards did not respond, so far as is recorded.

Richards also had little sympathy for the "artist-builder" concept—the idea that an organ was an integrated art-work in which pipes, mechanism, and structure were inextricably interlinked and should issue from the mind and (figuratively) the hands of a single master artisan (1964/12). After all, he could hardly be expected to encourage a species[28] whose proliferation would spell the extinction of the organ architect. He believed strongly in the need for a disinterested expert to mediate between the organ builder and the purchasing committee—the organist, he felt, should have nothing to do with the design of the instrument he was to play (1943/203).[29] The true artist was the architect

26. Of the Nason Flute in Ernest White's residence organ Richards wrote that it "spits like an outraged cheetah." He could not see why some "foreign experts" cultivated these "speech imperfections" (1943/81).

27. *The History of the Organ in the United States*, p. 412. As late as 1953. Harrison would argue against slider chests and tracker action (*The Organ Institute Quarterly*, Summer, 1953, 9).

28. Of which Charles Fisk was one of the greatest examples!

29. See also 1929/274, 276, 410.

who planned every detail of the instrument with due regard for budget, space, and musical needs over the long run. This might on occasion be the proprietor of a firm—he allowed Henry Willis III this honor—but then of course he would not be disinterested. In practice, of course, Richards did not let this position interfere with his admiration for Harrison (partly, one suspects, because of his own contributions to Harrison's thinking); and indeed, after daily exposure to Steinmeyer's point of view during his first German tour, he came perilously close to decrying the whole genus of organ experts: "If the German builder surmounts the manufacturing problem [heavy taxation and rigid government supervision], he still has to contend with the 'organ architect' in its most virulent form" (1931/342).

The account of the German tours came to an end with article number eight (1935/145) and the promise, never fulfilled, of more. The articles went on, nevertheless, through number fifteen (1935/413). Richards had done nothing less, it appears, than to write a full biography of Bach—one directed especially at organists—for that 250th anniversary year of his birth. The remaining German articles were excerpted and condensed by Buhrman from the "complete manuscript," which according to an editorial note (1935/196) had been placed at TAO's disposal.[30] Even this series broke off, however, with Bach's visit to Buxtehude and a note, "to be continued." Buhrman believed Richards "to be one of America's outstanding authorities on Bach" (1933/154). "He'll argue all week on Bach," said Buhrman. In a piece weighted with leaden Victorian humor recounting a stay on Richards's island in Moosehead Lake in Maine (in company with Skinner, Poister, Barnes, and Steinmeyer, who was in the country to install a big organ in the Catholic Cathedral of Altoona, Pennsylvania) Buhrman had Richards delivering an impromptu lecture "on Bach, Bach's choral music, Bach's organ music, Bach's views, Bach's spare time, Bach's lack of a job during the last twenty years of his life [sic], and the general depression that has resulted from too much of Bach's organ music" (1931/566). It is abundantly evident from Richards's writings that he devoured everything he could hear or read about Bach and that he knew not only the organ music but also (long before he could have heard many of them on records) "the instrumental pieces, and the marvelous, almost incredible combinations of voice, chorus, and orchestra." These, he often reminded his readers, vastly outnumbered and often outshone the works for their instrument (1933/155, 1935/16). One of his startlingly prescient observations occurred in a review of a Philadelphia performance of "O ewiges Feuer," BWV 34a, by Alexander McCurdy (1936/25). Regretting that a gamba had not been used in preference to a solo cello, he wrote, "the modern orchestra has not altogether gained by the elimination of some of the older strings." And this in 1936, only three

30. I have been able to find no evidence that the book was ever published.

months after Challis had announced the revival of the harpsichord to the
readers of *TAO* (1935/380).[31] No less surprising was his name on an article
entitled "Bach's Art of the Fugue" (1942/107), one of the few serious and
reasonably informed discussions of a musical composition ever to grace the
pages of *TAO*—and this by a lawyer whom its technical editor (Barnes) once
characterized as "a political boss" (*The Diapason*, January, 1964). The Senator's
knowledge of music and music history was not inferior to that of many who
have taught the subject and his ability to write about it, far superior.

∿

In 1927 Richards had written, "There is a Renaissance on the way in organ
design" (228). In 1935 he felt able to declare that "the Renaissance of the
American organ has arrived" (236). The revolution he led had succeeded and
now needed only to be consolidated and refined. With this victory came a shift
of emphasis in his articles (which had not yet reached their halfway point in
volume or total timespan), away from discovery and evangelizing and toward
the critical, the analytical, and the didactic. The occasion for his declaration
was a critical assessment of the new three-manual Harrison organ in Trinity
Church, New Haven—another tragically dead room. In spite of the "un-
friendly conditions," low pressures and brilliant upperwork had helped produce
"another milestone in the progress of the classic organ in America" (1935/235).
The article constituted a kind of quiet acknowledgment that the leadership in
the march toward the American Classic Organ had now passed to Harrison. It
began with a review of the "remarkable revolution in organ design" of the last
decade, in which his own role was passed over in silence and all attention was
directed to the transformations wrought by his friend. From this time on, a
substantial portion of his articles were reviews of new Aeolian-Skinner organs:
Church of the Advent, Boston (1936/304), Harvard's Germanic Museum
(1938/89), Columbia University and the Temple of Religion at the New York
World's Fair (the latter a failure) (1940/139, 171), Curtis Institute (1942/11),
Ernest White's private organ (1943/81) and his big one in St. Mary the Virgin,
New York (1943/105, 129, and 152), the Boston Symphony organs in Tangle-
wood and Boston (1940/299, 1949/294, and 1950/17), and one or two others.
In all of these his praise for Harrison was unstinting, though he did not hesitate
to say when he disliked some detail.

Two additional Aeolian-Skinners were designed by himself. One was his
immense residence organ (1946/79 and 1948/112–13), burned, alas, in 1958
along with his home and bathing establishment, and the other was a modest
instrument for the Methodist Church in Millville, New Jersey, designed by

31. The same year also saw an event at the opposite end of musical taste: the announcement of the
Hammond Organ.

him probably in 1946, and with whose rebuilding he occupied himself in his last years, seeking to preserve as much as possible of the work of Harrison, who had died in 1956 (1947/286; 1964/12).

The other principal facet of his writing from 1937 on was didactic: an attempt to educate the readers of TAO in some basics of organ design. An introduction to the subject of mixtures (1937/119) was followed eleven years later by a five-part series entitled "Mixtures—The Conclusion" (1948/13, 47, 79, 111, 143). In 1944 (256) there was a brief article on "Principals or Diapasons," and in 1941 another five-part series on chorus reeds appeared, written in collaboration with Harrison. The first four of these had actually been completed in the summer of 1938, the last was new.

In February, 1937, Buhrman wrote an article on "Clarity and its Development." Although principally devoted to an appreciation of the accomplishments of Harrison, it bestowed credit where credit was due.

> The Hon. Emerson Richards started the clarified-ensemble idea. He had no factory to put out of business by arguing for something nobody wanted to buy, so he argued; he tried to sell the clarified ensemble to all of us.

Burhman then went on to quote Richards's own summing up:

> "Because I realized that the organ as we were building it was not a real musical instrument I turned to the English recipes, and in 1923 put my first Diapason chorus into an organ—in the Atlantic City High school. These English recipes were an improvement, but they were not right. My 1925–1929 experiments with harmonic reenforcement did not furnish the answer. Then just in time to save the Auditorium organ I found the answer was in the mixtures. This was confirmed by a German visit in 1930 and justified by the Atlantic City Great in 1931.

> The Great is really what started it. It was the demonstration of a theory. When Mr. Harrison heard it he said, referring to a noted English organ [Liverpool Cathedral?] 'That is what they hoped for, but it didn't come off.' I am probably an impossible musician (I belong to the union) but I'm Welsh-Quaker enough to be stubborn about my opinions. So when the whistles wouldn't play music, I dug into their innards to find out why. Between bluster and Bach, I chose Bach. I believe the organ should be built to play music, not foment camp-meeting emotions."

Richards's love for music and his knowledge about it never failed to inform his thought about organ matters. It was this that ultimately distinguished him from other writers. If Audsley, the other great dilettante organ architect and evangelist,[32] cared a whit for the music that his big dream-schemes were meant to play, there is no evidence of this in the five hundred pages of his *Organ in the Twentieth Century*. For sheer literary talent, Richards also stood head and shoulders above his fellows. To be sure, his articles vary greatly in the quality of their finish. I suspect that they were often dictated, and went through the publishing process with greatly varying amounts of attention from him and from Buhrman, who, to all appearances, cared nothing for the niceties of text-editing. But when Richards took care, as he did with the Bach biography and certain other articles, like the one on slider chests, there was plenty of polish at little or no cost in verve. Candor—regarding changes of mind, the sources of new ideas, the existence of other seekers along the same paths, the possible value of opposing views—was not a notable characteristic of his utterances, nor would one expect it in one whose principal occupations were law and politics. He seemed also curiously indifferent to French organs, though he clearly had been to France. The big Gonzalez in Rheims cathedral was dismissed along with French elevators and plumbing (1939/123), Cavaillé-Coll was often invoked but not often aptly; and I have found the name of Clicquot but once in Richards's writings. But whether or not without him American organ building would have attained its present state of grace, as embodied in the instruments of Charles Fisk and those he trained, it was first set upon the path toward the way-station we call the American Classic Organ by the Honorable Emerson L. Richards, New Jersey State Senator from Atlantic City.[33]

32. And the designer of the instrument that became the nucleus of that other "world's largest organ," only a two-hour drive from Atlantic City.

33. I never knew Emerson Richards, though I visited Atlantic City in 1943 and even heard the big organ. But if he read his March 1945 issue of *TAO*, he would have known me as the author of the most egregious errors about the divisions and manuals of organs—errors I would not have made if I had been born soon enough to read his article on the Choir organ in 1925.

4-2. Summer, 1931. Emerson Richards at his island in Moosehead Lake. Back row: Hans Steinmeyer and Ernest M. Skinner. Front row: Richards, Arthur Poister, and William H. Barnes.

CREDIT: The American Organist, 1931, p. 567.

4-3. Christmas Day, 1943. Front row: Richards with his bride. Standing (left to right): G. Donald Harrison, best man; the bride's sister; Mrs. Harrison; Mrs. T. Scott Buhrman; a friend of the bride; and the bride's brother.

CREDIT: Mrs. Richards.

4–4. Emerson Richards with the boot of the 64' Diaphone at Atlantic City, one of only two full-length 64's in the world.

CREDIT: Barbara Owen and David Junchen.

CHAPTER FIVE

The Wellesley Organ's "Breath of Life" As It Affects the Music of Buxtehude

OWEN JANDER

PART OF CHARLES FISK'S GREATNESS lay in his ability to span wide gaps. He was both scientist and artist, pragmatist and dreamer, historian and prophet. All of these characteristics of Fisk's makeup found simultaneous expression in his fascinating essay, "The Organ's Breath of Life," which was first published in *The Diapason* in 1968 and is reprinted in the second volume of this memorial publication.

Fisk's premise in that article—"The organ has to *seem* to be alive"—has become famous in our time. My own favorite passage in "The Organ's Breath of Life," however, occurs in the middle, where Fisk says, "The whole subject of the wind is fascinating and elusive, and this writer makes no pretense at a thorough understanding of it. He can, however, put forth questions which, either in this country or abroad, might provoke further thought." The six questions which then follow are a remarkable demonstration of the old rule that the people who arrive at the best answers are those who ask the best questions. Again and again in his efforts to answer his own questions, Fisk is concerned not merely with technical matters of organ construction but with the end result: the effect of the "organ's breath of life" on the *music*.

In the seventeen years since the publication of that highly controversial article by Charles Fisk, three marvelous organs which can be pumped by calcants have been built in America: the two-manual instrument for Fairchild Chapel at Oberlin College, by John Brombaugh, dedicated in 1981; the three-manual instrument for Houghton Memorial Chapel at Wellesley College, by C. B. Fisk, Inc., dedicated also in 1981; and the four-manual organ for the chapel at Holy Cross College, by the firm of Taylor and Boody, dedicated in 1985. (There may be others of which I have not heard.)

These three instruments represent strikingly different conceptions—evident in the stoplists, the tuning systems, and the acoustical spaces for which they were designed. But these instruments also breathe very differently. The differences are enough to make us cautious about making generalizations concerning historical wind systems. This is an important caveat to the reader of the following pages.

In these pages I shall discuss various passages in the organ music of Buxtehude as they are affected by the wind system on the Fisk organ at Wellesley College. I have observed these effects during my many hours of service as calcant during chapel services and organ recitals at Wellesley. It is important that the reader be aware that I am describing the behavior of a single instrument—and a modern one, at that (albeit an instrument which in many ways seeks to get close to history).

Nonetheless, our experience at Wellesley is sufficient to allow us to ask an important question. To what extent are these effects—all of which involve unstable wind—mere accident, and to what extent are they consciously built into the music itself? Built into the music, to be sure, by an organist-composer who understands such an early wind system, and knows how to manipulate it to artistic ends.

Regular Wind

The normal tone of the Wellesley organ is quite regular. Music that has an even texture draws wind from the bellows in a steady stream. If one occasionally hears some unevenness, the cause is merely human error: the calcant is not attending to his (or her) job.

The Wellesley organ can be pumped by electricity, in which case the modern blower feeds into a single bellows, the second bellows remaining deflated and shut off. When a calcant pumps the organ, much of the time the outflow valves of both bellows are open, and there is a subtle intercommunication of the air in the two bellows. In most musical situations I hear no difference in the sound when the electric blower is on, or when the instrument is powered by a calcant. Some organists, however, insist that they can detect a difference at the keyboard. As Mireille Lagacé worded it, when the blower is turned on, the sound "flattens out."

The Tremulant

The Wellesley organ has only one tremulant device, affixed to the main wind duct on its way from the bellows to the instrument itself. Although this tremulant affects all three manuals, it affects each in a different way. The Oberwerk is affected only slightly—so slightly that when an organist performs on the Oberwerk *plenum* with the tremulant on, most listeners are unaware of that fact. Again quoting Mireille Lagacé (who performed a Byrd fantasia on the Oberwerk, with tremulant), the tremulant in this case only adds a subtle warmth to the *plenum* that helps offset the rather unreverberant acoustics of Houghton Chapel.

On the Wellesley organ, the Brustwerk is only slightly more responsive to the tremulant. The Rückpositiv, on the other hand, is throbbingly affected by this device.

In 1968 Fisk wrote, "In the Rückpositivs of some old organs, where the wind ducts are particularly undersized, the wind supply gives actually a little *port de voix* at the beginning of each note." The Wellesley organ has one of those "undersized" wind ducts leading to the Rückpositiv—and that is one of the most fascinating features of this instrument. On this organ, for example, if one plays an ornamented chorale melody on the Rückpositiv, accompanied on the Oberwerk Spillpfeife—and with the tremulant drawn—the two sounds are in phase with one another, but in the accompaniment the tremulant is very gentle, in the solo voice very emphatic.

The Wind-Sensitive Rückpositiv

Because of its long, "undersized" wind duct, the Rückpositiv at Wellesley is responsive not just to the impulses of the tremulant device, but to every irregularity in the total wind supply. For the organist unfamiliar with such wind-irregularity, this unsteadiness can create embarrassing problems. For the organist who understands the instrument, however, this unsteadiness permits new opportunities for expressive music making.

Take, for example, the final phrase of Buxtehude's setting of "Ach, Herr, mich armen Sünder." Assume here that the melody is being played on the Rückpositiv, the left-hand part on either the Spillpfeife or the 8′ Principal of the Oberwerk.

"Ach, Herr, mich armen Sünder"   BuxWV 178

In chorale settings of this type, Buxtehude is careful how he writes active lines in the pedal part under sustained notes in the melody—for the simple reason that an active pedal line (if the registration includes a wind-gulping 16′ sub-bass) will shake that long note in the melody. In this passage, however, such a shaking of the notes in the solo part seems to be Buxtehude's intention. The effect is so poignant, so beautiful, that one is reluctant to dismiss this as accident—the strange behavior of an instrument with a particularly unstable wind supply. In a case like this I am inclined to give the composer credit for knowing exactly what he was doing.

Undulated Wind

In Buxtehude's organ music one often finds passages like the following, where repeated patterns draw on the wind supply in waves, sometimes extending over several measures:

Praeludium in C   BuxWV 136

Unlike the situation with the tremulant stop, where the undulations of the organ tone are induced mechanically, in passages of this sort the texture of the music itself sets the wind system pulsating. (Of course, on a wind-sensitive pipe organ such pulsations can be maximized or minimized by the performer through touch, and by choices of registration.)

Another instance of this effect follows:

"Wie schön leuchtet der Morgenstern"   BuxWV 223

If this passage is played on the Rückpositiv at Wellesley (especially with a not-too-heavy registration), the activity of the bass line is reflected in a tremolo in the suspended thirds of the treble lines. The result is exquisite.

Appulsive Wind

A more extreme application of this principle of drawing on the wind in uneven amounts occurs in passages where very full registrations are appropriate. Here the wind is drawn on in great gulps, especially evident since the large pipes of the pedal division are involved.

Praeludium in D Minor   BuxWV 140

In the most dramatic climaxes this "bounce" in the organ sound can be intensified, of course, by coupling the Rückpositiv to the Oberwerk.

The Recoil Factor of the Bellows Levers

A particularly interesting discovery that we have made at Wellesley involves the role played by the bellows levers in certain loud passages that involve this "appulsive wind." The two long levers on which the calcant places his or her weight (alternately inflating each of the two pairs of bellows) are themselves very heavy. When the organ is being played with a particularly full registration these levers move up rather quickly, and when a chord is suddenly released the levers stop abruptly. Such is the effect of inertia that a series of quick, loud chords will induce a slight recoil and set the levers to bouncing—this, in turn, affects the pressures in the wind supply. The result is an effect that can be artistically controlled, and which, in a passage such as the following, can be gripping in its excitement:

Praeludium in D   BuxWV 139

The Expressive Use of the Wind System
As an Element of Musical Structure

In some instances in Buxtehude's organ music, the dramatic exploitation of flexible wind is so striking as to persuade the listener that this is a part of the composer's structural plan. A favorite example at Wellesley is the Toccata in F Major, BuxWV 157. In the exposition of the fugue with which the toccata concludes, as the subject is answered in the second voice Buxtehude introduces a singularly lively counter-subject. This counter-subject features an eighth-note anacrusis, then two leaps of a third, each of which is reiterated. (In this quotation the *Luftpausen* are my own.)

Toccata in F   BuxWV 157

In the last twenty measures of the fugue, the subject assumes a secondary role and Buxtehude builds up his counter-subject in a four-voice stretto. The first time this occurs, the F major triad is outlined, but then lingers on the dominant:

Toccata in F   BuxWV 157

In this stretto, as the voices enter one after another the reiterated notes—which now become chords—set the whole wind system pulsating. (This effect, we have learned at Wellesley, is maximized if the calcant has inflated both bellows just as this passage is about to occur—thus allowing for maximum "lever recoil.")

Ten measures later, Buxtehude repeats this wonderful passage, this time up on a B-flat triad moving to the final tonic pedal point.

If at this marvelous climax—just as this stretto begins to pile up—the organist couples the Rückpositiv to the Oberwerk and adds the 16′ Posaune to the Pedal, the pulsations of the wind system are greatly intensified. The excitement of this passage is eloquently revealed by the behavior of the bellows levers, which dance with a strange, stilted grace. Whenever I hear this passage—especially when I experience it from the calcant's ladder at Wellesley—I think, "Now that's what Charlie Fisk had in mind when he talked about 'The Organ's Breath of Life!'"

And I add, "This *must* have been part of Buxtehude's plan."

Out of respect for history, however, a caveat is in order. The organ on which Buxtehude performed at the Marienkirche in Lübeck no longer exists—nor do we have much information regarding its winding system. Are the observations that we make about Buxtehude's music at Wellesley, vis-à-vis the links between musical textures and flexible wind, in line with what Buxtehude knew at the Marienkirche? This question can probably never be answered.

This much we do know. The emotional range in Buxtehude's organ music is vast. In this music there is rhetorical contrast, there is poignancy, there is dance, there is color, there is excitement. When this music is performed on a fine organ by a sensitive musician, all of these qualities are present in full measure, and the music becomes a celebration of the sensuous effects that can be drawn from a splendid instrument.

This much can be demonstrated at Wellesley: when an organ has a flexible wind system, then Buxtehude's music has *more* rhetorical contrast, *more* poignancy, *more* dance, *more* color, and *more* excitement. In our sense of discovery it would be presumptuous to imagine that we are finding dimensions of this music that were not there from the moment of conception. These are not effects produced by the instrument on its own; these are effects produced *by the music itself*—but we become aware of their presence only if we perform this music on an instrument that can allow these things to happen.

Back in 1968 one of Charles Fisk's concluding remarks was this: "We need to apply our own minds and our own ears to the task of discovering what makes organ music come alive under the player's fingers." In the organ that he built for Wellesley College, Charles Fisk applied his mind and his ears to just that task.

CHAPTER SIX

New German Organ Tablature: Its Rise and Demise

CLEVELAND JOHNSON

GERMAN ORGAN TABLATURE, termed *Buchstaben Tabulatur* in German because of its use of *Buchstaben* or "letters" instead of *Noten*, was technically outdated as soon as letters of the gamut ceased to be inscribed on organ keys. Yet for three centuries or more, this notation proved itself remarkably versatile and resilient in the hands of German organists who used it as their primary tool in the composition, arrangement, or transcription of everything from medieval dances to the elaborate, concerted pieces of the Baroque. Tablature adapted to changing musical trends most conspicuously in the mid-sixteenth century as the so-called "old" German tablature gave way to the "new,"[1] but it failed to respond to a further need for revision in the eighteenth century and was gradually replaced by more popular notations. This later evolution, from the introduction of "new" German keyboard tablature around 1550 to the eventual extinction of tablature two centuries later, is the subject of this discussion.

The Impending Change

From its inception, "old" German tablature had been an intrinsically practical notation capable, most notably, of indicating the proper division of music between the left and right hands. The apposition of the discant voice, notated mensurally on a staff, and the lower voices, notated in letters below the staff, divided the music (and the keyboard) into two distinct regions: the "busy" discant region (from about middle C and above) and the lower accompanimental region. There was also a clear reason for writing the upper voice in mensural notation since it was consistently the most rhythmically complicated and the most melodically embellished of all the voices.

Hardly had the notation reached a level of relative sophistication in the Buxheim Organbook (completed 1465–75)[2] than its practicality began to be

1. Willi Apel, *The Notation of Polyphonic Music: 900–1600,* 5th revised ed. (Cambridge, Mass.: The Mediaeval Academy of America, 1953), p. 22.

2. Munich, Bayerische Staatsbibliothek: Mus. ms. 3725. Facsimile ed. by Bertha Antonia

compromised. In the ninth fascicle of this source (ff. 122–167v), signs of the impending change to "new" German tablature are already evident. For example, the division into left- and right-hand regions (or discant and accompanimental regions) began to dissolve as the discant voice wandered more frequently below the previous middle C division. In order to accommodate the discant's lower tessitura, the c-clef was forced upward on the staff: placement on the third line (from the bottom) was very common, and some instances of fourth-line placement can also be found. The separation of left- and right-hand regions was also destroyed in the letter-notated lower voices where the octave division no longer occurred between b-natural and c but between a and b-flat, or even between g and a.

Further inadequacies appear in the Buxheim source where the texture was increased from two or three voices to four. During the first half of the sixteenth century, as voices were treated more equally and as melodic embellishment began to be applied to all parts, the rationale for writing the discant in a separate notation simply disappeared. Although rhythmic notation remained fairly consistent during this period,[3] the order of voices fluctuated from source to source. Arrangement with the bass line directly beneath the soprano, SBAT, was the standard practice, but several tablatures organized the voices consecutively by pitch, SATB.[4] Regarding the letter notation of the lower voices, organists also failed to agree on where the octave should be divided: the divisions b♮/c', b♭/b♮', a/b♭', and even e/f'[5] can be found.

The New Tablature

At the midpoint of the sixteenth century, the time was right for change. The logic behind the old system had dissolved and the antiquated notation had become more a hindrance than a help. The curious decision reached, however,

Wallner, *Das Buxheimer Orgelbuch*, Documenta Musicologica, series II, vol. 1 (Kassel: Bärenreiter-Verlag, 1955). Modern ed. by Bertha Antonia Wallner, *Das Buxheimer Orgelbuch*, Das Erbe deutscher Musik, vols. 37–39 (Kassel: Bärenreiter-Verlag, 1958).

3. The printed notation in Arnold Schlick's *Tabulaturen etlicher Lobgesang und Lidlein* (Mainz: 1512) is the main exception to the standard rhythmic practice of this half-century. See Cleveland Johnson, *Keyboard Intabulations Preserved in Sixteenth- and Seventeenth-Century German Organ Tablatures: A Catalogue and Commentary*, 2 vols. (D. Phil. thesis, Oxford University, 1984), vol. 1, p. 41.

4. SATB order is seen in Fridolin Sicher's tablature (St. Gallen, Stiftsbibliothek: Ms. 530), Johannes von Lublin's tablature (Cracow, Polish Academy of Sciences: Ms. 1716), and in the "Holy Ghost" tablature (Warsaw, National Archives: no catalog number).

5. This unusual division is used in the single tablature example in Sebastian Virdung's *Musica getutscht* (Basel: Michael Furter, 1511), ff. Ji^v–Jii. Facsimile ed. by Klaus Wolfgang Niemöller, *Musica getutscht*, Documenta Musicologica, series 1, vol. 31 (Kassel: Bärenreiter-Verlag, 1970).

was not to abandon the cumbersome letter notation (which required two symbols for every note: one to indicate pitch and one to indicate rhythm) but to discard the staff notation of the upper voice. There was apparently no interest in experimenting with a notation in which all voices were mensurally notated on staves, even though this concept governed the contemporaneous keyboard notations in all non-Germanic countries except Spain. Instead, modern or "new" German tablature was born. The reason for this triumph of letters over notes is, most likely, the familiarity and security which German organists felt for their *Buchstaben*. The suggestion that new German tablature developed as a byproduct of the printing industry (letters, even with the separate rhythmic signs needed, were easier to print than notes on a staff)[6] is made less plausible by early manuscript examples.

The first extant tablature to have abandoned the mensural staff notation of the discant voice and resorted to the use of letter notation in all voices is Ms. GV 4/3 in the Kärntner Landesarchiv of Klagenfurt, Austria. Dating from approximately 1550, it predates the first printed example of this notation by two decades. Except for the changeover from staff to letter notation in the upper voice, this source resembles earlier tablatures in many ways (see 6–1.).

The rhythmic symbols used in GV 4/3 are drawn identically like those in the tablature books of Hans Kotter, Leonhard Kleber, Fridolin Sicher, and others. This similarity is most striking in the shape of individual flagged signs and in the barring of successive rhythms. Most German tablatures are characterized by this "fence-like" barring of adjacent rhythms, but unlike later sources where the cross-strokes begin *before* the first down-stroke, ‡‡‡ , the Klagenfurt tablature and many predating it have cross-strokes beginning *at* the first down-stroke and extending beyond the last downstroke,‖‖‖ . One common notational shortcut seen frequently in earlier sources, that of providing only the first rhythmic sign in a group of equal-valued notes, is not found in the Klagenfurt MS.

The most significant relationship of GV 4/3 to the earlier tablatures is its voice arrangement, SBAT. This arrangement, though not used consistently in the half-century leading up to the Klagenfurt MS, is common enough to be regarded as characteristic of sources in the old tablature notation. The SBAT order, however, is not found in *any* tablatures in the new notation except for GV 4/3.

The Klagenfurt tablature, which consists totally of intabulated vocal compositions,[7] adds frequent embellishment to the original lines. This ornamentation shows no resemblance to that of the "colorists," Ammerbach, Paix, or Schmid, but follows more closely the practice of Paul Hofhaimer and his disciples. One

6. Apel, p. 32.

7. Except for the first work, a six-voice "Praeambulum" by Ludwig Senfl.

6–1. Klagenfurt, Kärntner Landesarchiv: Ms. GV 4/3 fol. 4r. The *secunda pars*, "Ave Maria," to Josquin's "Pater noster."

CREDIT. *Josquin Desprez: Werken*, ed. Albert Smijers *et. al.*, Amsterdam 1921–, *Motetten*, deel ii, aflevering 36.

particular similarity is the use of a "whip-like" ornament, characterized by its snatching rhythm, ♫♫ , which is seen often in earlier sources but which fell from use soon after mid-century. Ornamentation is also less pervasive and less flowing than in the ornamented tablatures of the later sixteenth century— essentially a difference between ornamentation (single figures applied individually) and diminution (melodic intervals dissolved into continuous rhythmic motion).

In addition to the Klagenfurt MS, one other early manuscript example of new German tablature survives, a single intabulation of an anonymous five-voice motet, "Respice in me miserere mei Deus."[8] In this composition, the notation had fully evolved into the new tablature which would continue in use for the next two centuries. All voices were written with letters and were organized consecutively by pitch level, SATB.

Elias Nicolaus Ammerbach's *Orgel oder Instrument Tabulatur* of 1571, even if not the first absolute evidence of "new" German tablature, is the first *printed* source of this notation. This print, in effect, legitimized the new notation. The "Kurtze anleitung vnd Instruction," with which Ammerbach begins, provides a brief but comprehensive summary of the notation. Significantly, this introduction is more substantial than similar sections in later tablatures, laying down the rules, as they were, for the first time. Although Ammerbach makes no mention that his notation is new or recently modified from the old, the provision of such copious information in this important new print is certainly neither coincidental nor purely commercial. Nevertheless, Ammerbach does not state or emphasize any of the differences between the old notation and the new—namely, the use of letters in all voices and the arrangement of voice-lines consecutively by pitch.

The notation remained flexible in the hands of German organists, although printed tablatures did much to standardize its use. Aside from the personal idiosyncracies which can be found in the tablatures of many individuals, there was also widespread disagreement on where the octave should be divided. The printed sources support a division between b♭ and b♮, but dozens of tablatures split the octave between b♮ and c or, as in the earlier case of Virdung's *Musica getutscht*, between e and f.[9] In the intabulation genre, there were also differing ways for arranging the voice-lines: in multichoir compositions the parts were either intabulated consecutively, SSAATTBB for example, or the multiple

8. This work was enclosed in a letter, dated 1554, from Johann Kellner to Valentin Pralle, the organist of St. Catherine's of Hamburg. A transcription of the motet is found in Hugo Lichensen-ring, *Hamburgische Kirchenmusik im Reformationszeitalter*, with a postface and bibliography by Jeffery T. Kite-Powell, Hamburger Beiträge zur Musikwissenschaft, vol. 20, Constantin Floros, ed. (Hamburg: Verlag der Musikalienhandlung Karl Dieter Wagner, 1982), pp. 153–54.

9. This e/f' division is found in MSS. F. IX. 49 and 50 of the Öffentliche Bibliothek der Universität Basel.

choirs were kept distinct, SATB–SATB.
Competition from "foreign" notational systems began in earnest with the rise
of the *basso continuo* in the early seventeenth century. In fact, the reintroduction of staff notation to German organists was largely the result of the filtering
in of the continuo practice. Michael Praetorius documents in volume three of
his *Syntagma musicum*[10] the introduction of thoroughbass in Germany and
hints indirectly at the lukewarm reception it received from musicians there. As
Wolfgang Caspar Printz states, "There are people who look down on it [figured
bass] and dare to say, 'It serves but to make the organists lazy and careless.'"[11]
In Germany, the need for harmonic accompaniment was not met by the
modern continuo practice but by the long-proven (though laborious) technique
of intabulation. Keyboardists preferred to prepare a tablature score from the
original composition rather than read a bass-line in staff notation and play from
figures. Heinrich Schütz, a staunch advocate of intabulation, spoke out against
the *basso continuo* in the preface, *Benevolo lectori*, of his *Cantiones sacrae* of
1625:

> I would beg the organists who wish to satisfy more sensitive ears, however,
> not to spare the pains of writing out all the parts in score or so-called
> tablature; should you wish to accompany in the usual manner, solely from
> the continuo part, I should find it misguided and clumsy.[12]

In many cases, especially where the original model had eight, twelve, or
more voice-parts, the intabulated score served merely as a guide from which a
simplified accompaniment was improvised. One common method of reducing
or arranging an original composition to serve as keyboard accompaniment was
to intabulate the outer voices only.[13] With this framework of soprano and bass,
figures were apparently not necessary to ensure that proper harmonic filler was
supplied (although a sharp- or flat-sign would occasionally be added to remind

10. (Wolfenbüttel: Elias Holwein, 1619). Facsimile ed. by Wilibald Gurlitt, Documenta
Musicologica, series 1, vol. 15 (Kassel: Bärenreiter-Verlag, 1958).

11. *Phrynis Mitilenus oder Satyrischer Componist*, 2nd ed. (Dresden and Leipzig, 1696), Part II,
p. 114. Cited and translated by Albert G. Hess in "Observations on 'The Lamenting Voice of the
Hidden Love,'" *Journal of the American Musicological Society*, Vol. V, No. 3 (Fall 1953), p. 222.

12. "Vos autem Organicos, qui auribus delicatioribus satisfaciendum judicatis, rogatos volo, ne
gravemini voces omnes in Partituram seu Tabulaturam, uti vocant, vestram transcribere. Siquidem
in hoc genere Bassum solum pro solido fundamento vobis struere, vanum atque inconcinnum
mihi visum fuit." Heinrich Schütz, *Cantiones sacrae* 1625, Neue Ausgabe sämtliche Werke, vol.
8, Gottfried Grote, ed. (Kassel: Bärenreiter, 1960), p. XXVI. English translation by Edward
Olleson, p. XVII.

13. Tablatures exhibiting this technique include Berlin, Staatsbibliothek Preußischer Kulturbesitz:
Mus. mss. 40075 and 40158; Lüneburg, Ratsbücherei: Mus. ant pract. K.N. 209 and 210;
Munich, Bayerische Staatsbibliothek: Mus. ms. 265; Warsaw, Biblioteka Narodowa: Mus. 326;
and Johann Woltz, *Nova Musices Organicae Tabulatura* (Basel: Johann Jacob Genath, 1617).

the organist whether a chord of the major or minor mode should be played). In retrospect, the remarkable tablature skills of German organists must have been stupefying to many skeptical observers. Daniel Gottlob Türk, writing at the turn of the nineteenth century, expressed such doubts in his own thoroughbass treatise:

> The accompanist had to determine, at a glance, the harmony in the [tablature] score before him. To do this with rapidity presupposes, as one can imagine, long training and not [just] general knowledge [of the technique].[14]

Even during its heyday, Michael Praetorius admitted that tablature was not an easy notation and, indeed, that it was already in decline:

> But meanwhile it is quite a difficult thing—and is also tedious—to play this [tablature] securely. The men who discovered and taught it have long since died or are at least quite old. . . .[15]

With the growing international acceptance of thoroughbass, it seems that performers from tablature were being pressured by composers and theorists to relinquish this archaic notation and to adopt a more universal standard. Praetorius recognized the need for German keyboardists to learn the new techniques of figured bass but admitted that many musicians would need to rely on their trusted tablature as a crutch,

> so it is best advised that, in the beginning, they transpose their *concerti* and songs entirely into their customary letters. . . .[16]

Although Praetorius supplied such assistance once in his book (by transcribing his table of modes into tablature), he suggested after an example of realizing a figured bass that

> those who are unfamiliar with staff notation could write it quite conveniently in the German letter tablature and observe how the inner voices have to be supplied.[17]

14. "... der Begleiter mußte die Harmonie in der vorliegenden Partitur aus den einzelnen Stimmen übersehen. Dies in der Geschwindigkeit zu thun, setzte aber, wie man sich vorstellen kann, eine lange Uebung und nicht gemeine Kenntnis voraus." *Anweisungen zum General-baßspielen*, 2nd enlarged ed. (Halle, 1800), p. 41.

15. "Aber dieweil es gar ein schwehr ding ist, vnd auch langweilig, dieselbe recht *secur* zuschlagen, vnd die Menschen so sie erfunden vnd gelehret waren, zuvor gestorben, oder auffs wenigste gar alt ist. . . ." *Syntagma musicum* III, p. 129.

16. "... So ist es wol zum besten gerathen, daß sie im anfang die *Concert* vnd Gesänge gantz vnd gar in ihre gewöhnliche Buchstaben *Tabulatur* absetzen. . . ." *Syntagma musicum* III, p. 126.

17. "Die nun der Noten *Tabulatur* nicht gewohnet seyn, die können es daraus gar füglich in die

For German organists, the seventeenth century was a time of increasing confusion. They were required to be "bilingual"—to be knowledgeable and fluent in two (or more) languages of notation—as the use of staves spread northward and eastward from Italy and France. The "imported" keyboard notations were gradually being learned by the Germans, but the comfort and familiarity of tablature were only grudgingly given up.

In playing from a figured bass, many German keyboardists never advanced beyond even the most elementary level of ability. There is absolutely no evidence, however, that the basic musical skills necessary for continuo accompaniment were lacking—most Germans simply felt more comfortable accompanying from a bass-line,[18] soprano/bass framework, or full score notated in their own familiar *Buchstaben*. Also, in frequent cases where transposition was required, it was apparently easier to intabulate the work at the transposed pitch than to use the method described by Praetorius.[19] His procedure, involving an imagined change-of-clef for the bass-line, would have certainly daunted the novice convert to staff notation.

Although the practice appears not to have been extremely widespread, some performers experimented with a hybrid system of tablature and staff notation. Excellent examples of this technique can be seen in Mus. ms. 40075 (c. 1630) of the Staatsbibliothek Preußischer Kulturbesitz, Berlin. In several instances the scribe sketched in an upper voice above the figured-bass staff by using a row of tablature.[20] Conversely, several tablature pieces in this source were supplied with figures to clarify specific harmonies which may have been obscured in the process of intabulating or reducing the work for accompaniment.[21]

The resistance of German organists to thoroughbass is documented by the fact that they continued to intabulate, but their sources extended beyond the traditional vocal repertory and included popular keyboard works in staff notation. For example, many keyboard compositions by Sweelinck and by the English virginalists—works which were composed originally in keyboard score—also exist in tablature copies.[22] Frescobaldi's *Fiori Musicali* was not

Teutsche Buchstaben *Tabulatur* setzen, vnd sich daraus ersehen, wie die Mittelstimmen darzu *appliciret* werden müssen." *Syntagma musicum* III, p. 144.

18. Mus. 326 in Warsaw's Biblioteka Narodowa is an unusually large source of intabulated bass lines.

19. *Syntagma musicum* III, p. 83.

20. See ff. 26, 36, 37, and 38.

21. See ff. 69, 79v–81, 92v–93.

22. The numerous tablature sources for Sweelinck's keyboard works are described in Jan Pieterszoon Sweelinck, *The Instrumental Works*, Gustav Leonhardt, Alfons Annegarn, and Frits Noske, eds., Opera omnia: Editio altera quan edendam curavit Vereniging voor Nederlandse Muziekgeschiedenis, vol. 1, fascicles 1–3 (Amsterdam: Nirota, Koedijk, 1968). An important tablature source of works by John Bull is Ms. 17771 in the Österreichische Nationalbibliothek, Vienna.

only intabulated but acquired copious embellishment when it was copied.[23] Even a fellow German's attempt at a compromise notation, Samuel Scheidt's *Tabulatura nova* of 1624, was partially copied in tablature.[24]

Printed editions of keyboard music in staff notation began to be published in Germany approximately fifty years after the first tablature publication of Ammerbach. Johann Ulrich Steigleder's *Ricercar Tabulatura* of 1624 is recognized as the first German print of keyboard music to abandon tablature notation. From the same year, Scheidt's *Tabulatura nova* presented a notation which preserved the contrapuntal clarity of tablature but which used a separate staff (rather than a row of letters) for each voice. These editions did not, however, signal an immediate demise of printed tablature: Johann Erasmus Kindermann's *Harmonia Organica In Tabulaturam Germanicam composita* (Nürnberg, 1645) and Christian Michel's *Tabulatura Darinnen Etzliche Praeludia Toccaten vnd Couranten uff das Clavir Instrument gesetzt* (Braunschweig: Godfridt Müller, 1639 and 1645) document that tablature publications were commercially viable for at least two decades after the landmark editions of Steigleder and Scheidt.

Handwritten tablatures continued to be compiled long after printed tablatures had become an anathema in the music market. With the geographical advancement of the foreign keyboard notation from France and Italy into neighboring German lands, the distant regions of the North and East avoided total conversion to the new standard until the first half of the eighteenth century. As succeeding generations of German organists were trained, however, staff notation gradually rose in status to that of tablature and eventually surpassed it throughout the land.

An enormously entertaining account of "the baneful effects of a reactionary adherence to the Organ Tablature tradition,"[25] and the tale of one fictitious organist's attempt to learn thoroughbass, is found in the foreword to Friderich Erhard Niedt's *Musicalische Handleitung* of 1700.[26] At a sylvan musical gathering, the allegorical organist, Tacitus by name, begins his autobiographi-

Instr. mus. hs. 408 (*olim* 108) in Uppsala's Universitetsbiblioteket is a tablature collection of keyboard works by the Englishmen Bull, Byrd, Philips, and Tomkins (as well as pieces by Sweelinck, Scheidt, Scheidemann, Schildt, Sibern, Anerio, Striggio, and Frescobaldi).

23. Turin, Biblioteca Nazionale: Giordano 3.

24. Several excerpted works are found in Budapest, National Szèchènyi Library: Mus. ms. Bártfa 27 and Lüneburg, Ratsbücherei: Mus. ant. pract. K.N. 208, 208a, and 209.

25. F. T. Arnold, *The Art of Accompaniment from a Thorough Bass as Practised in the XVIIth and XVIIIth Centuries* (London: Oxford University Press, 1931), p. 217.

26. (Hamburg: Nicolaus Spieringk, 1700). The majority of the foreword is cited by Oliver W. Strunk in his *Source Readings in Music History from the Classical through the Romantic Era* (New York: W. W. Norton and Company, 1950) pp. 454–70. Specific portions of the foreword relevant to continuo and tablature performance are also cited in Arnold, pp. 214–22.

cal narrative in response to a statement by Fidelio (a less experienced organist) by recounting that "there was a famous master who thought nothing at all of the laborious German tablature, and could, nevertheless, in a short time teach a sensible person Music so thoroughly that he need not be ashamed to be heard by anyone."[27] Tacitus, whose experience in learning thoroughbass had been far from expedient, cites his own painful history to temper (yet substantiate) Fidelio's enthusiasm.

It seems that, despite years of instruction, Tacitus developed little competency at playing from figures, learning at most "how to put the thoroughbass into tablature."[28] At his first audition for a position as an organist, he was fortunate that "there was an old cantor in this place who had not forgotten much about Music because he had never been very well versed therein, so that it was a case of 'birds of a feather,' as the proverb says, and I [Tacitus] did not have to submit to being worried with thoroughbass (which I dreaded like the hangman)."[29] Tacitus was soon overwhelmed by his new position, however. The old cantor died, and Tacitus, in accompanying a candidate for the vacant position, was asked to play from a figured bass. "There I stood like butter in the sun,"[30] Tacitus said and complained that he would have preferred to have had the music ahead of time in order to transcribe it into tablature or at least to look through it at leisure. As a result of this embarrassment, Tacitus resigned his post, retained a reputable teacher (Prudentius), and perfected his thoroughbass skills.

Prudentius avoided tablature altogether and instructed his students in thoroughbass from the very beginning, "that they do not need to trouble their heads about that troublesome tablature, and, after many years' study, remain 'paper-organists' after all, but that they become, in short time, good sound musicians."[31] Florimon, another member of the musical company, added that, after thoroughbass, Prudentius' students advanced quickly to complete compositions in staff notation:

> [T]hey find that much easier than learning the German tablature; and I do not heed what some say to the contrary, to the effect that one should keep to the old ways. The old Germans deserve all respect, and, in their time, attained a very high standard with tablature: 60 years ago, or a little more, one hardly ever saw a German organist who played from a thoroughbass or from notes. But since a better and truer, and an easy way has been

27. Cited by Arnold, p. 216.

28. Ibid., p. 218.

29. Ibid., p. 219.

30. Ibid., p. 220.

31. Ibid., p. 221.

found, why should not the old humdrum be abandoned? The Italians have never used any German tablature, but, for untold years, nothing but notes, and this very fact is the real reason why they have, for so long, undoubtedly borne the palm above us Germans.[32]

Florimon, after an interruption by the senescent organist, Negligentius (who favored "keeping to the old ways"[33]), points out that

> many German organists are now not far behind the foreigners in their art, if they do not, in certain matters, excel them; but the fact remains that the reason of it is that they have accustomed themselves to play from a thoroughbass so much earlier than use to be the case, whereas, according to the doctrine of Prudentius (who can never be praised highly enough), this should come at the very beginning; for then one would notice the splendid effect on pupils, and, finally, no one would any longer be able to say shamelessly that people who had not been learning for nine or ten years, but had acquired their art in a short time, must have been to school with a magician.[34]

Shortly after Niedt's publication, Andreas Werckmeister began to comment, in his own writings, on the declining role of tablature notation in Germany. His *Harmonologia Musica oder Kurze Anleitung zur Musicalischen Composition*[35] of 1702 alludes to the diminishing use of tablature. Discussing the examination of candidates for positions as organists, Werckmeister suggests that "[t]hen the exam in thoroughbass must be undertaken; also something from tablature [should] certainly [be played] just to see if he understands it."[36] Had Werckmeister been a contemporary of Michael Praetorius almost a century earlier, the priorities in this statement would most certainly have been reversed. Tablature competency in the eighteenth century, however, was primarily of retrospective importance, giving the performer access to the vast repertory of earlier compositions:

> In so saying, I do not deny that it is very good when one can play a piece from tablature; and I hold good tablature creations in high esteem because one can observe what other accomplished organists have composed. One

32. Ibid., p. 222.

33. Ibid., p. 217.

34. Ibid., p. 222.

35. Frankfurt and Leipzig: Theodor Calvisius, 1702. Reprint ed. Hildesheim: Georg Olms Verlag, 1970.

36. "Dann muss auch das Examen im General-Basse vorgenommen werden, auch wohl etwas von der Tabulatur, das man nur siehet ob er auch dieselbe verstehet. . . ." Andreas Werckmeister, *Harmonologia Musica*, p. 69.

can see their good style and imagination, which can be put to use, and can get some [good] ideas through further study.[37]

Five years after his *Harmonologia Musica*, Werckmeister warned that, if improvements and simplifications could not be made, tablature was doomed to imminent extinction. As a last-ditch effort at reform, Werckmeister used his *Musicalische Paradoxal Discourse*[38] of 1707 to discuss specific problems in tablature notation and suggest how they might be resolved:

> [I]t appears nevertheless that one could finish sooner using lines and notes than with the present German tablature which has entirely too many varied characters such as twenty-paned windows and five-barbed hooks . . . the same with its many octave indications. One could, however, considerably obviate these [rhythmic signs]. If one commonly wrote:

```
Ce   gfed   cc   f   ed   ed   c
```

[this] could be rendered more concisely as:

```
8      16     4    4.16    2    1
Ce    gfed    cc    fed    ed   c.
```

The values are thereby classified according to their arithmetical equivalents.

Whereas one must make many ♯'s and ♭'s in the staves, one makes only a little tail or stroke on the letters, requiring but a single movement. Instead of the one- and two-line octaves, one could choose an alternative. First, one sets the lower octave in large German characters, the unlined [octave] in large Roman characters; the one-line [octave] could be in small German, and the two-line octave in small Roman as follows:

```
C  Cis  D  Dis  E  F  Fis  G  Gis  A.  B  H. │ ungestrichen

c  cis  d  dis  e  f  fis  g  gis  a   b  h.  │ eingestrichen

c  cis  d  dis  e  f  fis  g  gis  a   b  h.  │ zwey gestrich:
```

---

37. "Ich verwerffe hiermit nicht, wann einer ein gut Stück aus der Tabulatur spielen kan, es ist sehr gut, und halte viel auf gute *Tabulatur* Sachen, denn man kan daraus sehen, was andere rechtschaffene *Organisten* gesetzet haben, und kan von denen gute *Manieren* und *Inventiones* sehen, und sich dieselben zu Nutze machen und weiter darauf nachdencken, und Zufälle davon haben." Ibid., p. 68.

38. Quedlinburg: Theodor Calvisius, 1707.

And thus one might not make so many kinds of strokes. In writing dots one could also have greater convenience. Formerly F̣. Ḟ Ḟ. Ḟ , one could
$$\begin{array}{cccc} g & g & g & g \end{array}$$
8.
alternatively write 8 with the dot, g g g g and so forth. I certainly do not want here to prescribe to anyone or to make innovations—whoever can formulate still better inventions is obliged to serve others therewith—I only offer here my nonbinding opinion, and each person will certainly avail himself for his convenience.

In the meantime, may it please the kind reader, before judging unfavorably, to observe and consider further. Regarding the scale degrees, I see no [system] more suitable than our abc's for letters must be repeated by necessity. Indeed, should other characters be used, a repetition must [still] be necessary, because whatever is in one octave must be in the other, *de octavis idem sit judicium.* Should we not wish to accept this repetition, we would again run into the multiplicity of the heathen characters and produce just such confusion. And by adhering to a temperament, we would have 48 [different] notes in the keyboard compass, while presently, by repeating, we have twelve. The Guidonian staff-system is also not much better than the heathen for if one should have a two-stave system with bass and treble signs going from low C to c''', we would already have 48 positions, each requiring an [individual] mental impression and name. The more ♯'s and ♭'s which are added, the more percepts we must make of the matter. Meanwhile, this practice is so ingrained that this system of lines will remain well until the end of the world.[39]

39. "... so scheint es doch, als ob man im schreiben der Linien, und Nothen eher fertig werden könte, als mit der jetzigen teutschen *Tabulatur:* Denn in derselben hat man gar zu viel bunte *Characteren*, als 16. biß 20. fache Fenster und 5. fache Hacken: *Item* die vielen Uberstreichungen: Diesen aber könte man auch ziemlicher maßen abhelffen, als wenn man insgemein setzet . . . könte etwa also, und *Compendiose* gesetzet werden. . . .

"Denn dadurch werden die *Valores* nach ihrer *Arithmetischen* Geltung abgetheilet: da man in den Linien viel ♯ und ♭ machen muß, macht man an die Buchstaben nur ein Schwäntz- oder Strichlein, welches in einem Zuge geschehen kan. Anstat der gestrichenen, und gedoppelt gestrichenen *Clavium* könte man andere nehmen. Erstlich sezzete man die unterste *Octava* in große deutsche Buchstaben. Die Ungestrichenen in große *lateinische.* Die eingestrichene könten wieder kleine Deutsche sein: Die 2. gestrichene wieder in kleine *Lateinische:* folgender maßen . . .

"Und also dürffte man so vielerley Gestreiche nicht machen. Mit den *Puncten* könte man auch viel bequemligkeiten im Schreiben haben. Als vor . . . Könte man nur 8. mit dem Puncte setzen. Als . . . Doch will ich keinen hierinn vorschreiben, und Neuerungen machen, wer noch beßer *Invention* haben kan, der ist schuldig seinen Nächsten damit zu dienen, ich gebe nur meine unvorschreibliche Meinung hiermit an die Tag, ein jeder wird sich doch seiner Beqvemligkeit bedienen. Indessen bitte, der geneigte Leser wolle es im besten vermercken, und ehe er *sinistre judiciret* weiter nachdencken. Was nun diese *Claves* anlanget, so sehe ich keine die beqvemer seyn, als unser a, b, c. da die Buchstaben nothwendig müßen *repetiret* werden, solten es auch schon andere *Characteren* seyn, so muß doch nothwendig eine *Repetition* derselben seyn, denn was in einer *Octava* ist, daß muß in der andern auch seyn, *de octavis idem sit judicium;* Wolten wir die *Repetition* nicht annehmen, so würden wir wieder in die Vielheit, der Heydenischen *Characteren* hinein lauffen, und eben solche *Confusiones* anrichten, und wenn wir schon die *Temperatur*

As Werckmeister had predicted, tablature became a total anachronism by the middle of the eighteenth century. Although some old-timers were still familiar with the notation and used it on occasion,[40] tablature had gradually faded out of general use. Writers of the period treated tablature as an historic curiosity and found need to explain the odd symbols to the reader. Johann Samuel Petri, writing in his *Anleitung zur praktischen Musik* of 1782,[41] assumed from his audience as little familiarity with tablature notation as Willi Apel and Johannes Wolf assumed of their twentieth-century readers.[42] Petri not only explained the details of the obsolete notation but also related some of its history:

> This same Viadana is the inventor of figured-bass for accompaniment or of the so-called Italian tablature which, however, was not commonly accepted by us in Germany until the end of the same century or even until the beginning of the present eighteenth [century]. Musicians stuck preferably with that which they had learned and mastered in spite of the fact that, with its numbers, the new discovery is much easier to learn. In short, *the introduction of Italian tablature came to pass with as much difficulty as the phasing out of solmization.* [emphasis mine]
>
> In order, though, that one can form an idea of the traditional German tablature (for which the term tablature suffices), I want to cite an example to show that, to the organist, the entire piece on his page would be portrayed as on a blackboard. I choose for this purpose an advent cantata by the Sorau music director, Telemann, as copied by the famous Wolfgang Kaspar Prinz of Sorau around 1709. It looks like this:

behielten, so hätten wir doch 48. *Claves* und *Characteren* in einem Clavier, da wir nun 12. haben, wenn wir *repetiren*. Das *Gvidonische* Linien-Werck ist auch nicht viel beßer, als das Heidenische, denn wenn man schon ein gedoppelt *liniarisch Systema* haben wolte, mit dem Baß- und *Discant*-Zeichen, und gehen denn von unterm C. biß c''' so haben wir schon 48. Stellen, da wir ein sonderlich *Concept* und Nahmen uns einbilden müßen. Je mehr ♯ und ♭ nun dazukommen, jemehr Einbildungen wir uns von der Sache machen müßen. Indeßen ist diese Gewohnheit so feste gesetzet, daß dieses *Systema* der Linien wol bleiben wird, biß an der Welt Ende. . . ." Andreas Werckmeister, *Musicalische Paradoxal Discourse*, pp. 70–72.

40. Tablature was a space-saving device for Johann Sebastian Bach, as can be seen in the autograph of the *Orgelbüchlein* (BWV 599–644): Berlin, Deutsche Staatsbibliothek MS P 283, pp. 9, 17, 22, 26, and 30.

Here are five voices: discant, alto, tenor, bass, and organ. The bass, along with the organ, begins the theme in 4/4 meter. The other voices rest; ⨦ indicates the whole rest, ⌐ the half, F a quarter, ⧣ two consecutive quarters, E an eighth, ⧎ four consecutive eighths. The tenor enters in the third bar.

In the recitative the pedal notes of the great octave are in Roman letters; the notes of the small octave, however, are written with German [letters]. The text and melody stand above them, the latter again with small letters and the F⋅ F⧎ showing the values of the notes. In the upper voices, the discant and alto, the letters always have a stroke [above them], which indicates the one-line octave, or two strokes, which indicate the two-line octave. But [in this example] no scales or notes occur in these voices.

Succeeding scores always stand, without further gap, immediately beneath the line which is drawn under the organ voice. Therefore the entire pages and folia look like tables.

This bit is enough about the actual old tablature. I will soon have more to bring up regarding the subsequent mix of Italian tablature with the old German, the eventual total acceptance of the first and the removal of the latter. . . .

To show the intermixture of German and Italian tablature, the following example might serve, originating several years later but coming likewise from Prinz's own hand. It is the beginning of a pentecost piece. The text is: "This is the day, which the Lord hath made."

41. Leipzig: Johann Gottlob Immanuael Breitkopf, 1782.

42. Apel. Johannes Wolf, *Handbuch der Notationskunde*, 2 vols. (Leipzig, 1919). Reprint ed., Wiesbaden: Breitkopf & Härtel, 1975.

43. "Eben dieser *Viadana* ist der Erfinder der bezifferten Bässe für das Akkompagnement, oder der so genannten italienischen Tabulatur, welche jedoch bey uns in Deutschland erst ganz zu Ende desselben Sekulums, oder gar erst zu Anfange des jezzigen achtzehnten ist allgemein angenommen worden, weil die Musiker gern bey dem blieben, was sie gelernt und gut inne hatten; ohnerachtet die neue Erfindung durch Ziffern viel leichter zu lernen ist. Kurz es ging mit der italienischen Tabulatur bey ihrer Einführung so schwer her, als bey Abschaffung der Solmisation.

"Damit man sich aber von der vorher üblichen deutschen Tabulatur (welche eigentlich Tabulatur genennt zu werden verdient,) einen Begriff machen könne, so will ich ein Exempel anführen, um zu zeigen, daß dem Organisten das ganze Stück auf sein Blatt, wie auf eine Tafel hingemalt gewesen sey. Ich erwähle dazu eine von dem berühmten Wolfgang Kaspar Prinz zu Sorau eigenhändig geschriebene, von dem Sorauischen Kapellmeister Telemann aber gesetzte Adventskantate, die Prinz ums Jahr 1709 abgeschrieben hat. Sie sieht also aus:

"Hier sind fünf Stimmen, Diskant, Alt, Tenor, Bass und Orgel. Der Baß nebst der Orgel fängt an im 4/4 Takte, die andern Stimmen pausiren; ⨦ bedeutet die ganze Taktspause, ⌐ die halbe, F ein Viertel, ⧣ zwey Viertel nacheinander, E ein Achtel, ⧎ vier Achtel hintereinander. Im dritten Takte tritt der Tenor ein.

"Im Recitative sind die Pedalnoten der großen Oktave mit lateinischen Buchstaben, die Noten der kleinen aber mit deutschen geschrieben, und Text und Melodie steht darüber, letztere wieder mit kleinen Buchstaben, und den F⋅ F⧎ , den Werth der Noten anzuzeigen. In den hohen Stimmen, als Diskant und Alt, ist bey den Buchstaben allezeit der Queerstrich, der die ein-, oder zween, die die zwogestrichne Oktave anzeigen. Aber keine Skale und keine Note komt in der

This [example] shows that the 4 above the two notes would have often indicated a trill as, for example, in the sixth bar from the end. Furthermore, wherever there were just numbers instead of letters, the vocal part has rests as the piece itself (the parts of which I also have from Prinz) shows.[43]

ganzen Stimme nicht vor.

"Die folgenden Zeilen stehn allemal ohne weiterem Zwischenraume gleich unter den gezogenen Queerlinien unter der Orgelstimme. Daher die ganzen Seiten und Blätter wie Tabellen aussehen.

"Dis wenige sey genug von der eigentlichen alten Tabulatur.

"Von der darauf erfolgten Vermischung der italienischen Tabulatur mit der alten deutschen, und endlichen gänzlichen Einführung der erstern, und Abschaffung der letztern, werde ich bald mehr anführen . . .

"Von der Vermischung der deutschen und italienischen Tabulatur mag folgendes Exempel zeigen, welches Prinzes eigne Hand ebenfalls ist, und etliche Jahre später geschrieben zu seyn scheint. Es ist der Anfang eines Pfingststücks. Der Text ist: Dis ist der Tag, den der Herr gemacht hat.

"Dis zeigt, daß die 4 auf zwo Noten auch öfters einen Triller angezeigt habe, wie z. E. im sechsten Takte vor dem Ende. Ferner, wo keine Buchstaben, sondern blos Ziffern waren, da hat die Singstimme Pausen, wie das Stück selbst zeigt, welches ich auch von Prinzen ausgeschrieben in Stimmen habe." Johann Samuel Petri, *Anleitung zur praktischen Musik*, pp. 88–92.

Transitional pieces such as this one showing the combined use of staff and letter notation are not as common as one would expect. True, German organists did occasionally use *Buchstaben* above a figured bass or use figures above a tablature bass line (see above, at notes 20–21), but the transition to the new staff notation occurred with a minimum of such assistance. More striking in Prinz's example is its resemblance to the "old" German tablature which blended two different concepts of notation into a single utilitarian system. The difference in this eighteenth-century example, however, is that the bass line, instead of the discant, is now the voice to be notated on the staff. Obviously, this reversal is attributable to the flourishing thoroughbass practice.

Probably the most fascinating aspect in the demise of German organ tablature is not how or why the extinction occurred but the continual lingering on of this outdated notation long after its practical usefulness had vanished. The use of letters, with their direct relationship to the keyboard of the medieval organ, originally had a specific purpose in the earliest tablatures. The juxtaposition of staff and letter notation in "old" German tablature also served the needs of the performer in a practical way, at least until the end of the fifteenth century. But with the rise of the "new" German tablature, the notation had lost touch with its roots and purpose; it survived as long as it did largely through the tenacity of the German organists. An international mandate, under the guise of the thoroughbass movement, spread the seeds of change in Germany, but these seeds (considered weeds by many Germans) were slow to mature. When then did tablature actually die? No clear delineation can be given, for it perished slowly as a new generation of organists gradually replaced the old. Few organists whose original training was in tablature would have ever totally abandoned their unique notation: it died with them.

CHAPTER SEVEN

Organ Acoustics:
Building Churches for Organs/
Building Organs for Churches

R. LAWRENCE KIRKEGAARD
& DANA KIRKEGAARD

As ENTHUSIASTIC PRACTITIONERS in acoustics, that "whitest of the black arts," we frequently are called upon to perform our magic in creating acoustically appropriate environments for organ. Occasionally we are privileged to work with sensitive architects and organ builders from the outset of new designs and, through constructive interactions, are able to achieve the magical effects we all seek. More often we try to transform existing spaces into acoustically more suitable environments.

Charles Fisk seemed to take delight in dredging up the most perplexing spaces he could find to challenge our acoustical magic and his own organ building skills. Project by project, we learned together, from each other and from others as well. It is my special privilege to describe some of the acoustical approaches and understandings we came to share.

Designing Churches for Organs—Acoustic Design Goals

Have you ever seen children sparkle with joy when they experience very reverberant spaces? When the sounds they make build and blend and linger in ways they rarely experience, they delight in the wonder of it all. I've seen adults who marvel at the same effects and sometimes are awed by such reverberant spaces, intimidated when their smallest sounds spring to flight and hover in the air around them.

Combine this joyful exuberance with awed reverence, add effective communication capabilities, surround them in a quiet hush, and one has the basic acoustical elements of an environment well suited for worship, an environment where organ and other instrumental music find uplifting support, where congregational and choral singing encourages and rewards participation, where communication can be appropriately easy and effective.

Conventional wisdom puts music and speech into alien camps, claiming at best an uneasy tension when they are forced together. In the extremes this view may be valid, but there is a peaceful middle ground where neither music nor speech need be compromised. The discussions which follow explore the contours and limits of this middle ground, describing the artful balance among the various goals to be met.

Reverberation and Other Delights

For organ and choral music the lingering after-ring of sound we call reverberation is as important as the leavening in bread, giving that sound an important three-dimensionality. Too often, though, as important as it may be, reverberation has been the dominant acoustical consideration and many other critical issues have been ignored. At least as important as the duration of sound are qualities such as frequency response, smoothness, evenness of distribution, spatial accuracy, warmth, purity, clarity/intelligibility, focus, fullness, and loudness, among others. These are less easily defined and difficult to measure, but are nonetheless critically important.

Instead of attempting to define or elaborate on these acoustical qualities, we may proceed directly to a description of the architectural characteristics that determine them.

1. Reverberation and loudness are both determined by volume and sound absorption. The greater the volume, the longer the reverberation and the weaker the loudness; the greater the sound absorption, the shorter the reverberation and the weaker the loudness. A rough rule-of-thumb suggests twenty feet of average height over an audience for each second of reverberation time desired, assuming no significant absorption other than listeners. For 2.25 to 2.5 seconds of reverberation, the "average" ceiling height (total volume divided by area of listeners) must be in the range of forty-five to fifty feet. Additional absorption—in the form of thick carpet, upholstery, or draperies, and even openings to organ chambers—must be added to the area of listeners in this calculation. This added absorption requires additional volume, at the rate of fifty to sixty cubic feet for every square foot of efficient absorption, if the reverberation goals are to be met. This added volume has penalties in terms of loudness. Also, the increased remoteness of surfaces diminishes clarity and presence. Obviously, when remodelling is involved and volume is fixed, removal of absorption is the only way to increase inadequate reverberation. This absorption may be in the form of *porous* materials (soft limestone, stone, concrete block, mortar, acoustical tile, fabrics, etc.), of thin, *resonant* materials (wood paneling, glass, furred walls, pews, suspended ceilings, wood floor

structures, etc.), and of *openings* into cavities and chambers (including the minute cracks between tongue-and-groove wood planking). All of these contribute absorption (some quite frequency-dependent) that diminishes loudness and reverberation.

2. Space/time distribution of sound is established by the primary shaping of walls and ceilings. Narrowness and/or proximity of reflective surfaces near the source provide the strong early-arriving sound energy that is necessary for clarity and definition in music and intelligibility in speech. When placed near ceilings or between narrow flanking walls, organs have greater presence, focus, and clarity. Pulpit canopies shape speech-sound distribution in the same way, promoting clarity and intelligibility by reinforcing early energy and limiting access of sound to portions of the space where reverberation can build.

3. Diffusion of sound at all frequencies is achieved by abundant use of large- and small-scale sculpting of wall and ceiling surfaces promoting smoothness of response and freedom from the harsh, disturbing echoes, flutter, and phase distortions that simple, unadorned geometries tend to generate.

4. Strong low-frequency support requires massive, solid surface materials for floor, walls, and ceiling.

5. Complete control of noise—whether from air conditioning systems, organ blowers, nearby classrooms, or exterior traffic or equipment—is essential to concentration and to the fullest appreciation of the entire dynamic range, down to the softest whisper and most delicate nuance. The three-dimensional landscape of speech and music cannot be appreciated or understood when noise floods all the valleys and flatlands.

6. Pews and pew cushions require special consideration. Normal pew cushions can stabilize reverberation when pews are unoccupied, but they do so at the sacrifice of congregational singing and responses. The concentration of absorption near the sound sources and the covering up of surfaces that would otherwise provide confidence-building sound reflections to support timid singers can significantly weaken congregational participation. So fragile is the willingness to participate that even seemingly minor factors, such as absorption, row spacing, and proximity of other persons can be crucial. It has been said in focused humor that churches that insist on comfort at the expense of acoustics have inverted ear-to-rear ratios. Nonabsorbent cushions may be the answer to enhancing comfort without discouraging participation.

7. Speech reinforcement systems can be designed to provide clarity, naturalness, directional accuracy, presence, power, and subtlety. Conventional wisdom understands that highly reverberant environments render speech unintelligible, and frequently counsels antiseptically dry, compromised acoustics to accommodate the spoken word. As mentioned earlier, our ancestors faced the challenge more creatively and achieved highly intelligible speech in reverber-

ant spaces through the use of pulpit canopies. The canopies shaped the sound of the voice, directing it toward the congregation and preventing its access to upper volumes where most of the reverberation process occurs. The results were natural sounding, accurately localized to the person speaking, and only slightly "bigger than life." The best of today's audio system designs serve acoustically as electronic pulpit canopies, emulating the quality that our ancestors experienced. Technology can provide exceedingly high quality speech reinforcement even in very reverberant spaces. The problem is that the understanding of technology and its tasteful application are not a part of "the conventional wisdom." Audio system capabilities also need to be comprehensive in scope, including wireless microphones, multichannel recording and playback, intercom, monitoring, and CCTV and videotaping feeds, as well as possible interfaces with radio and television broadcast. An enlightened church would do well to seek out design expertise for its audio systems as carefully as it would select an organ builder to construct a fine instrument. Excellence rarely is achieved by accident or benign neglect; it is the goal and reward of good judgment and perseverance.

The Pitfalls

The best examples of historic churches were built with precedents of form, vocabularies of design, and traditions of construction that incorporated the essential aspects of this list. Architects today face serious challenges in their efforts to design significant, acoustically appropriate churches. 1. Budget constraints dictate tight volumes, 2. *Thermal* energy considerations produce furred *sound* energy-absorbing construction approaches for walls and ceilings, 3. Trends of style and taste preclude the richness of acoustically desirable sculptural treatment of volumes and surfaces, 4. Unsophisticated clients guided by the expedience of abundant free advice fall prey to inappropriate audio system designs, 5. Well-meaning committees seek to make upholstered living rooms of their sanctuaries, losing sight of a rich vocabulary of traditional materials that had beauty, durability, design opportunity, and acoustical integrity. "If it moves, mike it; if it doesn't move, carpet it," is too often the operative principle.

Designing Churches for Organs

One can most successfully design a church by artfully balancing the requirements of all the elements and functional relationships it is expected to accommodate. Ultimately, one designs for people in support of their worship . . . support in terms of sight and sound, involvement and participation, privacy and communication, reverence and celebration, individuality and community.

The acoustical design must enhance these aspects and provide a supportive environment for speech and music, prayer and response, congregational and choral singing, organ and instrumental performance. When there is a confident knowledge that all those aspects can be achieved without severe compromise, the too-common adversarial roles can become advocacy relationships.

University of Michigan Organ Recital Hall. At the time of this writing, the recital hall and Fisk organ are just being completed, so the finished products are yet to be heard. There has been a problem in construction of the space that should be shared to help others avoid the same difficulty. In order to provide ample diffusion of sound at all frequencies and strong bass response, we worked with the architects to develop a highly modulated wall shaping using a very rough-surfaced split-faced concrete block. The block was laid in randomly staggered vertical rows following a gross undulating geometry. The block was heavy enough, in combination with a concrete ceiling and audience risers, to sustain strong bass response. The block is very porous and, unless thoroughly sealed, absorbs sound quite efficiently. That's the pitfall! Those who recall the acoustical remodeling of Duke Chapel may remember that it was constructed of a porous artificial stone. The original intention was to cure the ills of excessive reverberation. Laboratory samples of the "stone" were tested and a sealant/ application technique was developed. After the sealant application was completed and the scaffolding was stripped away, reverberation had increased by only a small amount, far less than the consultants and the University had anticipated. All the pores had not been sealed! This same condition has occured at the University of Michigan and the third round of sealing is about to be undertaken.

In testing Rockefeller Chapel, the University of Chicago's equivalent to Duke Chapel, we have learned that very porous materials can become even more absorbent as they are being sealed. Apparently the increased flow resistance produced by the reduced porosity increases molecular friction, thereby absorbing sound energy by transforming it to heat. Until the pores were completely sealed the surface was not reflective.

Caution must be exercised when it comes to sealing very fine-scale porosity in spaces lacking diffusion. The resulting increase in high frequency reflectivity could create excessive brilliance, particularly in smaller spaces. Many older spaces have lost their patina when contemporary paint covered old plaster or whitewash.

Oberlin's Warner Concert Hall Revisited. Warner Concert Hall at Oberlin offers a useful example of the interaction between an organ and an appropriate—or inappropriate—space. Many musicians will remember the original Holtkamp organ and their disappointed expectations when it

7–1. The University of Michigan Organ Recital Hall. A highly modulated wall shape was created using rough-surfaced split-faced concrete blocks laid in randomly staggered vertical rows.

was replaced with an instrument by the Flentrop firm.

Warner Hall had reasonably appropriate reverberation time and gross geometry, but had some major flaws which affected all musical forces, including the organ. There was a nonstop flutter echo between the stage floor and the gently vaulted ceiling overhead. A single handclap on stage was repeated by the room a dozen or more times as it fluttered between stage floor and ceiling. The tyranny of the T-square created a proliferation of parallel surfaces that sustained high frequency interreflections, while thin construction materials caused absorption of low-frequency sound by resonant motion of the thin materials in response to sound-energy-destroying low-frequency support. The resulting conditions were strident, harsh, tinny, and cold. Worst of all, though, was the lack of definition and presence created by the floor/ceiling flutter echo. The organ sound was remote and indifferent; other instruments and musical forces experienced the same problems.

A major reconstruction, in 1984, included reshaping of wall and ceiling surfaces, replacement of flat, thin plaster wall surfaces with massive sculptured masonry, covering of thin glass windows with articulated heavy plastic shields, quieting of the air-handling system, the addition of adjustable absorptive banners to tune the room to various uses, and incorporation of performance space-shaping recital shell towers. All of these combined to create a warmly resonant, articulate, compelling acoustic environment that enhances all the musical forces the hall is called upon to serve. In the case of Oberlin, the Flentrop organ could not have been designed to cope with the flaws of the room; the room had to change.

Designing Organs for Churches

The variables available to the organ builder when designing an organ for a space are finite: disposition, voicing, wind pressure, doubling, and scaling in the instrument itself, and placement within the space. Each of these is restricted in the scope of its influence and accommodation, especially after the instrument has been installed. At best, the organ builder is greeted with all the ingredients for success: location, budget, musical taste, adequate reverberation and appropriate shape and finish, and proper relationships, among others. Typically, though, the constraints are more apparent than the opportunities, and the builder must practice the "art of the possible." The proper role of the acoustician is to provide to the organ builder as supportive and neutral an environment as possible, and where utterly impossible remodeling constraints pose potential problems, to advise the organ builder accordingly.

One can begin to define the limits of the possible by knowing the rule-of-thumb that says each one second of reverberation time requires twenty feet of average height above the congregation in an otherwise acoustically reflective space. If the perceived reverberation is significantly lower than such a calculation would predict, it is likely that unsuspected surfaces are absorbing sound— thin panelling, porous stone or block, minute cracks between planks of a wood roof deck or floor, extensive glass areas with thin glass and/or leaky cames, generations of accumulated dust and debris. Such conditions present opportunities for improvement and suggest need for professional advice and/or admonishment. Ideally that advice would include both actual and predicted values of reverberation, steady-state loudness levels, and narrow-band frequency response to guide the organ builder in his efforts both to scale the instrument and to set a disposition suitable to the special characteristics of the space. The process of designing and constructing an organ is treacherous enough; such information can reduce anxiety and add a modicum of certainty in an unavoidably uncertain world.

During the summer of 1983 we undertook an extensive study of some fifty churches and recital halls across the country in order to add to our understanding of the relationships among loudness, reverberation, and frequency response. The study was initiated in the hope of finding ways to give the organ builder more acoustical information about a space so that the basic design decisions regarding scaling and disposition could be made most appropriately and so that the initial voicing could be more accurate. The amount of time that our finest organ builders spend in voicing their instruments during installation is a testimony to their dedication, but a major sacrifice of their time.

The study included sound measurements in the set-up areas of five builders' workshops and measurements in spaces they selected, either as desirable or problematic. As unsponsored studies are often given back-burner status, this study has yet to be finished. We believe it will benefit all builders when we have completed it and published the results. The work will be dedicated to Charles, whose restless curiosity and patient inquiries helped initiate the effort.

CHAPTER EIGHT

Reflections on the Esthetic Evolution of the Cavaillé-Coll Organ

KURT LUEDERS

SLOWLY, ALMOST IMPERCEPTIBLY, the domain of "early music" is creeping toward and into the nineteenth century. The music world, having assimilated historically based performances of Baroque music, is coming to grips with the same treatment for the Viennese classical school. It is a matter of time before a similar approach to performance touches upon Beethoven, throwing the door open to the entire romantic movement.

If we subtract the "rediscovery" element—that is, the exciting resuscitation of virtually entire repertoires such as characterized the beginnings of the early music movement—it could be claimed that the nineteenth century holds as many secrets for us as previous eras. To be sure, the tangible link of sound recording mitigates the obscurity, but does not eliminate the need for careful historical study. We need to grasp the spirit as well as the letter of this music, to seek the inner causes as well as the outward effect.

In the realm of French organ music, one no longer has qualms about having an organ built "in the French classical style," shunning even the stylistic compromises that characterized previous decades. The same evolution is bound to occur for Cavaillé-Coll and the French-romantic school, especially since the corresponding repertoire has never totally ceased to be performed. As was the case with the French classical organ revival, the first instruments claiming openly to be "in the tradition of . . ." are basically "neo-classical" organs (in the contemporary French sense) with a more or less pronounced bow toward the nineteenth century in their specifications. (One German builder has even gone so far as to afix the Cavaillé-Coll nameplate to his instruments, changing only the wording.) Which serious organ builder of our era does not carry around, in mind and ear or even pocket, that haunting model specifica-tion from nineteenth-century France!

In this context, it is this writer's hope to convey—within a few paragraphs— something of the spirit and lasting value of Cavaillé-Coll's work. Books could and should be written about the technical aspects of the great builder's work, but even these are only one step: let us be wary of settling for an artistic goal which can be summed up with "The medium is the message." If this brief essay only helps to short-circuit possible misconceptions, then it will already have largely fulfilled its purpose.

"This man, pursuing such a lofty ideal, always accomplished a perfect realisation thereof, and every organ nurtured in his mind and emerging from his hands, from the smallest to the largest, was always a masterwork."

ALBERT DUPRÉ[1]

"All Cavaillé-Colls are alike. That is not the least of their shortcomings."

NORBERT DUFOURCQ[2]

It is easy to speak or write of "the" Cavaillé-Coll organ, forgetting that the builder's creative life spanned sixty or more years and encompassed several hundred instruments of from four to one hundred stops.[3] As the above statements suggest, for some this productivity means unending variety, for others unending monotony. In a way, each viewpoint carries a certain weight, since the technical and tonal perfection and durability of this master's works left scant leeway for valid divergence from the norm he established. The late André Marchal once commented to this writer, *"Cavaillé-Coll nous a tous écrasés."* A pregnant remark that shows to what extent "le père Cavaillé" could be perceived as a father figure in an unfavorable as well as in an affectionate sense! One fact has, however, stood out for decades, even among those who feel "crushed" by the pervasiveness of Cavaillé-Coll's style: without it, the organ world would be much poorer in musical literature. César Franck's debt to Ste. Clotilde and conceivably to the Trocadéro is universally recognized; Charles-Marie Widor asserted, "If I had not felt the seduction of these timbres, the mystic spell of this wave of sound, I would not have written any organ music";[4] and Louis Vierne echoes, "Who among us, when writing organ music, does not do so under the

N.B. Translations of original French texts into English are by the author unless otherwise indicated.

1. Albert Dupré, *Etude sur Aristide Cavaillé-Coll.* Rouen, 1919, p. 29.

2. Norbert Dufourcq, *L'Orgue* (Collection *Que sais-je,* No. 276), 4th ed. Paris: Presses Universitaires de France, 1970, p. 55.

3. The four-stop specification was *Montre* 8, *Bourdon/Flûte harmonique* 8', *Prestant* 4', and *Trompette* 8', all divided into basses and trebles (i.e., eight drawknobs). Cavaillé-Coll actually delivered a one-stop enclosed (!) positive organ (cf. Ton van Eck, "Het Cavaillé-Coll orgel van het St-Willibrorduscollege te Katwijk," in P. Begheyn and H. Tromp, *Katwijk 1831–1981,* Zeist, 1981, pp. 91–96).

4. Charles-Marie Widor, "Les Orgues de Saint-Sulpice," in *L'Eglise de Saint-Sulpice.* Paris: Blaud & Gay, 1931, p. 138, quoted and translated in John R. Near, *The Life and Works of Charles-Marie Widor,* doctoral dissertation, Boston University, 1984, p. 61.

spell of the flutes, gambas, principals, oboes, and trumpets made by the celebrated company?"[5] How did there evolve such sounds as to capture the imagination of an entire school of organ composition?

It is generally emphasized that Artistide Cavaillé-Coll was rooted and trained in the classical tradition. However, it is equally apparent that he had a progressive spirit from the start. His celebrated first project for Saint Denis, and even more so the actual instrument as completed, were not principally intended to showcase updated classical organ building; the intention was to build the organ of the future, progress incarnate. We forget this too easily when we concentrate our attention on the *jeux de tierce*, *grand plein jeu*, or *grand ravalement* elements. There can be little doubt that the concept of the novel *grand choeur* superceded these in importance, and it was for his tonal and technical *innovations* that Aristide wished to be known. When in 1846 he remarked to Hamel,[6] "I am more than ever aware of how far we have to go yet in our craft," it was with tacit reference to already progressive instruments such as Saint Denis and the Madeleine. (Moreover, Cavaillé-Coll never spurned the chance to modernize his own early instruments decades later when an overhaul was due.) Obviously, the newcomers to Paris could not get away with simply doing what their rivals did, only better, even though old Dominique would probably have liked it that way.

Until 1850 the partnership was equal on paper, including the father Dominique, his wife Jeanne Autard, and the two sons, Vincent and Aristide. Even conceding that Dominique played a determining role in the construction of the Saint Denis masterpiece, his position in these early years seems to have increasingly been as a check against Aristide's progressiveness, with poor Vincent caught in the middle. The older brother, exceptionally talented at voicing, continued to exercise his skill in a conservative manner, characterized by mild strings, refined, flute-like principals, and reeds rich in overtones. With respect to principals and reeds, the Madeleine organ—often regarded as Aristide's definitive break with the classical tradition—may equally well be interpreted as a superbly imaginative realisation of classical tonal ideals adapted to the musical situation of the 1840s. In instruments such as the 1848–49 organ of Saint Paul in Nîmes, the *Salicional* 8' is still a hardly masked version of the classical *Second Huit Pieds*, and one can, for instance, barely distinguish the combination of *Bourdon* 8' and *Doublette* 2' of the *Grand Orgue* from harmonic flutes 8' and 2' of the *Récit*. This was soon to change, with the arrival of new voicers (in particular the Reinburgs). Musicians such as Berlioz[7] and

5. Louis Vierne, "Quelques réflexions sur les orgues," in *Le Courrier Musical*, Vol. XVI, No. 1 (January 1, 1913), p. 11.

6. Fenner Douglass, *Cavaillé-Coll and the Musicians*. Raleigh: At the Sunbury, 1980, p. 555.

7. According to Albert Dupré (p. 24), Berlioz banteringly labeled the too-conservative Cavaillé-

Neukomm[8] were pressing early on for a more fundamental-oriented specification; it became necessary for the foundation stops simply to put out more sound.

Two days before New Year's Eve 1849, the family partnership was officially dissolved, ratifying a situation that had existed in practice for months. "The new activities which this company was engaged in, to wit the construction, sale, repair, maintenance and rental of organs of all types, shall be continued by Mr. A. Cavaillé-Coll *fils*. . . ."[9] This ushered in the quasi-industrial era in a more symbolic way. As soon as 1854, the workshop moved to a factory of sorts, with a proud erecting room where prestigious concerts could take place. (It was presumably at this time that the firm name changed, again significantly, to A. Cavaillé-Coll *and Co.*) Dominique receded into petty and ineffectual bickering with his now-celebrated son.[10] Vincent followed his own wayward paths—concretely speaking, southward to the family homeland around Montpellier—basking in the nostalgia of the "good ol' days" when organs sounded like organs, as he might well have put it. He kept on voicing more or less *à la* 1840, and his esthetic/technical "innovations" were models of superficial, abortive novelty with little or no organic *raison d'être* (for example, splitting up the common eight-stop *"petit Récit"* into two separately enclosed four-stop manuals,[11] or installing pedal and even manual couplers sounding at the fifth!)[12] How tempting it is to speculate that Aristide could have wound up basically the same way had he been content to "follow the 'right' paths and stay 'within tradition.'"[13] Once again, within the concept of "tradition" there exist the letter and the spirit, and to deny Cavaillé-Coll the developments of the second half of his

Coll as "an escapee from the Middle Ages and a torturer of the ears." (Cf. also *Journal des Débats*, December 29, 1844, and the *Grand traité d'instrumentation*, p. 169.)

8. Sigismund Neukomm's diatribe against compound stops is quoted in Didier Decrette, *Le grand orgue historique de la Chapelle Royale de Dreux (La Flûte Harmonique*, No. 27/28, 1983), p. 59.

9. Archives of the City of Paris, D32 U3 30, No. 1857.

10. Cécile and Emmanuel Cavaillé-Coll, *Aristide Cavaillé-Coll: Ses origines, sa vie, son oeuvre*. Paris: Fischbacher, 1929, reprinted 1981, p. 74. Cf. also Fenner Douglass, pp. 287 ff. It is as ironic as it is tragic that in his old age, Aristide Cavaillé-Coll had to deal with the same kind of serious family discord coming from his son Gabriel. Whereas Dominique must have been appalled at his offspring's esthetic and commercial audacity, Gabriel apparently found his father not progressive enough! He espoused the up-and-coming electric action and tried to supplant Aristide by setting up a rival firm in 1892. The attempt did not succeed, but one might assert that the future of the organ world hung in the balance for a few now-forgotten weeks. See especially Constant Pierre, *Les facteurs d'instruments de musique* (Paris: Sagot, 1893; reprinted Geneva: Minkoff, 1971), pp. 218–20, and Christian Lesaulnier, "Le Grand-orgue de l'église Saint-Médard d'Epinay-Sur-Seine," in *La Flûte Harmonique* No. 36 (1985), pp. 32–38.

11. Yves André, "L'Orgue V. Cavaillé-Coll de La Grand' Combe (Gard)," in *La Flûte Harmonique* No. 31/32 (1984), pp. 44–47.

12. Archives of the church of Notre Dame in Oloron-Ste.-Marie (Pyrénées Orientales).

13. Cf. Peter Williams, *The European Organ, 1450–1850*. Bloomington: Indiana University Press, 1978, p. 203 (quoting a judgment of Norbert Dufourcq).

life would be like asking a gifted child not to grow up, for fear that the gift might take "the wrong paths." As a matter of fact, in examining the progression of this builder's later works—and in certain respects the works themselves[14]—it seems remarkable to what extent he actually remained faithful to the grand French tradition in spirit, furthermore imposing it upon his colleagues, such as Merklin, Stoltz, the Abbeys, and several provincial builders, often his pupils.[15]

The turning point of 1849/1850—is it purely chance that it comes exactly at mid-century?—constitutes perhaps the only clear break in Cavaillé-Coll's career. The temptation has always been great to divide this career into neat periods; however, there is not unanimous consensus on this matter, which theoretically ought to be clear-cut. All depends upon which criteria one takes as most crucial. Figure 8–1 summarizes the major landmarks of Cavaillé-Coll's career, whereby the complex interaction between events and esthetic transformations may be better perceived.

In the course of his youth and the early years of his professional career, Aristide Cavaillé-Coll grew out of the Revolutionary era's desolation and into a new age, right along with his very homeland. It may or may not be true that life begins at forty; for Cavaillé-Coll, the early 1850s constituted a new start in several significant ways—personally, professionally, and esthetically. After braving—and surviving—the hardships of 1848, the company output rebounded. From the mid-1850s until the debacle of 1870–71, roughly the equivalent of a seventeen-stop organ left the shop each month.[16] (The same pattern was repeated until 1890, after which production fell off sharply, certain years chalking up barely a few dozen registers.)

A little-known major instrument completed in 1855, and virtually as important as the Madeleine ten years earlier, was the rebuild of Saint Omer in northern France (Cathedral at the time, now parish of Notre Dame). Here, Cavaillé-Coll attained one of his most stunning conceptions (above all in view of the historical context), fusing classical clarity with monumental and compelling romantic grandeur. A more subtly balanced *tutti* than this cannot be conceived! In addition to exquisite solo reeds and equally refined variety of fluework, we find the first *"grand Récit"* based on a double 16'. For its novelty and its intrinsic quality, the stoplist merits quoting in full.

---

14. Cf. especially François Sabatier, *La palette sonore de Cavaillé-Coll (Jeunesse et Orgue*, special issue 1979), *passim*.

15. Sometimes it was expressly specified that an organ was to be voiced "according to Cavaillé-Coll's standards," etc. (Cf. Abbé Paul Farinez, "Henri Didier était-il un facteur d'orgues 'faussaire'?", in *La Flûte Harmonique* No. 26 (1983), pp. 19–28.

16. Estimate based on Gilbert Huybens, "Liste des travaux exécutés par Aristide Cavaillé-Coll," in *ISO Information* No. 23 (August 1983), pp. 47–52.

1855, A. Cavaillé-Coll
St. Omer

Grand Orgue:
    Montre   16′
    Bourdon   16′
    Gambe   16′
    Montre   8′
    Bourdon   8′
    Viole de Gambe 8′
    Prestant   4′
    Flûte octaviante 4′
    Grand cornet   V

Bombarde:
    Flûte harmonique 8′
    Octave   4′
    Doublette   2′
    Fourniture   V
    Cymbale   IV
    Bombarde   16′
    Trompette   8′
    Hautbois   8′
    Clairon   4′

Pédale:
    Flûte   16′
    Flûte   8′
    Flûte   4′
    Bombarde   16′
    Trompette   8′
    Clairon   4′

Positif:
    Montre   8′
    Bourdon   8′
    Salicional   8′
    Prestant   4′
    Flûte douce   4′
    Dulciane   4′
    Nasard   2⅔′

Doublette	2'
Cornet	V
Plein jeu	V
Trompette	8'
Cromorne	8'
Clairon	4'

Récit Expressif:

Bourdon	16'
Flûte harmonique	8'
Viole de Gambe	8'
Voix céleste	8'
Flûte octaviante	4'
Viole	4'
Octavin	2'
Bombarde	16'
Trompette	8'
Basson-hautbois	8'
Voix humaine	8'
Clairon	4'

This is probably the last instrument of Cavaillé-Coll to be in full contact with his *débuts*. Two years later, he received the contract to rebuild what remained of Clicquot's masterpiece at St. Sulpice, and the course of organ building changed forever.

Much has been made of Cavaillé-Coll's "conversion" to progressive, non-repeating mixtures in the late 1850s, and even more of his "re-conversion" to classical compositions some fifteen years later. Indeed, this characteristic affords the handiest compartmentalization of his career. Although other facets of change may be more conclusive or significant, it has become customary to speak of three periods, delimited by mixture style. In practice, the essential sound of both types of mixture in Cavaillé-Coll's work is similar.

The *plein-jeu harmonique*—in German, *Progressivharmonica* after the latin-ate *progressio harmonica*—was used by Joseph Merklin in his instrument for Saint Eugène in 1855–56. Among those impressed with this organ was Louis Niedermeyer, who was on the reception committee. It may have been Niedermeyer who convinced Cavaillé-Coll to adopt this mixture at Saint Louis d'Antin two years later,[17] since the latter organ was linked closely with the

17. Parish archives of Saint Louis d'Antin; K. Lueders, "Die Merklin-Orgeln in Paris, St.-Eugène, und in der Kathedrale von Murcia," in *Ars Organi* No. 57 (October 1978), pp. 433–41. Further

activities of the *École de Musique Religieuse*. It was the "grave," "religious" character of the low-pitched, non-repeating mixture, compared to the "Gothic" formula of the classical *plein jeu*, that gave it particular appeal at this time. The famous "ascending voicing" was being developed, much abetted by the imminent adoption of slotted flues. Also, by now the old construction of reed stops—with bevelled shallots and thin tongues—had been abandoned; a fuller, more substantial tone through more generous curving replaced the somewhat acid sound of the former chorus reeds. This in turn, within the *tutti*, necessitated a "livening" of harmonics in the treble, hence the "progressive" mixture:

	8	$5\frac{1}{3}$	4	$2\frac{2}{3}$	2	$1\frac{1}{3}$
C				$2\frac{2}{3}$	2	$1\frac{1}{3}$
f_o			4	$2\frac{2}{3}$	2	$1\frac{1}{3}$
f_1		$5\frac{1}{3}$	4	$2\frac{2}{3}$	2	$1\frac{1}{3}$
f_2	8	$5\frac{1}{3}$	4	$2\frac{2}{3}$	2	$1\frac{1}{3}$

The climax of this development was reached at Notre Dame in 1868:[18]

Grand Orgue

	$10\frac{2}{3}$	8	$5\frac{1}{3}$	4	$2\frac{2}{3}$	$2\frac{2}{3}$	2	$1\frac{3}{5}$	$1\frac{1}{3}$	1
C				4	$2\frac{2}{3}$	$2\frac{2}{3}$	2			
c_o			$5\frac{1}{3}$	4	$2\frac{2}{3}$	$2\frac{2}{3}$	2	$1\frac{3}{5}$		
c_1		8	$5\frac{1}{3}$	4	$2\frac{2}{3}$	$2\frac{2}{3}$	2	$1\frac{3}{5}$	$1\frac{1}{3}$	
c_2	$10\frac{2}{3}$	8	$5\frac{1}{3}$	4	$2\frac{2}{3}$	$2\frac{2}{3}$	2	$1\frac{3}{5}$	$1\frac{1}{3}$	1

(Fourniture harm. II-V)   (Cymbale harmonique II-V)

Positif

	16	8	$5\frac{1}{3}$	4	$3\frac{1}{5}$	$2\frac{2}{3}$
C				4	$3\frac{1}{5}$	$2\frac{2}{3}$
c_o			$5\frac{1}{3}$	4	$3\frac{1}{5}$	$2\frac{2}{3}$
a_o		8	$5\frac{1}{3}$	4	$3\frac{1}{5}$	$2\frac{2}{3}$
f_{s_1}	16	8	$5\frac{1}{3}$	4	$3\frac{1}{5}$	$2\frac{2}{3}$

(Plein jeu harmonique III-VI)

Cavaillé-Coll continued to use progressive mixtures in his smaller instruments. However, it is as if the Notre Dame experiment—conclusive as it was, and slated for renewal in the unrealized monumental project for St. Peter's in Rome—ran him into a dead end. Furthermore, with the nomination of Gigout, Widor, and Guilmant to key posts in Paris (Saint Augustin 1863, Saint Sulpice 1870, Trinité 1871), the organistic ambiance that inhabited the master

evidence of Niedermeyer's *desiderata* may be found in the lack of a *voix céleste* stop at Saint Louis d'Antin and in Cavaillé-Coll's reluctance to install a free-reed *Clarinette* there.

18. Jean-Louis Coignet, "Le grand orgue de Notre Dame de Paris de 1868 à nos jours," in *La Flûte Harmonique* No. 14 (1980), p. 7.

builder's ears changed. Lefébure-Wély, Cavallo, Schmitt, and their operatic "*Grand Offertoire*" style gave way gradually to a more authentically symphonic compositional style, which demanded the availability of every tessitura at every dynamic level for the purposes of musical development. This the progressive *plein jeu* could not deliver. Let us reiterate, however, that the actual *sonority* of Cavaillé-Coll's mixtures changed little or not at all; even when the composition is virtually identical with that given by Dom Bédos, the sound of the principal chorus is virile, almost reedy, sometimes downright Germanic, having little in common with the sparkling, calm majesty of the French classical *plein jeu*. Considerations of "historical authenticity" for early music, often cited as the reason for Cavaillé-Coll's return to classical mixture compositions,[19] came after the fact, if at all. Indeed, many a principal chorus is almost too strong to be used alone, and, even after Lemmens' arrival on the scene, it was far from obvious that contrapuntal textures should be played on the mixtures: foundation stops alone—with or without crescendo to full organ—or even the traditional *grand jeu* concept often took precedence.

In order to give a further boost to the "ascending" voicing, now that the basses were acoustically enriched, Cavaillé-Coll borrowed an idea from the Germanic builders. The free-standing harmonic *Picolo [sic]* of the late 1850s and the 1860s doubtless had little justification after the demise (at least in Cavaillé-Coll's eyes) of Lefébure-Wély and his "brilliant" school of playing. Thus it was incorporated with the mutation ranks of the *Cornet*, $2\frac{2}{3}'$ and $1\frac{3}{5}'$, into the *Carillon III*.[20] In certain cases, cost perhaps being the deciding factor, the *Carillon* remained progressive, beginning with only the $2\frac{2}{3}'$ rank. It is significant that, despite its apparent vocation as a *tutti* stop, organists clearly enjoyed the picturesque aspect of the *Carillon*. Most notably among several examples, Guilmant used it with *Bourdon 8'* in the famous *Basse et Dessus de Trompette* of Clérambault.

It may be deduced from internal evidence that Cavaillé-Coll was no particular friend of *Cornets*. To be sure, in his large rebuilds, he retained at least one *Cornet* from the preceding instrument, and even in his new organs, a *Cornet* as unique compound stop above 4' was not totally unknown (for example, Church of the Lazarist Fathers in Paris, twenty stops, 1862—perhaps a client's

19. Cf. for instance William Sumner, *The Organ: Its Evolution, Principles of Construction and Use*. London: MacDonald, 1952, p. 211.

20. Cavaillé-Coll may have taken note of Bätz's *Carillon* in the Cathedral of Utrecht during his study visit there in October 1844, or he may have been further informed about the idea by his employee Neuburger. In any case, Merklin was already using a similar stop, called *Clochettes*, in the 1860s. (Cf. Maartin A. Vente, *Orgels en organisten van de Dom te Utrecht van de 14ᵉ eeuw tot heden*. Utrecht, 1975, p. 56; Fenner Douglass, pp. 659–61; K. Lueders, "Die Orgel der Basilika St. Epvre zu Nancy," in *Mitteilungsblatt der Internationalen Bruckner-Gesellschaft* No. 13 (May 1978), p. 9–10.

special condition?). Nevertheless, since this stop was used almost exclusively in the *grand choeur,* the crucial question must have been whether its sonority enhanced and complemented the reed-plus-flue chorus. Here, a familiarity with Cavaillé-Coll's very small instruments (those of four to nine stops, or those of ten to fifteen stops that have no mixture), whose *tutti* always sound astoundingly grandiose and "complete," gives a precious clue to the ideal or absolute sound the builder was aiming for: whereas the *Cornet* timbre can conceivably complement the rather tart reed sound alluded to above in connection with the earlier instruments, in later organs the ear intuitively perceives a mixture-like harmonic development. The smaller the organ, the more the *Prestant* 4' becomes the keystone of its tonal structure; without resorting to aggressiveness, it supplies the proper "nudge" in harmonics, like a soft mixture, assuring a warm *grand choeur* without sacrificing power. A few of Cavaillé-Coll's best-known organs do not contain any tierce rank (for example, La Madeleine, Ste. Clotilde, Luçon, Epernay); in other cases a sole *Cornet* is relegated to the symphonic *Récit* division, where it has the function of "sealing" the reeds to the flue sonority. One may speculate that Cavaillé-Coll associated the *Cornet* color with Germanic tonal schemes, personified by the rival firm Merklin, whose *Cornets* predictably stand sovereign over the full organ, next to a rather puny three- to five-rank *"fourniture."* This, aside from inevitable chauvinistic considerations,[21] may have been one reason why commentators regarded Merklin as more inspired by Germanic tendencies than by French.

   Toward the end of Cavaillé-Coll's career—even approximate dates cannot be put forth, due to as-yet-insufficient research and documentation—his voicers applied the technique of the *contre-tournure* to lend chorus reeds still more stability and brilliance while retaining reasonable wind pressures and voicing style. It was a simple principle, the tongue being given a convex curve at the point of contact with the tuning wire. Indeed, it was perhaps *too* simple, for, under Cavaillé-Coll's successor Charles Mutin, the practice seems to have been generalized, transforming it from an artistic fine point into a banal crutch, with a resulting blatant, undifferentiated chorus reed sound.

   A similar situation—once again with proper reserve, pending valid, specialized study and investigation—may be observed concerning nicking of flue pipe languids. That Cavaillé-Coll was aware of the procedure at a very early date is beyond doubt.[22] In any case, the slowing down of the speech of French symphonic *fonds* has often been noted by specialists. Aside from the general trend toward long, relatively unarticulated musical lines in the nineteenth century, there are at least two reasons for making pipes a bit less prompt in attack.

21. Cf. for instance *Le Monde Musical,* Vol. III, no. 44 (February 28, 1891), p. 4–5.

22. C. and E. Cavaillé-Coll, p. 58.

First, the adoption of Barker lever assistance necessitated avoiding even the possibility of overly violent speech. The Barker lever mechanism as perfected by Cavaillé-Coll is astonishingly sensitive to nuances of touch; but activated vigorously by corresponding finger action at the keyboards, the pneumatics were sooner or later bound to produce a sharp pallet opening, and this had to be provided for in the voicing.

A second reason may be sought in an aspect of mid-nineteenth century organistic style that has only recently come back into "favor" among organ composers: it is difficult for us to imagine how pervasive the practice of repeated chords was at the time, from the dabblers right through to the major composers. A handful of examples, culled almost at random, will illustrate this:

C. Franck: Fantaisie en la (1878)

Th. Dubois: Offertoire (1886)

One can imagine the effect of such passages rendered with rapid and highly articulated pipe speech.[23] In addition to organ music, outright piano repertoire such as Chopin's E-minor *Prélude* or the D-minor Fantasy of Mozart remained on every music rack until composers began wending their way toward an autonomous style. The voicing practices remained, however, once again to be allowed to slip into the grotesque at the hands of Charles Mutin (for example, deep nicks as a matter of course).

Without a doubt, Aristide Cavaillé-Coll was not a pure empiricist, and for this he was particularly praised by his contemporaries. One is reminded of the "infernal machine," as it was affectionately called by co-workers: a "mannequin" or model chest upon which stood thirty-two pipes representing the harmonic series of a fundamental note, all of which could be added or subtracted at will—a veritable tonal synthesizer! Visitors at the shop marveled at the metamorphosis of one timbre into another, but this was, of course, anything but a toy: Cavaillé-Coll was held in as high esteem by the scientific community as he was by the artistic. He possessed the perfect fusion of intuition, the feedback of concrete observation, and good taste. This was passed on to his voicers, most of whom grew up with him, professionally speaking, and served the company for decades. (A photograph from the Mutin shop clearly

23. Only passages predominantly on flue registrations have been chosen, since it might reasonably be argued that repeated chords on reeds necessarily have a sharper attack. Even in the case of reeds, the attack became slightly slower as Cavaillé-Coll's career advanced.

shows young children working alongside master craftsmen at the voicing tables.[24] One began early on, *chez Cavaillé!*) The care lavished on subtle tonal finishing must have been one of the main factors in the firm's high prices, but more than one contemporary writer emphasized the pitfalls of trying to pin a figure on such unequalled quality.

In this context, one perhaps misses the point by stigmatizing nineteenth-century voicing as "imposed by the boss."[25] Of course, if measured against the present "norm" of a handful of craftsmen collaborating and interacting freely, Cavaillé-Coll's system had drawbacks, on the sociological if not on the artistic level. Naturally, there was division of labor and specialization. Catalogues were indeed published with standard series organs for a fixed price, whose variety was by definition limited. It would, however, hardly be more fair to criticize a fine series organ than it would a fine lithograph, simply because there are several copies. (On the other side of the fairness coin, let us admit that there exists a small percentage of Cavaillé-Coll organs that are good organs but not exciting.) Furthermore, the work of any great artist contains constants making it immediately recognizable, without diminishing the esthetic pleasure it engenders. Would anyone think of claiming that, say, "All Mozart piano concerti are alike"...?

Cavaillé-Coll's uncanny knack for fitting each organ to the edifice housing it[26] makes for unending variety in subtle tone colors, particularly in the foundation stops. The different personalities of the company's voicers only enhanced this aspect. Just as we can identify and name the various colors of the spectrum without being able to pinpoint the transition from one to the next, so the relatively few names given to foundation stops fail to convey the breadth of timbres available among the master's organs. One could, without undue "stretching," outline the Cavaillé-Coll "spectrum," using as reference points the five basic *fonds* included on the *Grand Orgue* division of his larger instruments:

thin Gamba with beard	*gambe* / "warm"
Viole de Gambe	
Violoncelle	
Viole d'Amour	
Salicional	
Diapason	

24. Published in Alexandre Cellier, *L'Orgue moderne*. Paris: Lelagrave, 1913.

25. Cf. Pierre Chéron, "Harmonie, création, liberté," in *Les Facteurs d'orgues français*, (Spring 1982), p. 34.

26. In this connection, it should be mentioned that we are accustomed today to hear French romantic organs in empty or near-empty rooms, whereas the builders created their tonal schemes assuming virtually full rooms.

Montre
Flûte (rare, in rebuilds)
Octave 4' (gemshorn form)
Flûte harmonique
Flûte octaviante
Flûte traversière
Bourdon
Cor de Nuit
Quintaton

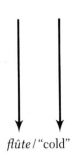

flûte / "cold"

With such finesse and variety, is it any wonder that Cavaillé-Coll felt solo mutations to be largely superfluous? If his technical means were different from those of the pre-Revolutionary builders, the basic ends were the same, namely the creation of the perfect tonal palette, carefully weighing quality and quantity of hues in search of that point at which the striving for one is not yet to the detriment of the other.

This builder, unlike many of his colleagues, knew where the point of diminishing returns lay with 8' stops. There is never one too many, but always a healthy, organic filling out in the 16' range and/or in harmonics. This was surely one of the secrets unlocked in part by the "mannequin," and accounts for the fact that a Cavaillé-Coll organ almost never gives the impression of being too loud. It is not exaggerated to say that, when other builders spoke of *puissance*, they meant "power," whereas for Cavaillé-Coll, the word connotated something like "strength," "intensity," or "richness." All the more reason to mistrust printed specifications! At this level, the close study of a one-manual, 6½-stop organ is hardly less rewarding than of Rouen's 64 or Notre Dame's 86 stops. Soon, the word *orchestral* used in connection with organ tone takes on a meaning at once deeper and more subtle. In addition, there is always the *petite surprise* waiting in the wings to scoff at the observer's hasty generalizations. (One example among many: the independent Quinte 2⅔' stop in the otherwise "standard" *Récit* of the 26-stop organ at Immaculée Conception in Elbeuf [1881], capable of transforming one's entire attitude and approach, not only to this particular instrument, but to Cavaillé-Coll's entire output.)

Compared to Cavaillé-Coll, the tone colors of the German organs, benefiting from much more diversified pipe construction, tended toward extremes. (Here the analogy, rather than to a spectrum, might be to a certain number of tubes of oil or watercolor paint.) Yet detailed registrations were rare—one finds "2 *od.* 3 *sanfte Grundregister*," "*dumpfe Stimmen*," "*mit hellen, doch nicht aufdringlichen Stimmen*," and the like. The well-known preface to Mendelssohn's organ sonatas points out the difficulty of giving more precise instructions. On the other hand, the French composers, able to count on certain tonal constants, could specify stop names in considerable detail. It is ironic that often, where the German organist marks *Grundstimmen* without being sure exactly how they will sound in any specific case, his French counterpart willingly forgoes the unambiguous and everywhere predictably sounding *fonds 8* in favor of writing out *Montres, flûtes, et Gambes 8'*. A fitting commentary on differing mentalities!

Nothing in the study of Cavaillé-Coll's work is as difficult as evaluating or even describing the organs of the last great period, from about 1872 onward. Selecting sample instruments for analysis already presents problems, so fascinating is each masterwork.

A celebrated pianist once remarked that, if asked to choose between the two Brahms piano concerti, his preference would have to go to the first: despite his admiration and fondness for the total mastery and flawlessness of the second, it was, in comparison to the stunning audacity of the first, almost *too* perfect. With the first, one senses a formidable wrestling with the material, and perhaps even more a struggle against the temptation to push ever further the limits of technique and innovation, possibly at the ultimate expense of artistic integrity. In the second, on the contrary, what an aura of total control over material *and* expression, creating an irresistably moving impression of assurance and strength! The miracle is that genius and fundamental maturity pervade the "youthful" work, just as there is ample freshness and fundamentally youthful life in the "mature" work.

These considerations apply perfectly to the *oeuvre* of Aristide Cavaillé-Coll, and shed light on the difficulty of describing his last instruments in words. During the past few years, a conventional terminology has, for better or for worse, been crystallized, according to which nineteenth-century French organs fall either into the category of *romantic* or into that of *symphonic*. While the literal application of these terms seldom works faultlessly (has the Trocadéro organ no romantic qualities, for instance, and what about the unquestionable symphonic elements at Saint Omer?), if we approach them from the standpoint of an analogy like the one above, they can lead to increased intuitive understanding.

The later, so-called symphonic works of Cavaillé-Coll are above all characterized by *balance*—horizontal balance, among the various isolated elements of the tonal spectrum centering on the 8' unison tone, and vertical balance, among the building blocks of the *grand choeur* ensemble. This balance results in a *homogeneity* of sound, which does not imply that a certain heterogeneity in his earlier organs is a fault. Quite the opposite is true. It is just that, between the perfection of the classical French *plein jeu/grand jeu* dichotomy, and the equal perfection of Cavaillé-Coll's definitive *grand choeur* ideal, a painstaking—if not painful—search had to be carried out, with the concomitant rejection of elements that, despite the efforts and sacrifices they implied, turned out to be inconclusive or still perfectible. This Cavaillé-Coll accomplished with characteristic courage, perseverance, integrity, and genius. At the risk of pushing analogy beyond the limits of plausibility, one might assert that the Cavaillé-Coll style went through the normal human stages of infancy, childhood (to c. 1856), adolescence (c. 1857–70), young adulthood (c. 1871–76), full maturity and productiveness (c. 1876–90), and old age (1891–99). The points of similarity, with reference to developmental psychology, are not as farfetched as one might suspect, but remarkably consistent, all the more in the light of the words of Cavaillé-Coll's actual children, who served as his biographers: "Cavaillé-Coll had toward his instruments a true fatherly affection [des entrailles de père]."[27]

As a representative of the last great masterful period, there follows the specification of Saint Etienne in Caen [1885]. The reader's conscientious examination will reveal the variety and subtle balance built into the instrument. Since the organ is the same size as St. Omer, a comparison of the two helps us understand the metamorphosis that occurred in the thirty years that separate them.[28]

1885, Aristide Cavaillé-Coll
Saint Etienne, Caen

Grand Orgue I:

Montre	16'
Bourdon	16'
Montre	8'
Bourdon	8'
Gambe	8'
Flûte harmonique	8'
Prestant	4'
Flûte octaviante	4'
Quinte	2⅔'
Doublette	2'
Plein jeu	VII
Cornet	V
Bombarde	16'
Trompette	8'
Clairon	4'

27. E. and C. Cavaillé-Coll, p. 125.

28. The choice of these two masterworks is not fully fortuitous, although other pairs of equally "typical" instruments could be found; the author has simplified his task by opting for his two favorite instruments!

Positif II:

Bourdon	16'
Principal	8'
Cor de nuit	8'
Salicional	8'
Unda maris	8'
Prestant	4'
Flûte douce	4'
Carillon	III
Basson	16'
Trompette	8'
Cromorne	8'

Récit Expressif III:

Quintaton	16'
Diapason	8'
Flûte traversière	8'
Viole de Gambe	8'
Voix céleste	8'
Flûte octaviante	4'
Octavin	2'
Cornet	III–V
Bombarde	16'
Trompette	8'
Basson-hautbois	8'
Clarinette	8'
Voix humaine	8'
Clairon	4'

Pédale:

Bourdon	32'
Contrebasse	16'
Soubasse	16'
Grosse flûte	8'
Bourdon doux	8'
Violoncelle	8'
Flûte	4'
Bombarde	16'
Trompette	8'
Clairon	4'

A corollary of the inter-manual balance and homogeneity of these last organs was multiple swell divisions (in cases where there was no dorsal *positif*, of course, although Cavaillé-Coll did at least once put a swell division in such a *positif* case).[29] This came toward the beginning of the 1870s, and accompanied the adoption of balanced, centered swell pedals demanded by English clients (like Mr. Hopwood of London, 1869).[30] The musical implications of this innovation have often been discussed in connection with César Franck, whose Ste. Clotilde organ retained the former, spring-loaded *cuiller* mechanism throughout his tenure there.[31] Vierne also assumed this system in his symphonies, in the case of *subito piano* effects, much more difficult to carry out with balanced pedals. Thus, a technique that at first was largely confined to rapid nuances and echo effects was swiftly transformed, taking on true symphonic dimensions. Cavaillé-Coll knew about enclosing the entire organ, but wisely left the *Grand Orgue* and *Pédale* divisions unenclosed.[32]

This latter characteristic illustrates the relative conservatism of Cavaillé-Coll straight through to his last years. During this period, competition was fierce, especially from Merklin and his high-powered publicity campaigns, centering on electric action, from 1885 or so onward. Debierre in Nantes was using a single, ingenious chest design for tracker/Barker, pneumatic and electric action, affording extraordinary flexibility *vis-à-vis* customers' special desires.[33] Above all, foreign firms such as Anneessens, Link, and Rieger were beginning an "invasion," thanks to the low prices of mass production and/or cheap nonskilled labor. Most other French firms did not hesitate to jump on the bandwagon, especially since the first signs of the impending separation of Church and State—with its catastrophic implications for organ building— could already be observed. Cavaillé-Coll never succumbed to the temptation of non-mechanical action, horizontal arrangement of divisions with cavernous cases, wind pressures above $3\frac{1}{2}$–$4\frac{1}{4}$ inches, unorganic specifications, under-

29. *La Flûte Harmonique* No. 1 (1976), p. 7, concerning the organ of the church of Saint Hippolyte in Poligny (Jura).

30. Claude Noisette de Crauzat, *Cavaillé-Coll*. Paris: La Flûte de Pan, 1984, illustration following p. 204.

31. Cf. Rollin Smith, *Toward an Authentic Interpretation of the Organ Works of César Franck*. New York: Pendragon Press, 1983, p. 50. (Intermediary stages by notches were not always included on such hitch-down swell pedals.)

32. Cavaillé-Coll's one-manual organs were usually fully enclosed except for the façade pipes. In the superb house organ he built for Charles Gounod, both *Grand Orgue* and *Récit* are independently expressive. Furthermore, in at least one case—the church of the Jesuit Fathers in Lyon, in which the organ is virtually hidden behind stone arches—there is a general swell box for the entire organ, within which is contained the *Récit expressif* division with its own swell box and a second swell pedal.

33. Among the extant examples of the three types of action are, respectively, Saint Lambert in Paris, La Trinité in Cherbourg, and the Cathedral of Vannes.

development of harmonics,[34] "pushing" individual stops at the expense of coherence and chorus integrity, octave couplers masquerading as tonal enrichment, dummy façades, and any number of further practices[35] that could only spell doom for the romantic organ and have unfairly been imputed to its original creators.

Hence, the debate over "Cavaillé-Coll vs. Tradition," most important to those who have an axe to grind, ought to be stilled in order to concentrate on the countless gaps and enigmas that remain in the study of his work. A short sampling:

1. The relationship between Lemmens, Fétis, Cavaillé-Coll, and Merklin does not seem yet to have been satisfactorily charted, nor has the esthetic stance of Lemmens been fully elucidated and publicized.[36]

2. The influence of the harmonium on nineteenth-century organ tone has perhaps been underestimated. Charles Fisk surmised that the popularity and ubiquitousness of the free-reed instruments may have made quasi-imperative the imitation of its tone in pipe organs.

3. It seems illogical that the normally tasteful and perspicacious Cavaillé-Coll, much more than his rivals, invariably installed the thunder pedal, even on relatively small instruments.[37] (It is true that we have lost all feeling for the place held in the nineteenth-century organist's arsenal by thunderstorm, earthquake, and related effects.)[38] Was it simply a means of adding an inexpensive

34. It is ironic that many contemporary rebuilds or "restorations" of Cavaillé-Coll's organs—particularly by the Alsatian builders—seem actually to have softened the nineteenth-century mixtures, destroying the tonal equilibrium desired by the original builder.

35. Of course, there are isolated exceptions to these observations, but do they not in fact sustain all the more the general rule?

36. Cf. for instance Georges L. J. Alexis, "Aristide Cavaillé-Coll et ses amis belges," in *Mélanges Ernest Closson*, Brussels, 1948, pp. 30–45; and the preface to N. J. Lemmens, *Oeuvres inédites*, Leipzig and Brussels, Breitkopf und Härtel, 1888.

37. The *effet d'orage* pedal was found to the extreme left of the pedalboard and progressively depressed the keys of the lowest octave of the pedal division (including any coupled manual divisions).

38. Some of the composers who published such pieces were Batiste, Blanc (Lunéville), Blanchet, Dallier, Joseph Franck, Grison (Reims), Hess (Nancy), Lefébure-Wély, Lemmens, Loret, Neukomm, and Schmitt. We cannot resist quoting in full one of the best evocations ever written of the organ's role as a reflection of nature:

> But already within our hearing, so many different voices capable of touching our soul, of moving it, of startling it, of terrifying it, of ravishing it, of transporting it from the cramped realm in which it lives, into the boundless regions of ideals and the infinite! Voice of the clouds, voice of the mountains, voice of the valleys, voice of the plain, voice of the deserts, voice of the forests, voice of the torrents, of the brooks, the rivers and the seas; voice of the living, you sing a hymn whose verses, grandiose and gracious in turn, enchant our souls even if we don't grasp its entire meaning, nor comprehend its secret harmony. I lend an ear to the thunder's rumbling, to the noise of the cataracts falling in sobs from the heavens, to the rush of avalanches and of torrents,

entry to the *Pédales de combinaison* list? Or a bow to the rabble? Did he himself even like the practice? A subtler explanation might be that, fully aware that such scenes were inevitable, he wished to preclude abuse and inadequate realizations thereof by standardizing—and thus in a sense neutralizing—the technique. In other words, Cavaillé-Coll may paradoxically have generalized this (to us) unmusical accessory on purpose, for overriding *musical* reasons.

∿

Every paragraph, sometimes every sentence, of this brief exposé of the Cavaillé-Coll organ esthetic could become the point of departure of a fascinating specialized study. Aristide Cavaillé-Coll created his instruments for the listeners of his time, whose attitudes were different than ours. He took part in the search for a proper *Art Catholique* within the framework of contemporary *bourgeois* society. As Stephen Morelot pointed out, the organ was anything but a passive witness to the social progress one felt was being accomplished or at least sought:

> The Church, by placing in its sanctuaries the instrument which is, so to speak, the tangible and material symbol of this new order, has thereby conferred the privilege of *bourgeoisie* upon the art that emanates therefrom, and by insuring its future, sounded the signal of its progress.[39]

Hence, Cavaillé-Coll and his colleagues may be counted in the forefront of the cultural and social metamorphoses of their era. The organ was a tool for actively shaping the future, a link between man and nature, and, ultimately and potentially, between the soul and eternity.

> The organ, properly understood, could perhaps tell us which regime is most appropriate to the governing of the things of this world. . . . Yet let us not dwell on this matter, but return to the sanctuary.

to the humming of the wind that makes the branches of the great trees sing like an aeolian harp's strings, to the rustling of the waters that flow slowly, caressing their banks, to the bellowing of the enraged waves that break on the haughty rocks, to those vague sighs, as of a sleeping giant, that you hear arise from the depths of a calm sea, to the joyous cries, to the lively and gentle songs, to the suave melodies, to the buzzing, to the murmurs of living creatures who, from the plains, from the air, from the trees, from every twig of shrubbery, greet the breaking dawn and the waning day; I tremble, I admire, I dream, am touched, I weep, I am exalted, and yet in all this there are numbers and relationships that escape me; I cannot say how these sounds, noises and voices come together to move my soul; but no matter, I have heard nature's *grand orgue*.

(from Le T. R. P. Monsabré, *L'Orgue, discours prononcé le 8 mai 1884 en l'église St. Godard de Rouen pour l'inauguration du grand orgue,* Rouen, 1884, pp. 7–8. See also P. G. Moreau, *Le langage religieux de l'orgue.* Paris and Poitiers, H. Oudin, 1895, pp. 8 ff.)

39. S. Morelot, "Des caractères de la musique d'orgue et des qualités de l'organiste," in *La Maîtrise,* Vol. I, no. 5 (August 15, 1857), p. 70.

Once the hymns are silent, once the organ fills the church with its religious harmony, it invites us to retreat into our innermost selves and to regard ourselves as living organs whose every stop should be singing the glory of God. . . .[40]

Here, then, was the profound ideal toward which Aristide Cavaillé-Coll was striving, and according to which he may most fairly be judged. He was most aware of his international vocation, giving and receiving freely of ideas and techniques.[41] The phrase, "Cavaillé-Coll has something to offer to everyone," is not simply a banal apologetic claim, but a valid statement of goals. Motivated and guided by a consummate union of ambition and integrity, spurning material gain, his life and career embodied a fundamental principle he shared with Charles Fisk: whatever the stoplist or "style" imposed, the task of the organ builder of quality is to trust his own inner aural image of the musical instrument to be created, and to find and use tastefully all the means at his disposal to realize it in actual sound.[42] The more numerous the available elements, the more demands are made on the artist to choose and mold them in a coherent and lasting way.

Despite the simplicity of this ideal, it remains elusive, except to those whose creativity and awareness of the spiritual needs of their eras, together with an innate sense of equilibrium, allow them to draw on the lessons of the past, without slavish copying or unconsidered rejection of valid elements. In this category may be placed the two master builders whose memory, directly and indirectly, the foregoing essay honors.

40. Le T. R. P. Monsabré, p. 20.

41. Cf. *Le Monde Musical*, No. 58 (September 30, 1891), p. 4, concerning Cavaillé-Coll's cherished wish to build for St. Peter's Basilica in Rome a monumental organ that would transcend all boundaries of nationalism. For an excellent discussion of foreign influences on Cavaillé-Coll's work, see Jesse E. Eschbach, "Aristide Cavaillé-Coll and Internationalism in Organbuilding in Nineteenth-Century France," in *The American Organist*, Vol. 19, no. 4 (April 1985), pp. 51–55.

42. Lecture by Charles Fisk given at Oberlin College on November 1, 1980.

Year	Commercial and personal	Paris Expositions	Principal organs	Organists/ Composers	Voicers, Foremen	Stylistic characteristics
1830	Move to Paris "Cavaillé-Coll père et fils"	1839	N—D. de Lorette Saint Denis	Benoist Neukomm Simon	V. Cavaillé-Coll Puig	Construction of Poikilorgues; subsequently gives up free reeds Barker pneumatic levers Classical mixture compositions New voicers
1840	European study trip			Lefébure-Wély		
1845	Title "Facteurs d'orgues du Roi"	1844	La Madeleine		Neuburger G. Reinburg	New voicers
1850	1848 Revolution "Légion d'Honneur" "A. Cavaillé-Coll fils" Marriage	1849	Ajaccio St. Vincent de Paul	Lemmens Franck	F. Reinburg Glock	Unequal temperament abandoned New reed construction Narrow-scaled stops more numerous; Voix céleste design "standardized" as string tone (Réc.)
1855	Move to new factory Merklin arrives in Paris "A. Cavaillé-Coll et Cie."	1855	Saint Omer	Loret	Thiemann	Progressive mixtures adopted Unda maris placed on Positif Slotting of flues begins
1860	Malines conference fixes norms		Sainte Clotilde Nancy Saint Sulpice San Sebastián Versailles	Saint-Saëns Dubois Liszt Widor Guilmant	Carloni Garnier Bonneau	Small series organs in production 56—note manual compass Coloristic elements in Positif division (Quintaton, Picolo, Clarinette . . .)
1865	Move to new factory	1867	Notre Dame Manchester	Chauvet		Complete mutation series at Notre Dame

8–1.

Date	Events	Location	Names		Characteristics
1870	War and the Commune				Balanced, centered swell pedals.
	Large-scale exportation begins				Gradual return to repeating mixtures in larger instruments
1875	"A. Cavaillé-Coll à Paris"				Carillon; independent Quinte $2\tfrac{2}{3}'$ even in smaller organs
	Officer of "Légion d'Honneur"				Two expressive divisions common
1878		Sheffield	Gigout	Mutin	
		Ketton-Hall			
		Amsterdam			
		Brussels			
		Trocadéro			
1880	Period of Prosperity: 1875–90	Orléans		Veerkamp	
	One large organ after another			Prince	
1885					Emphasis upon careful equilibrium among divisions
1889		Lyon	A. Chapuis		Introduction of chamades in larger instruments
		Caen	Pierné		
		Paris-American Church			
		Amiens			
		Toulouse			
1890	Serious financial difficulty;	Rouen	Boëllmann		
	Rival firm of son Gabriel				
1895	Support from private patrons	Saint-Sever	Marty	Mertz	
	October 13, 1899, death of A. Cavaillé-Coll	Chât. Ilbarritz	Vierne	Perroux	
		Azcoitia		Gonzalez	
1900	Mutin becomes company director	[Moscow]			Stylistic stability

Note: The placement of names with reference to the time scale is approximate in these two columns.

CHAPTER NINE

The One-Manual Anglo-Breton Organ
of the Seventeenth Century
and its Musical Implications

BARBARA OWEN

In the spring of 1983 I spent a week in Brittany at a study conference of the British Institute of Organ Studies, the purpose of which was to examine, document, play and discuss some little-known but historically important organs. On my return I spent an afternoon with Charles Fisk, describing the instruments we had seen. With typical enthusiasm, he expressed lively interest in this newly-opened window into what was for him the ever-fascinating variety of the organ's heritage. And inevitably questions were raised concerning musical usages, for with Charles Fisk the music was always the "bottom line"—the ultimate consideration, whether one built, played, or studied the organ. This essay is an attempt to expand on that critical element with regard to the organs in question. I am greatly indebted to Stephen Bicknell, Cecil Clutton, Michel Cocheril, Martin Goetze, Dominic Gwynn, and many other friends in the British Institute of Organ Studies for the generous sharing of their own insights and the fruits of their extensive and ongoing research.

The fortunes of the organ, its makers, and its players traversed a very uneven road during England's protracted Reformation period, which extended from the first Edwardian Act of Uniformity in 1549 to the collapse of Oliver Cromwell's Commonwealth in 1660. Depending on whether the stern Puritans or those with "Popish tendencies" were in control of church and state, church music (especially on the cathedral level) was either encouraged and supported at something approaching its pre-Reformation opulence, banned outright, or maintained at various levels between these two extremes. Things did not start out well for the organ: in 1552 Archbishop Cranmer decreed that the authorities of St. Paul's Cathedral in London "should leave the playing of the organs at the divine service,"[1] and the use of organs had been abandoned in other places before this, some organs having even been torn down and sold for scrap. Matters temporarily improved after the accession of Elizabeth I in 1558. There

1. Peter Le Huray, *Music and the Reformation in England 1549–1660* (London, 1967), p. 26.

was a revival of music in the cathedrals and the Chapels Royal which produced some of the greatest choral literature of all time, and a corresponding surge in organ-building activity. Prior to the Reformation, in the period 1510–30, records can be found which show that at least a dozen organs were built in each of these years, after which there was a sudden lapse. Between 1550 and 1560 four organs per year are recorded—significant activity, if not up to earlier standards. Between 1570 and 1590 there is almost no organ-building activity, although five organs were built in 1590, and volume increased again after this year.

Church music saw another flowering in the early years of the seventeenth century. William Byrd was connected with the Chapel Royal until his death in 1623, and his successor was Thomas Tomkins. But there were troublesome stirrings in the early decades of the seventeenth century; a Puritan revolution was brewing which would eventually overthrow not only the Church of England, but the Monarchy itself. When Cromwell's troops began their depredations in 1646, they attacked with particular visciousness the symbols and ornaments of the despised Church of England, and the tales of their smashing of windows, tearing down of rood-screens, and destruction of organs, statuary, and vestments are too well recorded to repeat here. Under Cromwell's Puritan Commonwealth, such things were equated with idolatry. Preaching was the only religious activity which mattered, and the only permissible music was unaccompanied psalm-singing.

The Puritan purge had been expected for some time, and many of those whose livelihood was threatened had made their plans accordingly. The elderly Thomas Tomkins simply retired when the choral services (and his employment) were ended at Worcester Cathedral in 1646, devoting the final decade of his long life to composing, copying, and revising his music. Younger men took more drastic steps, particularly if they happened to be Catholics, for while a certain amount of tacit tolerance had been unofficially shown by the Church of England to adherents of the "old faith" in the early years of the seventeenth century, the Puritans had less charitable views. For the sake of their lives as well as their livelihoods, many found it prudent to leave their native soil for the more hospitable climate of Catholic Belgium or France.

Among those who fled the threatened Puritan persecution were members of a distinguished organ-building family which, since the time of Elizabeth, had enjoyed royal favor and whose work had graced a number of prominent cathedrals, colleges, and city churches. In 1642 the forty-year-old Robert Dallam, with his six children and his son-in-law Thomas Harrison, crossed the English Channel to Brittany, probably going from Plymouth to Morlaix as other English Catholics had done before. There was in fact a strong cultural connection between the peoples of southwestern England and of Brittany, for the Celtic, Bretons and Cornish shared a common heritage and language. Breton churches had long welcomed persecuted English Catholics, and one finds evidence of their presence everywhere. In the graveyard of the Ursuline Convent of Morlaix (where we B.I.O.S. pilgrims stayed) there are many stones bearing English names. In Roscoff, the present landing-place of voyagers from Plymouth, the parish church had an organ built by an Englishman, John Bourne, a half century before Thomas Harrison erected an instrument there in 1649, and parts of an ancient English-made altarpiece still exist.

Considerable research on the Dallam family has been done in recent years by Stephen Bicknell, Michel Cocheril, B. B. Edmonds, and Betty Matthews, and much of what has been unearthed points fairly conclusively to the Dallams having been recusant Catholics. When Robert arrived in Brittany he carried a letter of recommendation from an exiled Catholic Bishop, and this may have helped to secure for him a substantial contract for three organs from Quimper Cathedral in 1643. A specification of the largest of these survives, recorded a century later, which delineates a full-fledged French classic organ consisting of *Grande Orgue, Positif, Récit, Echo,* and Pedal. While it is possible that any or all of the three last-named divisions were added between 1643 and 1750, the two main divisions are very similar to other Dallam/Harrison organs of the period in their dispositions, and their 48-note compass suggests that they had suffered no change. If the stoplist was French, however, the case design was English, bearing a strong resemblance to the one built in 1605–06 for King's College, Cambridge, by Robert's father, Thomas Dallam.

In a recent article Michel Cocheril raises the question of how and when Robert Dallam learned to make French organs, since, as he correctly observes: "All the information available about organs made by him in England shows that he made English organs in England—and everything suggests that he made French organs in France."[2] My own feeling is that the discrepancy between the two styles may not have been all that great, nor the transition particularly difficult. Evidence is fast mounting to support the theory that English organ-building practices in the sixteenth century, like those of France, derived directly from Flemish practice. Not only did English, French, Flemish, and Spanish musicians travel freely in each other's territories, but so did organ-builders. John Bourne's early work in Roscoff has already been mentioned, and other English organ-builders are found in France and Flanders in this period, including a Scot who is credited with building a substantial organ in Rouen. An inscription inside the impressive case of the organ in the Cathedral of Saint-Brieuc indicates that the original instrument was imported from England in 1540. Because of the particularly French style of its architecture, however, Michel Cocheril thinks it more likely that the original interior

2. Michel Cocheril, "The Dallams in Brittany," *B.I.O.S. Journal,* Vol. 6 (1982), p. 63.

of the organ was made by an expatriate Englishman, or that the organ was the gift of an English Bishop or benefactor.[3]

On the other side of the coin, Flemish organ-builders traveled widely during the sixteenth century, and their presence has been recorded throughout coastal Europe from Spain to Denmark. Not surprisingly, therefore, the researches of Andrew Freeman and others have turned up evidence of several Flemish organ-builders in England in the sixteenth and early seventeenth centuries. Among these we find Gyllain or William Treasorer, a Fleming who was "Regall maker" to Edward VI,[4] and Jasper Blankard, a member of the Flemish Blancart family of organ-builders. Recent research has unearthed the fact that Michael Langhedul, a member of a celebrated Flemish organ-building family, did extensive work at Salisbury Cathedral in 1530.[5] The question may even be raised (although documentation is presently totally lacking) as to whether there was any connection between the prolific Howe family, which is recorded as having built a significant number of organs in England between 1485 and 1570, and Hendrik van den Houwe, who was active in Malines in the early sixteenth century.

Complete stoplists of English organs before the beginning of the seventeenth century have yet to be discovered, but from the various clues and general descriptions available of English organs in the early and middle sixteenth century a picture begins to emerge of a typical Flemish-style organ, sometimes of good size, which may have contained such things as *Trompes*,[6] Regals,[7] and Mixtures, at least those of the "Cimball" type[8]—all of which seem to have disappeared from the English organ by the early seventeenth century. Peter Williams makes an excellent case for the interpretation of the enigmatic Anthony Duddyngton contract for All Hallows, Barking in London (1519) in the light of contemporary Flemish practices.[9] Indeed, if the "Principal" is interpreted in its early Flemish meaning of "*Blockwerk*," the "few other" stops could then have been the flutes and mutations of either a Chaire/Positif or an upper chest played from the same manual, and the result might well have been similar to the organ built by the Fleming Charles Waghers for the Abbey of

3. Michel Cocheril, *Les orgues de Bretagne* (Rennes, 1981), p. 15.

4. Andrew Freeman, "Records of British Organ-Builders 940–1660" in Mate, *Dictionary of Organs and Organists* (London, 1921).

5. Betty Matthews, *The Organs and Organists of Salisbury Cathedral* (Salisbury, 1972), p. 3.

6. Barbara Owen, "The Evidence for *Trompes* in the Sixteenth Century English Organ" in *Visitatio Organorum* (Buren, 1980).

7. Barbara Owen, "The Henrician Heyday of the Regal," *Continuo*, Vol. 7 No. 10 (September 1984).

8. Francis W. Galpin, *Old English Instruments of Music* (London, 1932), p. 293.

9. Peter F. Williams, "Diapason," *Musical Times*, Vol. 108 (1967).

Saint-Jean of Valenciennes in 1515.[10] Indeed, the term "Chaire" itself now appears to have Franco-Flemish roots (Valenciennes had a *"chaire,"* the 1510 organ of St. Michel in Bordeaux had a *"cheiere,"* etc.).

The above digression is given in support of the contention that the basic type of pre-classical Franco-Flemish organ which Dallam and Harrison found when they arrived in Brittany was, despite its retention of chorus mixtures and acquisition of full-length reeds and tierces, not unlike what they were familiar with in England with regard to such basic matters as construction techniques and scaling. The fact that many of the organs which they found there would have been old, and that even the newer ones in the northern coastal area were not as advanced as the Parisian ones, would tend to strengthen this.

Robert Dallam received his training from his father Thomas, whose first recorded work dates from 1599. Thus far the most assiduous researchers have been unable to unearth the exact source of Thomas's training, but they have determined with reasonable certainty that he was a native-born Englishman, probably from the Lancashire area, and one must thus assume that his background in the organ-building craft derives from the Anglo-Flemish tradition of the sixteenth century. Certainly he would have had ample exposure to older English organs, for he and his father had repaired, rebuilt, or added to numerous older organs in places such as Hereford Cathedral, Exeter Cathedral, Magdalen College, Westminster Abbey, Trinity and King's Colleges, and three of the Chapels Royal. Rather than having to assimilate a whole new style and methodology upon his arrival in Brittany in 1642, it is thus more reasonable to assume that Dallam simply grafted on to his established practices the reeds and mutations required by French usage to produce a type of pre-classic instrument which, if not completely in line with the advanced work being done in Paris, was nonetheless in accord with the more conservative norm for the coastal area northwest of that center.

Because the style of this area was more conservative, one must look not to contemporary Paris for instruments which correlate most closely to it, but to French and Belgian organs from the late sixteenth or early seventeenth century. An instrument which has many similarities to Dallam's early Breton one-manual organs such as the one now awaiting restoration in Lanvellec (1653) and its larger near-twin in St. Jean du Doigt (1652; unfortunately destroyed by fire in 1955) is the recently-restored early-seventeenth-century organ in Lorris-en-Gatinais (Loiret). Dallam's early small instruments have the same type of "Gothic" case construction—already archaic by the 1650s—with the wind-chest bungs accessible from the case front and a flat façade. The single-pipe segments of the Lorris case also find a correlation in later Breton work. The

10. M. A. Vente, "L'influence des Flamands sur les Français en matière de construction d'Orgues," *L'Orgue,* Vol. 48 (1948).

stoplist is virtually identical to that of many Breton organs of similar size, and the division of the reed stops at d$^\sharp$^{1}/e^1 is particularly significant.[11] Smaller French organs or cases from the sixteenth century are rare. One such, even earlier than Lorris, is found in Levroux. This case, empty and abandoned for many years, has recently had a new organ placed inside it, but the old front pipes (not used in the new organ but stored behind it) exhibit another unusual characteristic which typified Breton and English organs of the mid and late seventeenth century—the decorative use of three different types of mouth construction.

When the Monarchy was restored in England in 1660, and the choral service of the Anglican Church revived, there was a critical need for church musicians and organ-builders. Most of those who had exiled themselves to the continent returned to find a plethora of work awaiting them—not to mention a little competition from a few immigrants such as the organ-builder Bernard Smith, now fairly conclusively proven to have been of Dutch or North German birth.[12]

Among those who returned was Robert Dallam, with his sons Ralph and George, as well as Thomas Harris (he had dropped the "son") and his young son Renatus—Robert Dallam's grandson. That Robert had no intention of abandoning the type of specification he had adopted in France is clearly seen in his 1662 proposal for New College, Oxford, which is replete with French-derived terms (*burdane, furnitor, flut de alman, cleron*, etc.) and some rather atrocious spelling.[13] The Dallam-Harris French contributions, melded with some of Smith's Dutch contributions (which, since the Dutch organ also had its roots in the Flemish tradition, were not all that different) set the stage for the familiar eighteenth-century style of English organ built by the successors of Harris and Smith.

Not all of the exiles returned, however. Robert Dallam's son Thomas remained in Brittany and prospered, building and repairing organs until the beginning of the eighteenth century and, with the help of a succession of four wives, fathering at least twenty children. At least two of these, Toussaint and Mark Anthony, later emigrated back to England, and the latter was still working at the organ-builder's trade as late as 1730. The organs built by Thomas Dallam, Sieur de la Tour, following the return of his father and brother-in-law to England, continued to be in much the same style as those of his father. Although later ones display indications (such as the domed *Flûte à biberon* construction of the chimney flutes) that Thomas was aware of developments in

11. Ch.-W. Lindow, *Historic Organs in France* (Delaware, Ohio, 1980), p. 40.

12. John Rowntree, "Bernard Smith (c1629–1708) Organist and Organbuilder, his Origins," *B.I.O.S. Journal*, Vol. 2 (1978).

13. Stephen Bicknell, working notes for 1983 Breton tour.

Paris, they are still essentially conservative and old-fashioned in their tonal and visual orientation.

The surviving organs and organ cases of Robert and Thomas Dallam and Thomas Harris in Brittany are of unique historical importance. They are among the few tangible links remaining between the legendary sixteenth-century Flemish school of organ-building and the French and English organs of the late seventeenth and early eighteenth centuries.

Of sixteenth- and early seventeenth-century French organ cases France has a great treasure, and, despite the depredations of Cromwell's fanatics, a few significant cases from this period still exist in England. But organs which are relatively complete are rare, and they are all small. In France, outside of Brittany, there is the previously mentioned one-manual organ in Lorris, restored in 1975 but said to contain about two-thirds old material which was little altered because the organ had been in ruins for a considerable time. What few other smaller instruments survive from this period have been rebuilt so many times that it is difficult to determine their true nature (still to be investigated are certain small seventeenth-century Belgian organs by builders such as Bremser and LeDou). In England there are two organs in this category, both of which could bear further study, since they appear to be pre-Commonwealth or early post-Commonwealth rebuilds of earlier instruments. One of these is the one-manual organ in Stanford-on-Avon, in ruins for more than a century, which may have been the Chaire of a larger organ prior to its rebuilding; the other is the recently-restored organ in Adlington Hall, Cheshire. This also survived change by virtue of being unplayable since the late eighteenth century, and is essentially a one-manual organ, although the double-channeled chest (a hint of the Flemings again?) accommodates two independent stops and one borrowed stop of a second manual.

Filling the gap, in a way, between the above-mentioned survivals, we find in Brittany the following organs:

Lanvellec. Robert Dallam, 1653, moved from Plestin-les-Grèves in 1864. In ruins, with some pipework missing, but apparently unaltered and restorable.

Ergué-Gaberic. Thomas Dallam, 1680. Seemingly unaltered; fully restored in 1980.

Ploujean. Thomas Dallam, c. 1680. Unaltered until 1936 when an incompetent Parisian organ-builder attempted to electrify it. Original chest and pipework are still reasonably intact, however, and it is restorable.

Guimiliau. Thomas Dallam, c. 1677. Damaged by the same builder as the above, but presumably restorable.

Although only one of these single-manual organs is playable, the other three are intact enough for study purposes, and, one hopes, eventual restoration. While the three organs by Thomas Dallam de la Tour date from the late seventeenth century, they bear a far greater resemblance to the earlier work of Robert Dallam (which was in itself somewhat archaic in style) than to either the fully-developed Parisian classic organ of the same period or the organs being built in England by his cousin Renatus Harris.

Much has been said and written concerning the usage of the larger, fully-developed French classic organ, which normally had at the very least two complete divisions and a third half-compass (treble) division for solo purposes. About the smallest French classic organ imaginable, the exquisite Louis Clicquot organ of 1734 in Houdan, manages to meet all of these requirements, even though its *Grand-Orgue* and *Positif* share the same double-channeled windchest and the *Récit* must be played from the *Grande-Orgue*. But here we have in Brittany four surviving single-manual pre-classic organs, and records of a half-dozen or so more, some of them of fair size—the one-manual organ built by Robert Dallam for Lesneven in 1654 was, according to the contract, four stops larger than the thirteen-stop Houdan instrument!

This sort of thing cannot be dismissed by suggesting that it is a reflection of Dallam's English background, although the Dallams certainly built their share of one-manual organs in their mother country. In Brittany they were building thoroughly French organs, in a thoroughly French tradition which had its roots in the single-manual organs of Flanders. The Lorris organ is not the only non-Breton survivor of this tradition. One might cite a much-altered 13-stop one-manual organ of 1635 in Malaucène and a 1690 instrument of the same size in Roquemaure—both in the south of France, it is true, but in out-of-the-way places where such things are likely to survive. These are country parish church organs, but, unlike in Holland and northern Germany, fewer of them have survived in France.

Playing the organ in Ergué-Gaberic, questions were raised as to the literature which would suit such an organ. Obviously most of the early French pre-classical school—Titelouze, and, somewhat later, Roberday and d'Anglebert—would work, for even though one can presume that Titelouze would use all of the resources of the large organ at Rouen, it is perfectly possible to play his music on a single manual. Roberday's *Caprices* and d'Anglebert's *Fugues* are surely single-manual music, although the latter composer's *Quatuor* is, according to his own statement, a piece whose "effect can only be achieved on a large organ with four different keyboards."[14] But Titelouze was in his grave long before these Breton organs were built, and following Roberday and d'Anglebert

14. Beverly Scheibert, "The Organ Works of Jean-Henry d'Anglebert" (chapter from unpublished dissertation).

came composers such as Nivers and Lebègue who were writing music which clearly demanded organs of two or three divisions—or did it? The Ergué-Gaberic organ has two reed stops, a *Trompette* and a *Voix Humaine* (which, incidentally, sounds more like a mild *Cromorne*), and, as in the other Breton organs which have been examined, these stops divide between d$\sharp^1$ and e^1. It also has a *Cornet* above middle c. Interestingly enough, the much earlier Lorris organ has these identical characteristics. It was then discovered that some, though by no means all, of the pieces by various classical composers which required a reed solo in the *basse* or *dessus* could be played without either the right or left hand crossing the d $\sharp$/e dividing line, still others would work if one slightly rearranged the accompanimental part, and, of course, some would not work at all. The same was true of *Cornet* solos, for although these almost never descend below middle c, the accompaniments often rise above it—yet pieces were also found where they did not. Interestingly, it was found that duos and trios could be played on single combinations of flutes and mutations on this organ, the space between the parts often being great enough to place them in registers where the color differed sufficiently to give the impression that two different registrations were being used.

The question naturally arises: Is there in fact a specific literature for the one-manual French organ, or did village organists simply either adapt from the existing literature or improvise? An examination of existing published music from the late seventeenth and early eighteenth centuries—using the criteria of the dividing-place of the reeds and the *Cornet* compass—indicates that there is.

The most obvious place to start the search was in the masses, but most of the organists of cathedrals and Parisian churches appeared to be writing for themselves. While occasional pieces in the masses of many composers can be found which fit within the compass limitations, their occurrence appears to be hardly more than accidental. However, an anonymous mass in G found by Almonte C. Howell in the Paris Bibliothèque du Conservatoire (Res. 2094)[15] is unquestionably meant for a one-manual organ of the Breton type. Its provenance is unknown, but Howell places it in the 1670–90 period, which would make it contemporary with the work of Thomas Dallam de la Tour. All of the *Basse, Dessus, Cornet,* and *Récit* movements adhere strictly to the d$\sharp$/e division, as does even a *Duo*. There are no manual indications, and no Pedal is called for—in fact nothing is required which cannot be found on the Ergué-Gaberic instrument. All the movements are fairly short and relatively easy. It is a mass for a village organist. One must naturally wonder how many other such masses, probably anonymous like this one, lie awaiting discovery in some library or church archive.

15. Almonte C. Howell, Jr., *Five French Baroque Organ Masses* (University of Kentucky Press, 1961), p. 18.

The composers who worked largely in the eighteenth century seem to have assumed that the players of their music would have organs of more than one manual at their disposal, and probably, after the middle of the century, most of them did. But at least two major late-seventeenth-century composers seem to have recognized the existence of the single-manual organ. Guillaume Nivers's *Livre d'Orgue*, published in 1667, contains a mass which requires an organ of at least two manuals, probably with a separate short-compass *Echo* and/or *Récit*. But the *Hymnes* which follow it are another matter. They are generally simpler in style. The *Plein Jeu* movements might require a Pedal *Trompette* to play the *cantus* in the bass, but in fact the compass never goes beyond the reach of two hands, and at any rate the *cantus* could always be played as André Raison suggests in the preface to his *Livre d'Orgue* (1688)—by a "third hand," i.e., a second player.[16] These movements are followed by a *Couplet* and sometimes a *Fugue*. The *Fugues* and *Plein Jeus* are, of course, meant to be played on a single manual, but the *Couplets* are for reeds or *Cornet*, and again one finds the d♯/e division rigorously adhered to, and no manual indications given. One interesting feature of the *Couplets* is that many of them will begin on a *Jeu doux* registration in both hands, but either descend or ascend to the appropriate accompanimental register before the solo enters in such a manner that the hand playing the solo is free to draw the solo stop in advance of the entry. In the midst of Nivers's *Hymnes* there occurs a *Prose* for the feast of St. Sacrement in twelve short movements. Ten of these call for solos on the *Cornet* or reed stops, and every one observes the d♯/e division. The brevity and simplicity of this *Prose* and the *Hymnes* might suggest that, in contrast to the more complex mass, this is again music for the village (or perhaps convent or monastery) organist.

A final example may be given from the works of Nicolas Lebègue, said to have been a close friend of Nivers. His *Première Livre d'Orgue*, published in 1676 and containing sets of pieces in the eight tones, is plainly intended for an organ of two or three manuals with pedal, such as he played at the Church of St. Merry in Paris. Although in his preface he claims to have included pieces which will "be of some use to organists who cannot come great distances to hear the numerous and diverse types of stops which have recently been in use here," he also admits that while some of the pieces can be "played on all sorts of organs" (including, indeed, one-manual ones) there are several (quite a few, in fact) "which are not useful to organists whose instruments lack the stops necessary for their execution."[17] But his *Second Livre d'Orgue* contains, according to his own title-page description, "short and easy" pieces in the eight tones, as well as a mass. Here again we seem to have a "village organist" mass,

16. Fenner Douglass, *The Language of the Classical French Organ* (New Haven, 1969), p. 105.
17. Ibid., p. 179.

although while a number of solo pieces can be played on a single manual with the d#/e division (one *Voix Humaine* piece which switches from *Dessus* to *Basse* even having built-in rests before the changes to allow for stop-changing) others require a two-manual organ, since one or both parts cross the d#/e boundary. Following the mass are several Magnificats, most of whose solo movements can be played on a single-manual organ with divided reeds or a *Cornet*, but a few also include *Dialogues*, which require two manuals. Thus all that can be said of Lebègue's *Second Livre* is that is intended for small one- and two-manual organs, although Lebègue's awareness of the requirements of the single-manual organ seems evident. His *Troisième Livre d'Orgue* again contains longer and more complex works intended for larger instruments.

With the opening of the eighteenth century, the existence of the smaller church organs seems to have been quite forgotten by composers. While Du-Mage's works contain a few pieces which will work on a one-manual organ, deGrigny's demand a large instrument with pedals, and it is quite obvious that the organists of the "parishes" and "convents" for which François Couperin wrote his masses had at least two manuals at their disposal. In the *Avertissement* Louis-Nicolas Clérambault wrote to his *Livre d'Orgue*, published in 1710, however, one finds this interesting statement: "I have composed these pieces in such a way that they can be played as easily on a cabinet organ with split stops as on a large instrument; that is why in the *Basse de trompette*, and in the *Récits*, the accompaniment does not pass the middle of the keyboard, nor the melodies of the *Dessus* or *Basse*."[18] One's hopes of finding recognition here for the existence of the older type of one-manual church organs are dashed, however, when perusal of the music reveals that the keyboard division required is not the old d#/e break, but the lower c/c# (or c#/d) break beginning to appear in Parisian domestic organs, and that Clérambault really has in mind (as he indeed says) the *Orgue du Cabinet* or chamber organ, rather than the one-manual church organ.

There has not yet come to light any firm evidence that the d#/e division was used in England, although this is highly possible. The Stanford organ has a rather "Breton" disposition, which includes a divided reed stop, but its place of division will remain a mystery until a reasonably non-damaging means can be found to remove the toeboards of the windchest (presently secured with large and very well rusted nails) to reveal the sliders.

Organs with divided keyboards were known and written for in England in the late seventeenth century, but the division occurred at c/c#. The well-known *Voluntary on the Old Hundredth*, variously ascribed to Purcell or Blow, is intended for such an organ, and is in fact a typical *basse et dessus* piece in the classic French style for a divided reed or cornet/sesquialtera stop, beginning

18. Ibid., p. 106.

with a *jeu doux* section on both staves which conveniently ascends to the treble in time to draw the bass half of the solo stop (and doing the same in reverse for the treble solo entry). No registration is given in any of the sources for this piece, but that a reed rather than a *Cornet* is the solo stop of choice is suggested by the fact that the final section is played by both hands with the solo stop drawn in both halves—as in certain French pieces for *Voix Humaine* or *Cromorne*. Another English work for a divided-manual organ is the anonymous and untitled Voluntary found in British Library Add. MS 31446, and almost certainly attributable to Blow.[19] This would appear to be a *Cornet* piece, as the solo line occurs only in the upper part. It is quite French in its construction, beginning with the usual *jeu doux* section before the appearance of the florid solo, which is interspersed with brief "echo" sections played below middle c ♯. While echo effects are more likely to bring to mind Netherlandish music of the Sweelinck school, at least one such echo piece—and a *Cornet* piece at that—is found in Nivers's *Second Livre d'Orgue*.

The substitution of the c/c ♯ (or, later, B/c) division for the older d ♯/e division in both French and English music at the end of the seventeenth century strengthens the case for the single-manual Anglo-Breton organ being a backward-looking survival of an earlier type of instrument, probably going back to at least the beginning of the century. If music from the middle and late seventeenth century can be found which was suited to the unique properties of such instruments, what of music from an earlier period? Titelouze, as previously mentioned, offers no clues; neither, on the other side of the channel, does Redford, which may not be surprising, since the former had an organ of more than one division at his disposal, and the latter, as organist of St. Paul's in London, may very possibly also have had more than one division to work with, although concrete proof is presently lacking. Bull, Byrd, and Tomkins likewise give us no clear clue that they had any familiarity with divided-manual instruments.

Divided-manual organs appear to have originated to the south of the geographical area under discussion. They were known in Spain, Portugal, and Italy by the end of the sixteenth century, and either Spain or Italy may have been responsible for the introduction of the concept to the north. There was a strong cultural connection between Spain and Flanders (the so-called "Spanish Netherlands") during the sixteenth and early seventeenth centuries. Flemish musicians were found in the Spanish court, and Flemish organ-builders (including members of the noted Brebos family) built organs for Spanish cathedrals. It is possible that the idea of dividing the keyboard of a one-manual organ was brought back to Flanders by such builders.

But the Spanish keyboard traditionally divided at c/c ♯ in this period; the

19. Robin Langley, *Organ Music in Restoration England* (London 1981), p. 14.

d $^\#$/e division seems to have been a peculiarly Flemish adaptation (although organs with half-stops beginning at e are found in Flemish-influenced Tuscany). Support for the thesis that this particular keyboard division existed in Flanders early in the seventeenth century comes, interestingly, from a musical source which includes pieces by both native Flemish composers and expatriate English writers: Christ Church MS 89, dating from c. 1620 and fairly well authenticated as to its Flemish provenance, although it has been in England since about 1700.

A recent article in the *Journal of the British Institute of Organ Studies*, Vol. 7, contains an excellent example of the type of divided-manual piece which occurs in Christ Church MS 89.[20] It is a three-part Kyrie with no manual or registration indications, but it begins with the typical *jeu doux* section characteristic of later pieces, with an ornamented and florid bass line beginning in measure four. From this point on, the lowest note in the upper (accompanimental) part is e, and the highest in the lower (solo) part is d. The *jeu doux* introduction characteristically rises up beyond the break to a range where its two parts can be played by the right hand, freeing the left hand to draw the solo stop which, since the solo occurs in the bass, is almost certainly meant to be a reed. This little Kyrie is but nineteen measures long, and was cited as an example of one of the several fingered pieces in MS 89. But its importance extends beyond even this significant fact, for in its style and construction it is a prototype of French music of the late seventeenth century and English music of the Restoration as well as a link with Spanish *Medio Registro* music and the early-seventeenth-century "double organ" voluntaries of Lugge and Gibbons.

This piece, possibly by the English expatriate William Browne, is by no means unique among the numerous liturgical pieces in Christ Church MS 89. A significant number of pieces in this MS can be played on a single undivided manual, and a few quite definitely require two manuals. But a cursory examination of the complete manuscript (as transcribed by Dr. R. Harrison Kelton) reveals at least twenty pieces which are clearly meant for a divided-manual organ. Space does not permit a detailed discussion of these pieces, but a few comments may suffice.

Most of the divided pieces—all anonymous, although many may be Browne and possibly also Peter Phillips—observe the d $^\#$/e division, save for a 3-part fantasie near the end (p. 300) which has been attributed to Pieter Cornet, and observes the Spanish c/c $^\#$ division. All are in three parts, with a definite and usually florid solo line in either the treble or bass. Some of the treble pieces (such as a *Gloria, p.* 64; *Pro elevatione*, p. 119), are marked "*per le Cornett*"; probably all of the bass solos are meant for reed stops, and a few (*Gloria*, p. 52;

20. Richard Vendome, "Spanish Netherlands Keyboard Music, 1596–1633," *B.I.O.S. Journal*, Vol. 7 (1983).

Magnificat, p. 253) contain dramatic octave leaps in the style of later French *Basse de Trompette* pieces. The bulk of these pieces follow the simple formula of a *jeu doux* introduction followed by an accompanied solo in either the treble or bass, but there are a few interesting exceptions. A *Kyrie* from a *Missa Beata Virginum* (p. 68) is obviously divided, but with a *cantus firmus* and a bass line in the left hand, and a free descant in the right. Toward the end of the manuscript is a *Regina Coeli* (p. 331) which anticipates the previously mentioned *Cornet* voluntary attributed to Blow in the manner in which it drops below the dividing-point to echo the solo. An interesting reversal of this occurs in a *Sanctorum Meritis* (p. 107), where the left hand leaves the solo to go to the treble accompaniment in the middle.

While Christ Church MS 89 is the richest Flemish source of this type of divided-manual music to come to my notice, it is not the only one. Liège MS 888 (the *Liber Fratrum Cruciferorum Leodiensium*, dating from 1617) is a remarkable testimonial to the international nature of organ music in the early seventeenth century, containing as it does pieces by Browne, Phillips, Gabrieli, Merulo, Scronx and Sweelinck as well as many anonymous works. Among these latter is a most interesting *Echo* (p. 34 in Guilmant/Pirro *Archives* edition) in which the upper and lower parts strictly observe the d#/e division, and the "echo" passages, as in certain other works already alluded to, drop below the division. Near the end of Liège MS 888 are two short untitled compositions which appear to be *Cornet* pieces (pp. 147, 149); both again strictly observe the d#/e division, and one has a few short "echo" measures which drop below the break.

It should be said here that the writer has by no means exhaustively researched the available resources of Franco-Flemish organ literature from the seventeenth century. That examples of music for a specific type of divided-manual organ come to hand so readily in the sources consulted suggests that a more thorough search might well establish clearer beginning and ending dates for the practice of dividing stops in single-manual organs at d#/e, as well as a sharper geographical locus.

Having established a rudimentary literature for the single-manual Anglo-Breton organ and its presumed Flemish prototypes, a few final words might be said concerning registration. Little needs to be added to what has already been said concerning the solo registrations, since the compass of the *Cornet* restricts it to treble solos, and the fact that only the reeds are divided requires them to be used for all bass solos and for treble solos where they are either specifically indicated, or where, in lieu of this, they are suggested by the character of the music. In the pieces in Christ Church MS 89 for example, it may be that reeds are intended in all treble solos not specifically designated for the *Cornet*.

For the *Jeu doux* which accompanies the solos, Nivers (1665) recommends the *Bourdon* 8' and *Flûte* 4', with the possible addition of the *Prestant* 4' and even *Doublette* 2' if greater strength is needed. Since these stops do not divide, they will of course also be sounding with the solo stop, but then it was customary to use the *Bourdon* with solo reeds even in organs of more than one manual.

For pieces intended for single, undivided registrations, most of the French conventions of the period are suitable. *Fugues graves*, for example, are frequently recommended (Nivers, 1665; Gigault, 1685) to be played on the *Trompette*, with or without the foundation stops. The opening segment of a mass or hymn usually is fairly homophonic, and requires the *plein jeu.* Mersenne's registration suggestions for the *Positif* (1636) also apply, since the specification of the one-manual organs is very similar to that of the *Positif* in a large organ. Some of these which would work in duos, lighter fugues, or plainsong pieces would include the *Jeu harmonieux (Montre* or *Bourdon* 8' with *Prestant* 4' and *Fleute d'Allemand* 4'), *Nazard (Bourdon* 8', *Prestant* 4', *Nazard* 2.2/3'), the *Bourdon* 8' with just the *Flûte* 4', *Doublette* 2', or *Flajolet* 1'; the *Bourdon* 8' with the *Flûte* 4' and the *Cymbale* II; the *Bourdon* 8', *Nazard* 2.2/3' and *Flajolet* 1', and the "strong Nazard": *Bourdon* 8', *Prestant* 4', *Doublette* 2', *Nazard* 2.2/3' and *Petit Nazard* 1.1/3'. One can probably assume that these are all intended for single-manual playing, since certain solo combinations are specifically designated "for playing on two manuals."[21]

The foregoing discussion has attempted to place the Dallam and Harris organs of Brittany (and, most importantly, the surviving ones, which should be carefully restored and jealously preserved) in the context of a link between the smaller Flemish organs of the sixteenth century and the style of organs which developed in both France and England at the end of the seventeenth century, both structurally and musically. In doing so, I realize that more questions have been asked than answered. More organs need to be studied in detail (not only in France and England, but in Belgium, and probably even in Italy) to document the course of the evolution of such things as pipe scales and general construction characteristics, and far more solid information is needed on the correlation between the organs and the music prior to the last third of the seventeenth century, both in England and France. The result of such study, however, should help to give us new insights into an important segment of early organ music.

21. Douglass, p. 174.

Specifications

1636, Mersenne's Positiv

Montre	8' or 4'	open, tin
Bourdon	8'	stopped
Prestant	4'	
Fleute		
d'Allemand	4'	chimney
Nazard	2⅔'	chimney
Doublette	2'	
Tiercette	1⅗' (?)	
Flajolet	1'	
Petit Nazard	1⅓'	
Fourniture	III (1')	
Petit		
Cymbale	II (½')	
Petit		
Cromorne	4'	

c. 1600, Lorris-en-Gatinais (Loiret)

Montre	8'	
Bourdon	8'	
Prestant	4'	
Nazard	2⅔'	
Doublette	2'	
Tierce	1⅗'	
Cornet	V	from middle c
Fourniture	III	
Cymbale	II	
Trompette	8'	divided d#/e
Voix Humaine	8'	" "

1653, Robert Dallam
Lanvellec

Bourdon	8'
Montre	4'
Flûte	4'
or	
Quarte	2'

Nasard	2⅔′	
Doublette	2′	
Tierce	1⅗′	
{ Flageolet	1′	
or		
Larigot	1⅓′	
Cornet	V	treble
Fourniture	III	
Cymbale	II	
Cromorne	8′	divided d #/e
Voix Humaine	8′	" "

1680, Thomas Dallam
Ergué-Gaberic

Bourdon	8′	
Prestant	4′	
Flûte	4′	stopped
Nasard	2⅔′	
Doublette	2′	
Tierce	1⅗′	
Cornet	V	treble
Fourniture	III	
Cymbale	II	
Trompette	8′	divided d #/e
Voix Humaine	8′	" "

c. 1600, rebuilt c. 1650–60?
St. Nicholas, Stanford-on-Avon

Op. Diapason	8′	c. 1600, embossed
St. Diapason	8′	
Princepel	4′	
Twelfth	2⅔′	
Fifteenth	2′	
Bs. Tierce	1⅗′	bass?
Cornet	IV(?)	treble
Trumpet	8′	divided

CHAPTER TEN

Psalm-Tone Formulas
in Buxtehude's Free Organ Works?

WILLIAM PORTER

IN 1972 there appeared a thought-provoking book by Murray C. Bradshaw, *The Origin of the Toccata*,[1] in which the author questioned several common assumptions concerning the nature of the classical keyboard toccata as it developed in the late sixteenth century, and as it was represented by the works of composers active in Venice. The assumptions which Bradshaw scrutinized were those which held that (1) the modality of the toccata at this time was apt to be ambiguous, and the practice of designating toccatas according to tone was done simply "for tradition's sake";[2] (2) the toccata is a "free" composition, in that it is not governed by a *cantus firmus*, and (3) the toccata exemplifies improvisational practice, i.e., the toccatas of the Venetians are examples of written-down and cleaned-up spur-of-the-moment music-making.

Bradshaw's thesis that the early toccata, far from being a "free" composition, is often governed by the presence of psalm-tone either as an "ideal" or "real" *cantus firmus*, is given credence in his study by a number of means: (1) he draws parallels between the toccata and the Spanish *falsobordone*, the Italian *intonationi*, and the earlier sixteenth-century German *preambulum*, all of which show the frequent governing presence of psalm-tone, (2) he draws attention to the supposed liturgical context of the early toccata, and (3) he provides analyses of numerous toccatas by the Gabrielis, Diruta, Merulo, and others, to demonstrate that in the "free" sections of these pieces (those characterized by rapid runs and chords) psalm-tone formulae are either present in long notes, or that the music itself constitutes a harmonization of a psalm-tone, and that the more strictly imitative sections often derive their thematic material from the psalm-tone.

In his analyses of free sections, Bradshaw is sometimes forced to suggest that in some pieces portions of the psalm-tone are repeated several times (with

1. *Musicological Studies and Documents* 28, American Institute of Musicology, 1972.

2. Murray C. Bradshaw, *The Origin of the Toccata* p. 16. This is Egon Kenton's view. See *Life and Works of Giovanni Gabrieli. Musicological Studies and Documents* 16, American Institute of Musicology, 1967.

occasional extra passing or neighboring tones) in order to support his contention that a *cantus firmus* governs these sections throughout, thus raising the question whether it is always possible to distinguish between a piece which is a harmonization of a psalm-tone and one which simply outlines the harmonic characteristics of its particular mode. If the cautious reader responds to such psalm-tone hunts in the more extended works of Andrea Gabrieli with a reserved "maybe," there can still be no doubt that Bradshaw's analyses have successfully challenged the first two assumptions mentioned above, while providing information which can lead us to increasingly informed speculation about the nature of keyboard improvisation in the sixteenth and seventeenth centuries.

Having established the frequent presence of psalm-tone in a wide variety of keyboard genres at this time (toccata, *intonationi, falsobordone, preambulum*), Bradshaw devotes his final chapter to a discussion of the role of psalm-tone in the free works of seventeenth-century keyboard composers, beginning with Sweelinck and Scheidt, but finds no significant continuation of the tradition among the Lutheran composers of the north. At this point the intensity of his scrutiny begins to fade. A closer look at the toccata style of Scheidt and of Scheidemann reveals the use by both composers of tone formulae for the Magnificat in their toccata writing, an association also found later in the two keyboard Magnificats on tone I by Dietrich Buxtehude. The unique treatment of liturgical melody in these last two pieces can also be detected in some of Buxtehude's "free" works, as will be shown below.

Bradshaw's discussion of psalm-tones in Scheidt's toccatas is limited to a consideration of the toccata in the Berlin Graues Kloster MS,[3] which he sees as containing four successive statements of the termination of psalm-tone II near the end of the piece.[4] The fact that this "ideal" *cantus firmus* (1) must take on strikingly different rhythmic shapes in order to fit, even though the rhythmic flow of the toccata at that point is quite consistent, (2) contains extra notes which alter the shape of the termination, and (3) alters Scheidt's harmony in several places, makes this example perhaps the least convincing of his arguments, though not demonstrably false. Perhaps more meaningful is the fact that within the concluding twelve measures of the toccata there occurs six times the figure which is even more clearly an outline of a

common termination for tone II. Whether the composer intended it to be perceived as such is another question, although the piece is in the right key for tone II and the shape of the figure is obvious enough. It is in any case true that the use of tone formulae in small note values treated sequentially and imita-

3. Printed in *Samuel Scheidt Werke* V. Hamburg, 1937, p. 12.

4. See Bradshaw, p. 69–70.

tively does occur among seventeenth-century composers, particularly in the north.

One of the earliest and most extended examples of this technique is found in Samuel Scheidt's *Toccata super: In te Domine speravi.*[5] This monumental work of 211 measures, which closes part two of the *Tabulatura Nova* (1624), has the following structural organization:

A(1–51)   Quasi-imitative beginning in long notes, after which the opening material is presented in diminution, double diminution (becoming increasingly figural), with octave echoes, inversion, and canon, finally dissolving into free figuration supported by chords.

B(51–82)   Closely knit imitative section.

C(82–124)   Figuration supported by chords, treated sequentially and with octave echoes.

D(125–162) Second imitative section, concluding with canonic writing over pedal points.

E(162–211) Sixteenth-note figuration, first alternating hands, then both hands together, culminating in sixteenth-note echoes employing *imitatio violistica.*

The melodic materials for sections A and D are derived from one of several three-part canons by Scheidt having the text, "In te Domine speravi, non confundar in aeternum."[6] But the most significant point about the toccata in the context of this discussion is that the first large imitative section contains seventeen measures of exactly the same music found in the first verse of Scheidt's *Magnificat VIII toni* in part three of the *Tabulatura Nova.* The melodic material treated is as clear a quotation of the ending of tone VIII as one can hope to find. This material is preceded in the toccata by twelve measures of paired imitation in which the notes of the mediant cadence of tone VIII are heard simultaneously with the termination (figure 10-1). Whatever the intended function of this piece may have been, it is noteworthy here that this is a German toccata, in tone VIII (though not specifically titled as such), in which psalm- (or canticle-) tone VIII is present as the subject of a major imitative section.

5. Bradshaw's assertion that "it is significant that Scheidt, educated in the Venetian tradition, wrote a toccata that was based on a vocal composition and one, moreover, that was a setting of a psalm text" is a curious one; it is probable that the text is drawn rather from the concluding verse of the *Te Deum* (see Christhard Mahrenholz's essay in *Samuel Scheidt Werke* VII, Hamburg, 1954, p. 47). Likewise, his view that the toccata is "actually a set of variations" (Bradshaw, p. 70) is difficult to understand, considering the architecture of the piece, in which each section has its own distinct thematic material.

6. See Christhard Mahrenholz, *Samuel Scheidt: sein Leben und sein Werk.* Leipzig, 1924, pp. 13–14, 43–44.

10—1.

It is curious that just as Scheidt left a complete Magnificat cycle for organ along with a large "free" work which refers to his *Magnificat VIII toni*, his contemporary Heinrich Scheidemann also composed a complete Magnificat cycle as well as an extended "Magnificat" toccata on tone VIII. This latter piece, which immediately follows Scheidemann's Magnificat cycle in the Zellerfeld tablature, is referred to as a fantasia by Breig[7] and is titled *Magnificat VIII toni* in the new Bärenreiter edition.[8] However, in the Zellerfeld tablature (the only extant source), the piece is untitled (and unascribed);[9] there is nothing in this piece to suggest that the appellation "toccata" is not equally apt. A single-movement work of 209 measures, this piece bears all of the characteristics of northern German toccatas written during the second quarter of the seventeenth century: an underlying simplicity of motivic material developed into rich colorated passage work in soprano and bass, often against block-chordal support, extended echo treatment, fugato sections, and sequences. The resemblance of this piece in compositional procedure to Scheidemann's *Toccata in G* (WV 43) is striking, and may be observed in the following table:

SECTION	"Magnificat toccata" MEASURE NO.	Toccata in G MEASURE NO.
A. Imitative introductory section, Rückpositiv line a colorated treatment of opening material. Cadence.	1–18	1–30
B. Continuation of colorated writing, but fragmented, with some canonic writing and octave echoes. Cadence.	29–73	31–59 (includes fugato section)
C. Echo section in all voices (polychoral effect) and in single lines. Cadence.	74–161 (includes fugato section)	60–105

7. Werner Breig, *Die Orgelwerke von Heinrich Scheidemann.* Wiesbaden, 1967, p. 65.

8. *Heinrich Scheidemann Magnificat-Bearbeitungen,* ed. Gustav Fock. Kassel, 1970.

9. Breig, p. 7.

D. Concluding section beginning   161–209   105–186
imitatively in all voices, but
Rückpositiv line increasingly
colored. Sequences, single-voice
echoes, cadential flourish.

The structural similarities between these two pieces are further emphasized by the prominence of the large echo section in each.[10] In both pieces this section is announced by a sharp textural contrast in a shift to homophonic, declamatory writing; in WV66 the second half of the canticle-tone first appears at this point, whereas here in WV43 the motive upon which the piece is based disappears for thirty measures. In each piece this section begins almost exactly one-third of the way through the composition and serves as a structural keystone for the entire toccata. Whatever titles (or absence of titles) may signify, the chief difference between these two pieces is not in structure, compositional procedure, or style, but in the fact that WV66 is based upon canticle-tone VIII and WV43 (apparently) is not.[11]

The association of psalm-/canticle-tone with the keyboard toccata in northern German practice is continued, albeit in a tentative way, by Mathias Weckmann. Bradshaw cites two examples from the Lüneburg tablatures, one from KN 207/22, the other from KN 147, in which tone I is present in the opening section as an ideal *cantus firmus*.[12] But it is Dietrich Buxtehude who provides us with the next examples of Magnificat toccatas, in two pieces titled *Magnificat primi toni*, BuxWV203 and BuxWV204.[13]

Had the larger of these two pieces (BuxWV203) survived in manuscript sources untitled, as the Scheidemann example, it is likely that the work would have been printed in modern editions as "toccata" or "praeludium." It is virtually indistinguishable in structure and style from Buxtehude's monumental "free" organ works, and as such is a supreme example of late seventeenth-century *stylus phantasticus* writing. Perhaps it was this strong resemblance to the free works which led Hedar to assume that no *cantus firmus* is present in either piece: "Keine der beiden Magnificatphantasien knüpft thematisch an die

10. A similar formal design is found in the large toccata of Delphin Strungk, preserved in Lüneburg KN 209.

11. The theme of WV43, which is similar to those of some English voluntaries and fantasias of the early seventeenth century (cf. Farnaby, Tomkins), resembles psalm-tone VIII in basic outline, but would require C♯ rather than C to make credible any association with the tone formula.

12. Bradshaw, p. 83.

13. Georg Karstädt, *Thematisch-systematisches Verzeichnis der musikalischen Werke von Dietrich Buxtehude*. Wiesbaden, 1974, p. 162.

liturgische Melodie an. 'Primi toni' ist ausschliesslich als Tonartbezeichnung zu betrachten."[14] On the contrary, the larger *Magnificat primi toni* (BuxWV203) consists of two complete statements of the canticle-tone, the smaller piece only one. The following chart indicates the organization of BuxWV203 and the portions of the canticle-tone upon which it is based. Bradshaw's statement that "the works of these Lutheran composers (Buxtehude, Kneller, et al.) are not in any way linked to a psalm tone"[15] is erroneous, as will be shown below.

	Measure numbers	Length of section (in measures)		
I.	1–11	(11)	Opening toccata, rapid figurations, pedal solo	Incipit: F–G–A
II.	12–29	(18)	Fugato	Mediant cadence: A–C–A–G–A
III.	30–49	(20)	Fugato	Second incipit: G–A–C–A
IV.	50–75	(19 + 7)	Fugato + coda (lento)	Termination: A–G–F–G–A–G–F–E–D
V.	76–91	(16)	Fugato (gigue-like, 12/8)	Incipit: F–G–A
VI.	91–102	(11)	Homophonic interlude (3/2)	Mediant cadence: A–C–A–G–A
VII.	103–124	(22)	Fugato	Second incipit: G–A–C–A
VIII.	125–146	(16 + 6)	Fugato + closing toccata	Termination: A–G–F–G–A–G–F–E–D

SECTION I: The incipit F–G–A appears in embellished form at the quarter-note level six times in the soprano and alto in the first seven measures, four times in invertible counterpoint (figure 10-2). At measure 8 it appears at the whole-note level in the soprano in syncopated repeated notes, concluding the section with a "plain" statement of the theme (figure 10-3). All sections except the third conclude with a relatively undecorated statement of the theme.

SECTION II: The subject of the fugato outlines the first two notes of the mediant cadence (figure 10-4), the entire theme appearing in the soprano at measure 25 to conclude the section (figure 10-5).

SECTION III: An extended fugato having a countersubject which outlines the second *incipit* (figure 10-6).

14. Josef Hedar, *Dietrich Buxtehudes Orgelwerke*. Frankfurt a. M., p. 282.

15. Bradshaw, p. 83.

10—2.

10—3.

10—4.

10—5.

10–6.

10–7.

10–8.

SECTION IV: Here the subject outlines the termination of the chant (figure 10-7a). The concluding *lento* presents the termination in incomplete form as canon between the alto and tenor, yet this seven-measure coda can also be perceived as a harmonization of the entire termination (figure 10-7b).

SECTION V: The chant begins again. The *incipit* is the subject of the gigue-like fugato (figure 10-8).

SECTION VI: The mediant cadence is given one complete statement in the soprano, interrupted by a short excursion to the subdominant (figure 10-9).

SECTION VII: This section is the thematic counterpart to section III, and the second *incipit* likewise appears first in the bass, though here as the subject (figures 10-10 and 10-11).

SECTION VIII: Here the termination, the first four notes of which form the melodic outline of the subject, is heard in its complete form only at the end of the section (figure 10-12).

10-9.

10-10.

10—11.

10—12.

In his *History of Keyboard Music to 1700*, Willi Apel recognized the presence of some sort of canticle-tone in this piece and located the termination correctly in several places, but was forced to conclude that "a unified plan in the sequence of sections does not seem to exist."[16] It appears that his conclusion is a result of having looked in the right places for the wrong tune: by assuming a common version of tone I which corresponds to that contained in the *Liber Usualis* rather than the version in common use throughout the seventeenth century in northern Germany, he misidentified the mediant cadence and apparently ignored the second *incipit*. Tone I as used by Buxtehude is the same as that used by earlier northern German composers and corresponds to that printed in Franz Eler's *Cantica Sacra* (1588).[17] The peculiar northern German practice of giving special treatment to the second *incipit* in keyboard Magnificats is also employed by Buxtehude, recognition of which is a key to making sense of the structure of both BuxWV 203 and BuxWV 204.

The smaller work, BuxWV 204, reveals an equally unified construction. In this four-sectioned work *incipit*, mediant cadence, second *incipit*, and termination are heard in succession.

Buxtehude's extensive use of liturgical melody in two compositions which are otherwise virtually identical to works titled "toccata" or "praeludium" raises the question of whether some of the "free" works might also have a basis in psalm- or canticle-tone. The Toccata in F (BuxWV 156) contains two fugues having thematically related subjects, as observant players have long been aware. It is possible to see the outline of the most common form of tone V in

16. Willi Apel, *The History of Keyboard Music to 1700*. Bloomington, 1972, p. 620.

17. Breig, p. 58.

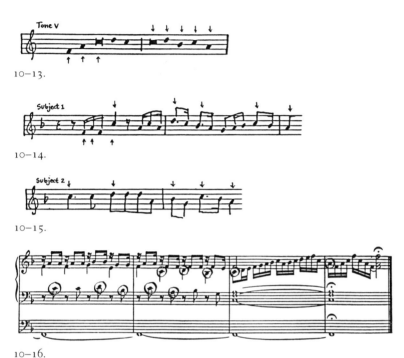

10-13.

10-14.

10-15.

10-16.

both subjects (figures 10-13 to 10-15). It will be remembered that the keys of F and C are those associated with keyboard compositions on the fifth tone. The common termination C-D-B[(b)]-C-A occurs frequently in the non-fugal sections of this piece as well (see as one example of this figure 10-16).

Is it possible that the Praeludium in E (BuxWV141) also has a psalm-tone basis? Here one observes a procedure similar to that found at the beginning section of the two Magnificats; in the opening toccata of BuxWV141 the soprano and bass appear to outline the first half of psalm-tone V (figure 10-17). The same treatment of the soprano occurs again in the toccata-like interlude at measure 54, exactly the midpoint of the piece (figure 10-18). The fugue subjects in this piece raise more questions. The subject of the first fugue,

bears melodic kinship to those of BuxWV145 (F major) and BuxWV136 (C major). Might this be an outline of the mediant cadence of psalm-tone V? Particularly since the fugue is surrounded on either side by toccata-like writing

10–17.

10–18.

based upon the same material? If the first three sections of this six-sectioned piece are related to the first half of psalm-tone V, what of the remaining three sections? The remaining sections are all fugal. A comparison of their respective subjects as they first appear in the soprano reveals a clear thematic relationship (figure 10-19). The circled notes reveal the common outline. Do these notes have anything to do with the termination of psalm-tone V? It is possible to make several observations concerning this. (1) Tone V historically has fewer variant endings than the other tones, but the common ending given above (figure 10-13) was not the only ending in use in the seventeenth century. (2) Variant endings for tone V frequently descend to the tonic. Keyboard pieces for this form of tone V are usually, but not always, in C rather than F. (3) Buxtehude's southern contemporary, Murschhauser, included two complete sets of versets

10–19.

for tone V in his *Octi-Tonium Novum Organicum* of 1696.[18] The first, *regularis*, in F, has its final on A; the second, *irregularis*, in C, has its final on C. Murschhauser reminds the reader of this in his preface to this volume.

Whether the pattern found in these three subjects, sol-mi-fa-re-ut, represents a termination for tone V known to Buxtehude must for the time being remain an open question. This is a termination form which was common in the nineteenth century, particularly in England, and which enjoys widespread use today. Its relevance to Buxtehude is uncertain. What is certain is that BuxWV141 bears strong resemblance to the *incipit* and mediant cadence in the first half of the piece, and is based in the second half on a melodic pattern which begins on the dominant and descends to the tonic, in accordance with the *irregularis* ending for tone V. If this is indeed a tone V piece, then the now-popular hypothesis that C major, rather than E major, was the original key for this piece has gained additional credibility, not for reasons of temperament but for reasons of tone.

It is just possible that the association of psalm-tone and toccata did not die with Buxtehude. The two fugues of the E major/C major Toccata of J.S. Bach (BWV566, figure 10-20) have an obvious resemblance to those found in BuxWV141. Might BWV566 also have been conceived as a tone V piece in C?

18. Printed in *Denkmäler der Tonkunst in Bayern* XVIII. Leipzig, 1917.

a.

b.

10—20.

CHAPTER ELEVEN

Bach and Buxtehude
at the Large Organ of St. Mary's in Lübeck

KERALA J. SNYDER

A delicately carved wooden balcony rail surrounds the console of the organ at the Hammond Castle in Gloucester, Massachusetts. It is said to have "once stood around the console of the organ of the Marienkirche in Lübeck where Buxtehude was organist, and his friend, Bach, often visited him." Charles Fisk and I inspected it together one summer afternoon. Following my own journey to Lübeck, I had come to Gloucester to seek his help as I tried to reconstruct in my imagination the organs which Buxtehude had played at St. Mary's in Lübeck.[1] The trip to the museum provided an interesting sidelight to the work at hand. We studied the design of the balcony rail and compared it with photographs of the lost Lübeck organs. Could it have formed a part of the instrument played by Dietrich Buxtehude and Johann Sebastian Bach?

So far as we know, Bach visited Buxtehude only once. It was a lengthy stay, however, beginning in the fall of 1705 and lasting about three months. Bach was then twenty, Buxtehude about sixty-eight. Bach must have recounted the visit often to his sons, for it figures prominently in his obituary:

> In the art of the organ he took the works of Bruhns, Reincken, Buxtehude, and several good French organists as models. While he was in Arnstadt he was once moved by the particularly strong desire to hear as many good organists as he could, so he undertook a journey, on foot, to Lübeck, in order to listen to the famous organist of the Marien-Kirche there, Diedrich Buxtehude. He tarried there, not without profit, for almost a quarter of a year, and then returned to Arnstadt.[2]

1. Kerala J. Snyder, "Buxtehude's Organs: Helsingør, Helsingborg, Lübeck—2: The Lübeck Organs," *The Musical Times* cxxvi (1985), 427-34.

2. Carl Philipp Emanuel Bach—Agricola—Mizler—Venzky: *Nekrolog auf Johann Sebastian Bach und Trauerkantate* (Leipzig, 1754; reprinted in *Dokumente zum Nachwirken Johann Sebastian Bachs 1750–1800, Bach-Dokumente* III, ed. Hans-Joachim Schulze [Kassel: Bärenreiter, 1972]), p. 82. Translation from *The Bach Reader*, ed. Hans T. David and Arthur Mendel (Revised edition; New York: Norton, 1966), pp. 217–18.

Unlike Bach's visits to Reincken in Hamburg, which may have occurred with some frequency during his Lüneburg years, the trip to Lübeck is documented by archival evidence, the proceedings of the Arnstadt consistory of February 21, 1706:

> The Organist in the New Church, Bach, is interrogated as to where he has lately been for so long and from whom he obtained leave to go.
>
> *Ille:* He has been in Lübeck in order to comprehend one thing and another about his art, but had asked leave beforehand from the Superintendent.
>
> *Dominus Superintendens:* He had asked only four weeks, but had stayed about four times as long.[3]

Bach's answer, "to comprehend one thing and another about his art," appears at first to be frustratingly vague. But if we expand his answer with words from the obituary, we can interpret it to mean that he understood his art at the organ to be multi-faceted, and that he had learned from Buxtehude in a variety of ways. In addition to the art of composition for the organ, he must also have learned something about performance. But the area of greatest growth may have been in his knowledge of the organ itself, for Buxtehude was an expert in organ construction, and his own art was intimately connected with the magnificent organ which he played.

The large organ of St. Mary's known to Buxtehude and Bach was removed in 1851 to make way for a new instrument, to be built by Johann Friedrich Schulze. The façade of the older organ remained in place until virtually the entire interior of St. Mary's was destroyed by flames following the bombing of Lübeck in 1942. The history of this instrument is unusually well documented, and it has been previously chronicled by Hermann Jimmerthal and Wilhelm Stahl.[4] But copies of their publications have become rather rare, and since some new material has come to light, it is useful to recount the history of this organ once again.

The large organ which Buxtehude played was the second or third to occupy its position on the west wall of St. Mary's. The church was completed in the mid-fourteenth century, and donations for the building of a new organ are

3. *Fremdschriftliche und gedruckte Dokumente zur Lebensgeschichte Johann Sebastian Bachs 1685–1750, Bach-Dokumente* II, ed. Werner Neumann and Hans-Joachim Schulze (Kassel: Bärenreiter, 1969), pp. 19–20. Translation from *The Bach Reader*, pp. 51–52.

4. Hermann Jimmerthal, "Zur Geschichte der St. Marien Kirche in Lübeck" (manuscript [1857] at Nordelbisches Ev.-Luth. Kirchenarchiv, Lübeck); Jimmerthal, *Beschreibung der großen Orgel in der St. Marien-Kirche zu Lübeck* (Erfurt & Leipzig: G. W. Körner, 1859); Wilhelm Stahl, *Die große Orgel der Marienkirche zu Lübeck* (Kassel: Bärenreiter, [1938]).

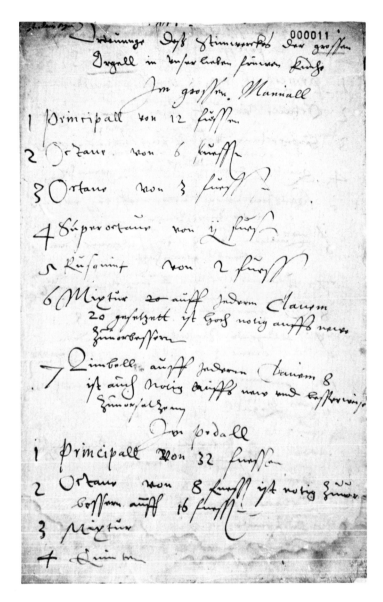

11–1. A stop list from the late sixteenth century for the large organ of St. Mary's Lübeck.

CREDIT: St. Mary's Church Archives (taken from that portion of the records now in custody of the Staatliche Archiv Verwaltung in Potsdam).

recorded for the years 1396–99.[5] This organ from the late fourteenth or early fifteenth century was in turn replaced by an instrument built by Master Bartold Hering during the years 1516–18. He was responsible for the magnificent two-story façade which survived until 1942. Its upper story contained five fields, the outer and middle fields containing Pedal pipes, the second and fourth those of the "large manual," or Werck. The prospect pipes were those of the 32′ Principal of the Pedal and the 16′ Principal of the Hauptwerk. The lower story contained two towers projecting to either side of the console, housing the large Positiv im Stoell, and two outer fields which contained the remainder of the Pedal pipes, including the 16′ Principal in the façade. Hering's organ was a pretentious instrument with two manuals and a very large Pedal division, including a 32′ Principal in its basic design. It was indeed a suitable organ for the Ratskirche of the imperial free city of Lübeck, Queen of the Hansa, still in the early sixteenth century near the height of her power and wealth.

The earliest preserved document listing the specifications for the large organ is a four-page manuscript entitled "ordenunge deß Stimwerckes der grossen Orgell in unser lieben fruwen kirche." It belongs to the archives of St. Mary's Church which are presently in the custody of the Staatliche Archiv Verwaltung in Potsdam.[6] Both its physical characteristics and its contents indicate that it was written in the latter part of the sixteenth century. The paper bears a watermark similar in design to that found by Briquet in documents from Hamburg dated 1586–87 and from Lübeck dated 1598,[7] and the style of handwriting is typical for this period (see figure 11–1). This document lists forty-two stops, including the Brustwerk division added by the Hamburg organ builder Jacob Scherer in 1560–61 but not the additions made to the organ by Gottschalk Borchert and Jacob Rabe in their major renovation of 1596–98. It may have been written shortly before that renovation, because the comments on the condition of the various stops indicate that it was written by an organ builder in contemplation of a renovation. The writer could have been either Hinrich Rölcke, organist of St. Mary's from 1572–78 and himself an organ builder, or Gottschalk Borchert, the master organ builder who began the renovation but died of the plague in 1597, leaving its completion to his journeyman, Jacob Rabe. The stoplist reads as follows:

5. Stahl, p. 5.

6. Lübeck, Archiv der Hansestadt, Marienkirche, vol. 13, "Acta die große Orgel betreffend" [new signature 15053], fols. 11–12.

7. Charles Moïse Briquet, Les filigranes: Dictionnaire historique des marques du papier dès leur apparition vers 1282 jusqu'en 1600. A Facsimile of the 1907 Edition, ed. Allan Stevenson (4 vols., Amsterdam: Paper Publications Society, 1968), #15936.

Im grossen Manual

1 Principall von 12 fuessen
2 Octave von 6 fuessen
3 Octave von 3 fuessen
4 Superoctave von ii fuessen
5 Rusquint von 2 fuess.
6 Mixtur auff jederm clavem 20 gesetzett ist hoch notig auffs newe zuverbessern
7 Zimbell auff jederm clavem 8 ist auch notig auffs new und besserweise zuversetzen

Im pedall

1 Principall von 32 fuessen
2 Octave von 8 fuess ist notig zuverbessern auff 16 fuess
3 Mixtur
4 Quinten

Im Mittelsten Clavier zum brust positiff

1 Principall von 8 fuessen
2 Octave von 4 fuess new gemachett
3 Superoctave von 2 fuessen new gemacht
4 Quinten darauβ Nasarden gemachet
5 Gemshorn ist auch notig auff besser masse new zumachende
6 Quintadena von 8 fuess darauβ ein gedackt gemachett
7 Blocfloÿten von 4 fuessen sein guedt
8 Mixtur auff jederm Clavem 8
9 klingende Zimbelln auff jederm clavem 3 mussen new gemachet werden
10 Krummhorner Mussen new gemacht werden
11 Regall ist guedt

Im Untersten Clavier zum grossen Positive Im Stoell

1 Principall von 8 fuess.
2 Octave von 4 fuess.
3 Ruβquinte
4 Superoctave auffs new gedubbell zusetzen
5 Mixtur auff jederm Clavem 8 new gemacht
6 Zimbell auff jederm Clavem 3 new gemacht
7 Grobe quintedena von 12 fuess darauβ ein gedackt zuintonieren
8 Hollfloÿten von 8 fuessen auff besserweise zu intonierende
9 Blockfloÿten von 4 fuess. davor offene floÿten gemachet

10 Trumeten mussen auffs new umb gemachet werden
11 Schalmeyen Mussen auch auffs new besser gemachet werden

Im Pedall auff beÿden seÿten im Stole

1 Principall von 16 fuess
2 Octave von 8 fuess.
3 Octave von 4 fuess.
4 Quinten davor delzken gesetzett
5 Mixtur zuvorbessern
6 Simbell zuverbessern
7 Baerpfeiff new gemachet
8 Bassuen new gemachet
9 Trumeten new gemachet

This document apparently escaped the attention of both Jimmerthal and Stahl. Stahl mentions a similar proposal for the renovation of the organ, presumably written by Gottschalk Borchert in 1596,[8] but Stahl's quotations clearly indicate a different document.

A detailed description of the organ following the renovation of 1596–98 survived in the account book of the church. The account book itself is not presently available, but Jimmerthal copied the description of the organ into his manuscript chronicle of the church,[9] carefully retaining the Low German language in which it had originally been written. It takes the form of a stoplist followed by notes concerning alterations (given in italics below), yielding the following list of forty-six stops:

Manuall

[1] Principal von 12 Voeten *is verbetert mit nien Zungen* [!] *up die nien Laden; dubbelt gemaket*

[2] Octave von 6 Voeten *ganz nie gemaket*

[3] Octave von 3 Voeten

[4] Super octave von 2 Voeten oder kleyn Octave *is nie gemaket duppelt*

[5] Quinte

[6] Mixtur

[7] Symbel

[8] Scharp

[9] Felt-Trummete v. 12 Veten

[10] *Zwe apene floiten, de eyne von* 8

[11]   *[apene floite]   de andre von* 4 *Voeten*

[12] *Ein Walthorn von* 4 *Voeten*

8. Stahl, p. 11.
9. Jimmerthal, "Zur Geschichte," pp. 197–99.

Im Pedall

[1] Principal von 32 Voeten
[2] Flaiten Baes von 8 Voeten u.
[3] [Flaiten Baes] von 16 Voeten
[4] Salmeyen Baes
[5] Corneten Baes
[6] *Cussan Basso v. 16 Voeten*

Im Brust Positiff

[1] Principal von 6 Voeten
[2] Gedackt von 8 Voeten
[3] Velt Pipen
[4] Gemβhoern von 2 Voeten
[5] Krumhoren von 8 Voeten
[6] Regael von 8 Voeten
[7] *eine nie Blockpipe . . ganz nie gemaket*
[8] *eine nie Zimbell*
[9] *Baerpeiffe* [im Basse] *und*
[10] *Clarith im Basse*
[11] *Corneten oder Zinken im dißkante*

Im stoele im Manuall, det stoell Positiff

[1] Principal von 8 Voeten, syn intoneret
[2] Octave v 4 Foeten is nie gemaket
[3] Super Octave von 2 Voeten is nie gemaket
[4] Groeff Gedect alias Borduen genannt up 16 Voeten . . nie gemaket [in
      place of Quint]
[5] Holpipen von 8 Voeten syn umb gemaket
[6] Kwerfloiten von 4 Voeten
[7] Dulcian von 8 Voeten
[8] Mixtur is ganz nie gemaket, det Scharff stehet in den Mixtur
[9] Trummeten von 8 Veten ganz nie gemaket
[10] Vassueten von 16 Voeten ganz nie gemaket
Tremolant

Im Pedall unden

[1] Gemßhoren von 2 Voeten
[2] Dubbelt Detzken foer de Baerpipe
[3] Mixtur is ganz nie gemaket

[4] Quinte Dene Baesse [in place of Symbelen] *von 4Voeten* [possibly in
    addition to an 8-foot Quintadena]
[5] Bassunen von 12 Voeten syn nie gemaket
[6] Felt Trummeten von 8 Voeten
[7] *Ein dubbelt groff Baes woldt sick nicht hoeren laten is deswegen
    dubbeltgesettet*

This list suffers from the fact that the man who originally wrote it, presumably the *Werkmeister* Gerdt Zöllner, probably knew nothing about organs, and
was very likely copying from information given to him by the organist or organ
builder. It was not until Franz Tunder's time that the positions of organist and
Werkmeister at St. Mary's were combined. The 1598 specifications published
by both Jimmerthal and Stahl differ from the list given above; perhaps they were
working from other documents which are no longer available. Jimmerthal's
published list varies only slightly, numbering forty-nine stops.[10] Stahl's list, however, contains fifty-five stops, adding *Quintadena* 8′, *Zimbel* II, and *Schalmei*
4′ to the *Stoell Positiv* (which he calls *Unterwerk*), adding *Oktav* 4′, *Quinte*,
and *Mixtur* VIII and substituting *Superoktav* 2′ for the *Velt Pipen* in the
Brustwerk, and adding *Quintbaß*, *Mixtur*, *Oktav* 8′, *Oktav* 4′, and *Quinte* to
the combined Pedal while omitting *Flaiten Baes* 8′ and *Gemshoren* 2′.[11]
   The specifications listed by Michael Praetorius in *Syntagma musicum*
(figure 11–2) have perplexed all who have studied the history of this organ.[12]
Jimmerthal presumed that Praetorius was unaware of the renovation of 1596–
98;[13] however, his list includes the reeds added to the Pedal at that time. Stahl
declined to print the Praetorius specifications on the grounds that they would
only make an overview of the history of the organ more difficult.[14] Praetorius'
greatest error lies in his apportioning of the stops between *Brustwerk* and
Positiv; a number of those he lists as belonging to the "*Rückpositiv*," such as (1)
Gemßhörner, (2) *Blockpfeiff* 4, (7) *Principale* and (8) *Feldpfeiffe* can clearly be
identified with stops belonging to the *Brust Positiff* in the 1598 list. Others,
such as (9) *Octava* and (18) *Mixtur* are found both in the late sixteenth-century
list and in Mattheson's list published in 1721; these could be omissions from
the 1598 list which might have been given correctly by Praetorius.
   The final stoplist which concerns us is that published by Mattheson in 1721,

10. Jimmerthal, *Beschreibung*, pp. 4–5.

11. Stahl, *Große Orgel*, p. 13; Stahl, *Musikgeschichte Lübecks, II: Geistliche Musik* (Kassel:
Bärenreiter), 1952, p. 37.

12. Michael Praetorius, *Syntagma musicum II: De Organographia* (Wolfenbüttel: author, 1619;
facsimile reprint edited by Willibald Gurlitt, Kassel: Bärenreiter, 1958), pp. 165–66.

13. Jimmerthal, *Beschreibung*, p. 6.

14. Stahl, *Große Orgel*, p. 14.

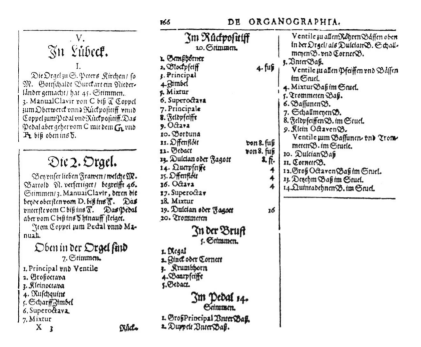

11–2. Disposition of the Lübeck St. Mary's organ as given by Michael Praetorius in 1619.

CREDIT: Michael Praetorius, *Syntagma musicum* II (1619), pp. 164–66.

given in facsimile in figure 11–3, which reflects the state of the organ at the time of Bach's visit.[15] The organ had just been renovated in 1704 by Otto Diedrich Richborn. Buxtehude had hoped for a major renovation of the organ by Arp Schnitger and had twice negotiated with him—in 1689 and again in 1702—for this purpose, but on both occasions the church had refused to give Schnitger the contract. The minor renovation subsequently performed by Richborn, a former journeyman to Schnitger, represents the only change to the stoplist of the large organ during Buxtehude's entire tenure at St. Mary's. Since his choices appear to have been so limited by financial constraints, the two stops added in 1704—*Vox humana* 8′ to the *Positiv* and *Sesquialtera* to the *Brustwerk*—probably represented his highest priorities for changes to the

15. Friedrich Erhard Niedt, *Musicalische Handleitung zur Variation Des General-Basses . . . Die Zweyte Auflage, Verbessert, vermehret, mit verschiedenen Grund-richtigen Anmerckungen, und einen Anhang von mehr als 60. Orgel-Wercken versehen durch J. Mattheson* (Hamburg: Bey Benjamin Schillers Wittwe und Joh. Christoph Kißner im Dom, 1721), pp. 189–90.

Anhang.   189   190

Die Orgel zu St. Marien, in Lübeck/ hat 54. Stimmen.		
4. Hohlflöte	4	13. Vox humana 8
5. Sesquialtera	2 fach.	14. Scharff 4 a 5 fach.
6. Feld-Pfeiffe	2 Fuß	
7. Gemshorn	2	Pedal.
8. Sifflet	1½	
9. Mixtura	8 fach.	1. Principal 32
10. Cimbel	3 fach.	2. Sub-Baß 16
11. Krumhorn	8 Fuß	3. Octava 8
12. Regal	8	4. Bauerflöte 2
Werck.		5. Mixtura 6 fach.
1. Principal 16		6. Groß-Posaun 24
2. Quintadena 16	Ruck-Positiv.	7. Posaune 16
3. Octava 8		8. Trommete 8
4. Spitz-Flöte 8	1. Principal 8	9. Principal 16
5. Octava 4	2. Bordun 16	10. Gedact 8
6. Hohlflöte 4	3. Blockflöte 8	11. Octava 8
7. Nasat 3	4. Sesquialtera 2 fach.	12. Nachthorn 2
8. Rauschpfeiffe 4 fach.	5. Hohl-Flöte 8 Fuß.	13. Dulcian 16
9. Scharff 4 fach.	6. Quintadena 8	14. Krumhorn 8
10. Mixtura 15 fach.	7. Octava 4	15. Cornet 2
11. Trommete 16 Fuß	8. Spiel-Flöte 2	
12. Trommete 8	9. Mixtura 5 fach.	Hiebey ein Cimbel-Stern/
13. Zincte 8	10. Dulcian 16 Fuß.	zwo Trummeln/zweene
Brust.	11. Baarpfeiffe 8	Tremulanten/ und 16.
1. Principal 16	12. Trichter-Regal 8	Bälge. Der Organiste/
2. Gedact 8	(Dieses wird auch wohl von keiner neu- en Inventen seyn.)	Christian Schiefer-
3. Octava 4		decker/ ist ein habiler
Aa 3	13. Vox	Mann.

11–3. Disposition of the Lübeck St. Mary's organ as given by Johann Mattheson in 1721.

CREDIT: Johann Mattheson, Appendix to Friedrich Erhard Niedt's *Musikalische Handleitung* (1721), pp. 189–90.

organ. These were both expressive stops, used for the playing of a solo line. In addition, the existing *Dulcian 16'* in the Pedal was renewed at that time.

The remainder of Mattheson's 1721 stoplist represents the state of the organ from the time of Friedrich Stellwagen's renovation of the large organ from 1637 to 1641, just prior to Franz Tunder's appointment as organist of St. Mary's. This had been an extensive renovation, but the changes in the specifications which he made were not itemized in the church records. It can be assumed, however, that stops named by Mattheson which appear in neither the 1598 list nor that of Praetorius can be attributed to Stellwagen. These would include the *Trichter Regal* and *Sesquialtera* in the *Positiv* and the 32' *Posaune* in the Pedal.

To judge from the information in the literature, it appears that the compass of neither organ in St. Mary's was sufficient for the performance of Buxtehude's music. Jimmerthal and Stahl both state unequivocally that D$^\sharp$, F$^\sharp$, and G$^\sharp$ were added to the bottom octave of the manuals and Pedal of the large organ only in 1733.[16] And yet the pitches F$^\sharp$ and G$^\sharp$ appear frequently in Bux-

16. Jimmerthal, *Beschreibung*, p. 7; Stahl, *Große Orgel*, p. 17.

tehude's organ music—and to a lesser extent in Tunder's—and most of them cannot be explained away as changes made in later sources. Furthermore, Gottschalk Borchert, who began the rebuilding of the large organ in 1596, had previously built a new organ for the neighboring St. Peter's church which included F# and G# in the Pedal,[17] and Stellwagen's 1636 rebuilding of the small organ at St. Jakobi had also included F# and G# in the Pedal.[18] It would seem odd if these pitches were available in the organs of two lesser parish churches and not at St. Mary's, the official *Ratskirche* of the city and the parish church of its most important citizens.

The sixteenth-century stoplists given above may provide a clue to the solution of this dilemma, offering some evidence that changes were made to the compass of the instrument prior to 1733 which are not noted in the literature. It is clear from the pipe lengths that the *Hauptwerk* was originally based on F, while the other divisions were based on C, and Stahl noted that the façade pipes of the *Hauptwerk* Principal 16′ began with F.[19] In Mattheson's list, however, the pipe lengths for the *Hauptwerk* are given in standard lengths based on C, suggesting that the compass of the *Hauptwerk* had been extended downward. This might have occurred during the 1596–98 renovation, which included a new chest for the *Hauptwerk*, or at least for its Principal. The Pedal, too, received a new chest "*im groten Werk*," presumably the upper story. The addition of these pitches to at least one manual and Pedal might also have taken place during Stellwagen's renovation of 1637–41, about which Jimmerthal wrote that "unfortunately one cannot tell what was done, but in any event many new things were added."[20]

So far as the wind system is concerned, Jimmerthal's chronicle tells us that in 1594 its twenty-one bellows were repaired, and that these bellows were most likely replaced by Stellwagen. In 1700 there were only ten bellows to be repaired.[21] The sixteenth-century bellows probably resembled those of the old organ in the cathedral of Halberstadt, which, as described by Praetorius, required one calcant for every two bellows.[22] According to the St. Mary's account books, there were only two calcants during Buxtehude's time; they each received 15 Lübeck marks annually for their regular work. One was a woman named Cathrin, and it was often she alone who received extra compensation for her services when repairs were being made to the organ. One calcant

17. Praetorius, *Syntagma musicum* II, p. 164; see figure 11–2.

18. Information received from Harry Hillebrand, whose firm restored the organ 1977–78.

19. Stahl, *Große Orgel*, p. 8; Jimmerthal says G ("Zur Geschichte," p. 198).

20. Jimmerthal, "Zur Geschichte," p. 238.

21. *Ibid.*, pp. 237, 296.

22. Praetorius, *Syntagma musicum* II, p. 103 and plate XXVI.

appears to have been sufficient for the purposes of tuning and voicing, while two would have been needed when the organ was actually played.

There is reason to believe that Buxtehude caused the temperament of the St. Mary's organs to be changed in 1683. That year, two years after Andreas Werckmeister had originally published his "first correct temperament,"[23] which he later designated as Number III,[24] thirty-six days were spent in a complete tuning of the large and small organs of St. Mary's.[25] Many of Buxtehude's free organ works exceed the limits of quarter-comma meantone, or "Praetorius," tuning which was standard for organs in Germany at that time. Indeed, the startling harmonic juxtapositions found in some of his best works, such as BuxWV 139, 146, and 151, may have been inspired by the possibilities opened up when a new tuning closed the circle of fifths on his organ.

The months spent with Buxtehude in Lübeck may have offered Bach his first opportunity to play a "well-tempered" organ. There is no evidence to suggest that the organ which he regularly played at the New Church in Arnstadt was not tuned in the standard Praetorius tuning, even though it had been completed only two years previously. There is no mention of temperament in the 1699 contract between the Arnstadt city council and the organ builder, J. F. Wender.[26] Some years later, in 1717, Wender was using an unequal temperament

23. Andreas Werckmeister, *Orgel-Probe Oder Kurtze Beschreibung Wie und welcher gestalt man Die Orgel-Wercke Von den Orgelmachern annehmen, probiren, untersuchen und den Kirchen liefern könne und solle, Benebst einem kurtzen jedoch gründlichen Unterricht Wie durch Anweiß und Hülffe des Monochordi ein Clavier wohl zu temperiren und zu stimmen sey, damit man nach heutiger Manier alle modos fictos in einer erträglichen und angenehmen harmoni vernehme* (Frankfurt and Leipzig: Theodorus Phil. Calvisius, 1681), p. 35.

24. Andreas Werckmeister, *Musicalische Temperatur, Oder deutlicher und warer Mathematischer Unterricht, Wie man durch Anweisung des MONOCHORDI Ein Clavier, sonderlich die Orgel-Wercke, Positive, Regale, Spinetten, und dergleichen wol temperirt stimmen könne, damit nach heutiger manier alle Modi ficti in einer angenehm und erträglichen Harmonia mögen genommen werden, Mit vorhergehender Abhandlung Von dem Vorzuge, Vollkommen und weniger Vollkommenheit der Musicalischen Zahlen, Proportionen, und Consonantien, Welche bey Einrichtung der Temperaturen wohl in acht zu nehmen sind: Benebst einem darzugehörig in Kupffer vorgebildeten deutlichen und völligem MONOCHORDO beschrieben, und an das Tages-Licht gegeben* (Frankfurt and Leipzig: Theodor Philipp Calvisius, 1691), chart between pages 38 and 39.

25. "Sonnabend [24 February, 1683], mit Consens Meiner HochgeEhrten H. Vorsteher, laut Memorial fol. 91. hat der Orgelmacher Michel Briegel mit der kleinen Orgel durch zu stimmen den anfang gemacht, und 4½ tagl. daran gearbeitet, à 3 mlub. thut 13/8/- ." "Sonnabend [17 November, 1683], Noch Meister Briegel dem Orgelmacher, so mit Consens der H. Vorsteher, laut Protocolli fol. 87:91, die beide Orgeln ohne die Röhr wercke gantz durch gestimmet, und hat Er an der großen Orgel 18½ tagl., an der kleinen 13 tagl. gearbeitet sind 31½ tagl. à 3 mlub. thut so bezahlet 94/8/-" Lübeck, Archiv der Hansestadt (presently in the custody of Staatliche Archiv Verwaltung, Potsdam), Nr. 5290 [St. Mary's Accounts, 1678–1685], fols. 245, 279. For a full discussion see Snyder, "Buxtehude's Organs."

26. Printed in Karl Müller and Fritz Wiegand, editors, *Arnstädter Bachbuch: Johann Sebastian Bach und seine Verwandten in Arnstadt* (2d edition; Arnstadt: Im Auftrage des Rates der Stadt, 1957), pp. 81–84.

which strongly favored the diatonic modes, according to Johann Kuhnau, who placed him in the same category as Silbermann (presumably Gottfried) in this regard.[27] The organs in Lüneburg were in a bad state of repair at the time Bach was there, which hardly suggests that they would have been tuned in the most up-to-date manner.[28] The rebuilding of the organ at St. Michael's in Ohrdruf was completed only in 1706.[29] Apart from the possibilities which its temperament may have offered him, the large organ at St. Mary's in Lübeck most likely provided Bach his first extended opportunity to play so large an organ, with such diverse colors and such a massive Pedal division.

Back in Arnstadt, following his journey to Lübeck, Bach was chastised by the consistory not only for overstaying his leave of absence but also for the manner in which he was playing the chorales: "Reprove him for having hitherto made many curious *variationes* in the *chorale*, and mingled many strange tones in it, and for the fact that the Congregation has been confused by it. . . ."[30] Is it possible that upon his return Bach had retuned his reeds in Werckmeister's temperament and was injecting previously unheard harmonies into his chorale settings? Buxtehude's chorale settings, or in any event those which have come down to us, contain many "curious *variationes*" but few "strange tones"; he seems to have reserved the latter for his free organ works. But it is worth noting that the Lübeck congregation was likewise confused by Buxtehude's chorale playing. The ministers decided on December 10, 1701, to hang boards with the hymn numbers in the church, because "from the organ playing beforehand, the hymns can be recognized by only a few, and the new hymns, whose melodies are not known, by practically no one."[31]

Two years after his return from Lübeck, Johann Sebastian Bach, not yet twenty-three, assumed the responsibility for drawing up the recommendations for the renovation of the organ at Divi Blasiikirche, Mühlhausen.[32] The question has been raised as to how he had gained sufficient expertise for this purpose so early in his career.[33] His knowledge of organ construction must have

27. Letter dated Leipzig, 8 December 1717, published in Johann Mattheson, *Criticae musicae tomus secundus* (Hamburg, 1725), pp. 229–39.

28. Gustav Fock, *Arp Schnitger und seine Schule: Ein Beitrag zur Geschichte des Orgelbaues im Nord- und Ostseeküstengebiet* (Kassel: Bärenreiter, 1974), pp. 102–104.

29. Werner David, *Johann Sebastian Bach's Orgeln* (Berlin: Berliner Musikinstrumenten-Sammlung, 1951), pp. 13–14.

30. *Bach-Dokumente* II, pp. 19–20; translation from *The Bach Reader*, pp. 51–52.

31. Cited by H. Gebler, "Beiträge zur Geschichte der Entwicklung des Kirchengesanges in Lübeck," *Sionia, Monatsschrift für Liturgie und Kirchenmusik* xxi (1896), p. 84.

32. *Schriftstücke von der Hand Johann Sebastian Bachs, Bach-Dokumente* I, ed. Werner Neumann and Hans-Joachim Schulze (Kassel: Bärenreiter, 1963), pp. 152–53; translated in Peter Williams, *The Organ Music of J. S. Bach, III: A Background* (Cambridge: Cambridge University Press, 1984), p. 142.

33. Williams, p. 139.

begun with his observation of the repairs to his brother's organ at Ohrdruf, which took place at the same point in J. S. Bach's life as the rebuilding of the organ at St. Olai, Helsingør, had occurred in Buxtehude's.[34] In Lüneburg he had the opportunity to observe Johann Balthasar Held rebuilding the Chorpositiv of St. Michael's Church in the summer of 1701.[35] Bach probably increased his knowledge of organ building with every organ he saw, particularly those in Hamburg. But the time spent in Lübeck with Buxtehude must have been especially important to his development as an expert on organ construction.

A number of Bach's recommendations for the rebuilding of the Mühlhausen organ directly reflect his knowledge of the large organ of St. Mary's and the additions to it which had occurred in 1704. His request for the addition of a Subbaß 32' to the Pedal recalls the very foundation of the Lübeck organ, with its 32' Principal in the façade. The modifications to the 16' Posaune to achieve greater Gravität suggests in turn Stellwagen's 32' Posaune in the Pedal. Reincken had also admired Buxtehude's 32' Pedal stops, and the contract for the addition of these same stops to the organ at St. Catherine's in Hamburg (1669) specified that they should be "at least as good as, if not better than, those of the large organ at St. Mary's in Lübeck."[36] Bach's admiration for these 32' stops in the St. Catherine's organ most likely dated from his 1720 visit.[37] Bach's request for a Fagott 16', "which is serviceable for all kinds of new musical ideas and sounds very pleasing in ensemble music," for the Oberwerk of the Mühlhausen organ may also reflect his Lübeck experience. Having timed his arrival to coincide with Buxtehude's Abendmusiken performances, Bach must have witnessed—or more likely participated in—numerous performances of ensemble music from the large organ. Bach might have served as an extra continuo player, performing in one of the side balconies on the 16' double regal which had been purchased in 1678 for use in the Abendmusiken.[38] Since Bach's new 16' Fagott extended only to middle C,[39] it was clearly a bass stop, which could also have been played with a coupler from the Pedal. Buxtehude had had his similar 16' Dulcian in the Pedal renewed in 1704. Bach's wish for a "perfect

34. See Snyder, "Buxtehude's Organs."

35. Fock, pp. 103–04.

36. Ibid., p. 57.

37. Jacob Adlung, Musica mechanica organoedi (Berlin: Friedrich Wilhelm Birnstiel, 1768; facsimile reprint ed. Christhard Mahrenholz, Kassel: Bärenreiter, 1961), p. 288, footnote a.

38. "Laut Protokoll fol. 81 haben meine hochgeehrten Vorsteher auf mein bittliches Ersuche, zur Ehre Gottes und zur Beförderung meiner festtäglichen- und Abend-Musik, ein doppelt 16 füßiges Regal der Kirchen zum besten für 16 Rtlr gekauft." Lübeck, Archiv der Hansestadt, Nr. 5290 [St. Mary's Accounts, 1678–85], fol. 4.

39. Adlung, p. 61: "Fagott, von C bis c." The dash to indicate c' is missing, probably due to a typographical error.

and beautiful" *Sesquialtera* on the new *Brustwerk* recalls the fact that Buxtehude had added a *Sesquialtera* to his *Brustwerk* in 1704; the addition of the
Brustwerk itself may have been prompted by Bach's experience playing a
three-manual instrument while in Lübeck.

Bach learned about organ building from sources other than Buxtehude, of
course, and Williams has convincingly demonstrated that beginning with the
Mühlhausen report much of Bach's language concerning organs was drawn
from Werckmeister's *Erweiterte und verbesserte Orgel-Probe* of 1698.[40] Three
years prior to Bach's visit, Buxtehude had contributed two dedicatory poems to
the *Harmonologia musica* of his friend Werckmeister. Was it Buxtehude who
introduced Bach to Werckmeister's writings? Bach's insistence that the stops of
the Mühlhausen organ which were to be retained be completely tuned anew
(*"von neüem durchstimmet werden"*) suggests a change in temperament which
could have come from Werckmeister through Buxtehude. The word *"durch-*
stimmet" is the same as that used in the Lübeck accounts of 1683; in itself it
neither implies a change of temperament nor excludes it. But the modifier *"von*
neüem" suggests a change to a different tuning, perhaps one which Bach had
come to know in Lübeck. Did Bach persuade Wender to adopt a new temperament?

Back in Gloucester, Charles Fisk and I decided that it was unlikely that the
balcony rail at the Hammond Castle had belonged with either of the organs
which Buxtehude and Bach had played at St. Mary's in Lübeck. Its delicate
filagrees did not match any of the wood carving which could be seen in the
photographs of these organs. It does appear to have been carved at about the
same time that the large organ was built, however, and it may have found a
place in some other part of St. Mary's Church—a side chapel, perhaps. If so, it
could have witnessed the glorious sounds produced on that organ by Tunder,
Buxtehude and Bach. But the balcony rail had no secrets to tell concerning the
conversations which took place between Bach and Buxtehude at the organ bench
of St. Mary's late in 1705.

40. Peter Williams, "J. S. Bach—Orgelsachverständiger unter dem Einfluß Andreas Werckmeis-
ters?", *Bach Jahrbuch* LXVIII (1982), pp. 131–42.

CHAPTER TWELVE

Notes on Tuning Methods in Fifteenth-Century Italy

LUIGI FERDINANDO TAGLIAVINI

As is well-known, until the second half of the fifteenth century musical intervals were calculated according to the Pythagorean system: that is to say, the notes were drawn from a succession of pure fifths (ratio 3:2). A series of six ascending fifths, from F to B, generates the seven notes of the *diatonic order*, to which the B♭ normally has to be added. The notes of the *chromatic order* may be obtained with a continuation of the ascending succession of fifths (B–F♯ – C♯–G♯–D♯–[A♯]) or, vice versa, with an extension of the series by means of descending fifths ([B♭]–E♭ –A♭ –D♭ –G♭). In 1413 Prosdocimo de Beldemandis suggested both methods, at the same time showing their limits. Four notes necessary to musical practice are lacking: B♭ and E♭ in the first chromatic series, and F♯ and C♯ (which serve as *subsemitonia modi*) in the second. The ideal solution for Prosdocimo is the presence of both series of chromatic notes, i.e., a seventeen-note octave containing the seven notes of the "diatonic order" plus the five ascending and five descending alterations.[1]

Nevertheless, the normal keyboards continued to be restricted within the limits of a twelve-note octave. Choosing the notes of the chromatic order, practical musicians seem to have given priority to the ascending alterations, the only exception being B♭. This fact is reflected in the nomenclature used for the notes in German-speaking countries, where the letters from A to H designate the notes of the diatonic order, including the B♭, called B (the B natural is called H), while for the notes of the chromatic order the same letters with the suffix -*is*—a suffix indicating an ascending alteration, i.e. a♯ —are employed. (The suffix -*es*, or -*s*, used at present for descending alterations, e.g., Es = E♭, seems not to have been used before the eighteenth century.) It is well-known that such alphabetic symbols served for the notation of the low and middle

1. We consulted the version of the treatise of Beldemandis contained in the Bolognese manuscript *Parvus tractatulus de modo monocordum dividendi quem Prosdocimus de Beldemandis patavinus Padue anno Domini* 1413 *compilavit* (Bologna: Biblioteca Musicale "G. B. Martini," Cod. 4 [A56], pp. 139–45). The treatise has been published, on the basis of the Bologna and Einsiedeln manuscripts, by E. de Coussemaker, *Scriptorum de musica medii aevi nova serie*, III (Paris: Durand, 1864; reprint, Hildesheim: Olms, 1963), pp. 248–58.

voices of keyboard music written in the German area during the fifteenth and sixteenth centuries (and for all voices in German tablatures of the seventeenth century).

When we compare the views of musicians—especially those of keyboard players—with those of theorists and instrument builders, we have an impression of a strange contradiction: if the first seem to prefer the ♯ , the others opt for the ♭ . In fact, the most widespread method for calculating musical intervals in the fifteenth century, based on the division of the monochord, derived the notes of the chromatic order from the descending succession of fifths, F–B♭–E♭–A♭–D♭–G♭ . In other words, the twelve usual notes were obtained through an ascending series of eleven fifths, from G♭ to B. This system was adopted by many theorists, e.g., Arnaut of Zwolle (about 1440),[2] Johannes Gallicus (+ 1473),[3] and the pupil of the latter, Nicolò Burzio.[4] The scaling of the pipes (which are still preserved) of the front and rear prospects of the organ built in 1470–75 by Lorenzo da Prato for the basilica of San Petronio in Bologna seems to have been calculated according to the same system.[5] This method became so deeply rooted in the organ builders' practice that as late as 1766 Dom Bédos followed it for his *diapasons* or pipe scaling.[6] (However, at the moment of tuning Dom Bédos had to adapt the pipe lengths to a completely different system, close to "meantone" temperament.[7])

The discrepancy between the views of instrument makers and players is only an apparent one: the system adopted by the makers and tuners actually turns into an advantage for the practical musician. In fact, four of the Pythagorean ♭ -notes, combined with notes of the diatonic order, create intervals which are very close to the pure major and minor thirds (ratios 5:4 and 6:5), i.e., to those intervals that as early as the beginning of the fourteenth century Walter

2. The treatise by Arnaut of Zwolle is preserved in Paris, Bibliothèque Nationale, Ms. latin 7295, fol. 128–32, and was edited by G. Le Cerf and E. R. Labande, *Les traités de Henri-Arnaut de Zwolle et de divers anonymes* (Paris: Picard, 1932).

3. The treatises by Johannes Gallicus (alias Legrensis) are preserved in the British Library (Add. 22315, fol. 1–60, and Harl. 6525) and have been edited by Coussemaker, *op. cit.*, IV, pp. 298 ff. (see especially chapters VII–X on the division of the monochord, pp. 318–23).

4. Nicolaus Burtius, *Musices opusculum* (Bononiae, 1487; reprint, Bologna: Forni, 1969), Tractatus 3, chapter XX: "De divisione monocordi."

5. On the organs of San Petronio in Bologna and their recent restoration, a monograph by Oscar Mischiati and L. F. Tagliavini is in progress. See also the writings of the same authors: "Gli organi di S. Petronio" in *Il restauro degli organi di S. Petronio* (Bologna: Alfa, 1982) (*Quaderni della Soprintendenza per i beni artistici e storici per le province di Bologna, Ferrara, Forlì e Ravenna*, 5), pp. 13–39, and "Gli organi" in *La Basilica di San Petronio*, II (Bologna: Cassa di Risparmio, 1984), pp. 313–22.

6. Dom François Bédos de Celles, *L'art du facteur d'orgues* (Paris: Delatour, 1766–78; reprint, Kassel: Bärenreiter, 1963–66), I, pp. 58, 60.

7. *Ibid.*, II, pp. 428–35.

Odington recognized as "suave consonances,"[8] unlike the harsh Pythagorean thirds (ratios 81:64 and 32:27). More precisely, the interval between D and G♭, E and A♭, A and D♭, B and E♭, corresponding to the ratio 8192:6561, is only one *schisma* (ratio 32805:32768 = nearly 2 cents) flatter than the "natural" major third (ratio 5:4). On the other hand, the interval between G♭ and A, A♭ and B, D♭ and E (ratio 19683:16384) is one *schisma* sharper than the "natural" minor third (ratio 6:5). Thus, the intervals that the theorists call diminished fourth and augmented second, deeming them dissonant, appear on the contrary to the musician to be perfectly practicable, since they serve respectively as excellent major and minor thirds—indeed, as the only really consonant thirds.[9] The pragmatic attitudes of the musicians and the instrument makers allow them to be free from theoretic prejudices and to change the names of notes easily, according to the notes' practical uses: then D♭, E♭, G♭ and A♭ can be named *Cis*, *Dis*, *Fis*, and *Gis* respectively.[10]

In the second half of the century the efforts to increase the number of "consonant" thirds became more and more frequent. One of the earliest evidences of these efforts is found in the contract stipulated on September 23, 1468, by the organ builder Andrea Molighi for the restoration of the organ at the Cathedral of Cesena: Molighi agreed to give the instrument "an excellent sonority and a gradation of sounds in conformity with the style, form and manner of modern times and new consonances." For this purpose he had to add "three semitones with perfect thirds":[11] certainly the addition of split keys

8. Walter Odington, *Summa de speculatione musicae*; edited by Frederick Hammond, s. l. (American Institute of Musicology, 1970) *(Corpus scriptorum de musica*, 14), pp. 70–71.

9. On this subject see the essay by Edward Pepe, "Pythagorean Tuning and Its Implications for the Music of the Middle Ages" in *The Courant* I, 2 (Ann Arbor: The Academy for the Study and Performance of Early Music, April 1983), pp. 3–16.

10. The discrepancy between theory and practice is reflected in some statements of the *Epistola* written between 1482 and 1486 by John Hothby (alias Johannes Octobi) against Ramos de Pareia. Describing the chromatic tetrachords B–C–C'–E and E–F–F'–A, Hothby observes that the notes C' and F' do not exist on the organ, yet the sounds corresponding to the "black keys" are used instead of these notes (C' "non è in organo e pero si piglia e nero in luogo suo"; F' "non est in organo et ideo accipitur nigrum loco sui"). Hothby, an advocate of the Pythagorean system, seems to point out with the words quoted that the notes produced by the "black keys" actually are D♭ and G♭, but are used in practice as C' and F'. Hothby's *Epistola* is preserved in Florence, Biblioteca Nazionale, Magl. XIX, 36, and has been edited by Albert Seay in Johannes Octobi, *Tres tractatuli contra Bartholomeum Ramum* (Rome: American Institute of Musicology, 1964) *(Corpus scriptorum de musica*, 10), pp. 79–92 (for the passage quoted see pp. 91–92).

11. "Vir egregius Magister Andreas quondam Iohannis de Molighis magister organorum civis et habitator Arimini inherendo se convenctionibus capitulis et promissionibus suis... factis circha revisionem reaptationem concimen et bonitatem perfectionem et manutentionem organorum per eum magistrum Andream organistam factorum in ecclesiis Episcopatus Cesene... promisit et convenit... diligenter et studiose revidere et reaptare et in bona et optima sonoritate et gradantia vocum iuxta stilum formam et modum moderni et novi temporis et modernas concordantias... et in illis noviter adiungere ac ponere tres semitonos cum tertiis perfectis vocibus et tonis...." This

was intended. Twelve years later, Domenico di Lorenzo of Lucca was engaged to build an organ endowed with supplementary keys for "*la terza del b quadro et la terza del fa delle f*" in the cathedral of his town.[12] The first note mentioned here certainly has to be explained as D♯, while the meaning of the second is rather obscure. Most scholars interpret it to be A♭,[13] but more likely it was intended to be A♯.[14] According to the latter interpretation, the chromatic order of the Lucchese organ was planned to include, besides the five traditional ♭-notes (from B♭, in a succession of descending fifths, down to G♭), two ♯-notes (D♯ and A♯) as well. These two supplementary notes would have been considered ascending alterations by the theorist (e.g., by Johannes Hothby, a convinced partisan of the Pythagorean system, who at that time was *maestro di cappella* at the Cathedral of Lucca), but to the organ player the same two notes certainly served as descending alterations (i.e., as E♭ and B♭ respectively).

Such a divergence between the views of the theorist and those of the practical musician seems to be a paradox. The custom of the keyboard players, who used Pythagorean diminished fourths and augmented seconds (which are very close to the *sesquiquarta* and *sesquiquinta* proportions, i.e., to the ratios 5:4 and 6:5) as major and minor thirds, should finally have brought the theorists to recognize that the aforesaid proportions, rather than the Pythagorean ratios 81:64 and 32:27, correspond to the real "consonant" thirds. But this step was not easy, since the Pythagorean doctrine of musical intervals was very deep-rooted. It is

contract, preserved in the Notarial Archives of Cesena, has been published by Carlo Grigioni, "Maestri organari nella Romagna" in *Melozzo da Forlì—Rasssegna d'arte romagnola* (Forlì, 1937–39), p. 159.

12. See Luigi Nerici, *Storie della musica in Lucca* (Lucca: Tip. Giusti, 1879) (*Memorie e Documenti per servire alla storia di Lucca*, XII), p. 143, and Franco Baggiani, "Gli organari lucchesi" in *L'Organo—Rivista di cultura organaria e organistica* XIII (1975), pp. 5–27 (especially pp. 15, 19).

13. See Wilhelm Dupont, *Geschichte der musikalischen Temperatur* (Kassel: Bärenreiter, 1935), p. 45; F. Baggiani, *op. cit.*, p. 19, footnote 6; and Mark Lindley, "Fifteenth-Century Evidence for Meantone Temperament" in *Proceedings of the Royal Musical Association* CII (1975–76), pp. 37–51. In Baggiani's article the phrase *terza del fa delle f* is interpreted as a third above f♭, while Lindley (p. 49) explains it as the minor third above f. According to both explanations, the note would have been a♭; thus, the Lucca organ should have had the pair of split keys d♯/e♭ and g♯/a♭, i.e., the pair destined to become the most common in the sixteenth century, since they enlarge the limits of meantone temperament in a logical way. The same hypothesis was already expressed by Dupont. Nevertheless, it is unlikely that in 1482 in Lucca—where under the musical direction of Hothby the Pythagorean system was in full vogue—the a♭ would have been considered a supplementary note (and the g♯ the normal one). In fact Hothby's *Epistola* quoted above (see note 10), seems to confirm that, according to the English theorist, the normal "black keys" of the organ correspond to the b-notes.

14. According to the solmisation extended to the *musica ficta* (an enlargement promoted by Hothby), the problematic *fa delle f* could be intended as f♯, i.e., as *fa* of the hexachord beginning from c♯; such a hexachord was possible on the basis of Hothby's theory. In fact, the "third order" of his division of the monochord contains seven ♯-notes, from f♯ in a succession of ascending fifths,

well-known that Bartolomeo Ramos de Pareia was one of the very first theorists to propose, in 1482, a division of the monochord[15] containing the ratios 5:4 and 6:5, together with other intervals not belonging to the Pythagorean system, which were only later accepted and recognized as "natural": the minor tone (ratio 10:9), the diatonic semitone (ratio 16:15), and the large "natural" chromatic semitone (ratio 135:128). The harsh polemics against Ramos and his followers—foremost among whom was Giovanni Spataro—show how difficult it was to embrace the new ideas. Nevertheless, Ramos and Spataro were not alone.[16] Considerable attention should be paid to a theorist who hitherto has passed almost unnoticed: Bonaventura da Brescia, whose treatise *La Venturina*, dated 1489,[17] shows a division of the monochord analogous to that of Ramos de Pareia, but which is at the same time closely linked to the traditional system. In fact, it is a sort of "correction" of the latter, which eliminates the difference of views between theorists and practical musicians. Bonaventura's division corrects the Pythagorean diminished fourths (D–G$^\flat$, E–A$^\flat$, A–D$^\flat$, B–E$^\flat$) and augmented seconds (D$^\flat$–E, G$^\flat$–A, A$^\flat$–B) into "natural" major and minor thirds (ratios 5:4 and 6:5 respectively; to that purpose, the fifth D$^\sharp$–A$^\sharp$

up to b^t. See J. Octobi, *Tractatus quarundam regularum artis musicae*, preserved in manuscript copies at Florence (Biblioteca Nazionale, Pal. 472) and London (British Library, Add. 36986). Thus, the third of the *fa delle f* would have been a^t. Incidentally it may be remarked that the divided keys a^t/b^b are documented again at Lucca (together with the pairs d^t/e^b and g^t/a^b) as late as the beginning of the seventeenth century in the organ built by Andrea Lucchese (i.e., very probably Andrea Ravani, 1575–1616) for the "Accademia" of Tomaso Raffaelli and described by Adriano Banchieri, *Conclusioni nel suono dell'organo* (Bologna: Rossi, 1609; reprint, Bologna: Forni, 1968), p. 15. See also F. Baggiani, *op. cit.*, p. 21.

15. Bartholomaeus Ramos de Pareia, *De musica tractatus* (Bononiae, 1482; reprint, Bologna: Forni, 1969), Prima pars, Tractatus I, Cap. II and Tertia pars, Tractatus II, Cap. III.

16. Divisions of the monochord containing the ratios 5:4 and 6:5 are to be found in anonymous treatises written in France and Germany in the second half of the fifteenth century. Among the small treatises of the Ms. lat. 7295 of the Bibliothèque Nationale of Paris published by Le Cerf and Labande (see note 2 above) there are three divisions of the monochord in fol. 128 bis: the first one shows a diatonic scale in *just intonation* starting from C (with the remark that A "discordans est cum D," since this fifth is one syntonic comma flat); the second one is a partial Pythagorean division, in which the E (placed over C at the interval of 81/64) is said to be "dissimile tamen e prius reperto"; the third method calculates the intervals of octave, fifth, fourth, major and minor third according to the ratios 2:1, 3:2, 4:3, 5:4 and 6:5 respectively, with the remark "sed istud non potest in omnibus reperiri." All the observations quoted show the full consciousness of the impossibility of reconciling all the "natural" intervals within the same system. The well-known treatise *Pro clavichordis faciendis*, preserved in Erlangen (Universitätsbibliothek, Ms. 729, fol. 202^v–203) and first studied by Dupont (*op. cit.*, pp. 20–22), shows a division in which four major thirds (C–E, G–B, D–F^t, and A–C^t) are calculated according to the ratio 5:4, two fifths (G–D and B–F^t) are one *schisma* flat and the "wolf fifth" (a syntonic comma minus a *schisma*, i.e., about 20 cents flat) is placed between A and E.

17. Bonaventura da Brescia, *Brevis collectio artis musice . . . quae dicitur Venturina*, 1489; copy in Bologna, Biblioteca Musicale "G. B. Martini," Cod. 105 (A57), Cap. 27 ff.: *De compositione monocordis regularis*. This treatise was recently edited by Albert Seay (Colorado Springs: Colorado College Music Press, 1980) (*Critical Texts*, XI).

is flattened one *schisma*. Otherwise Bonaventura's cycle of eleven fifths (from F♯ to B) is the traditional one: it cannot be "closed" by a twelfth fifth, B–F♯, this last being too narrow; but instead of being one "Pythagorean comma" (ratio 531441:524288, i.e., about 24 cents) flat, the "wolf fifth" is one "syntonic comma" (ratio 81:80, i.e. about 22 cents) flat. Four major thirds (C–E, F–A, G–B and B♭–D) and as many minor thirds (E–G, A–C, B–D and D–F) remain Pythagorean (ratios 81:64 and 32:27); four more major thirds—or, depending on the notes' denominations, four diminished fourths (D♭-F, E♭–G, G♭–B♭, A♭–C)—and three minor thirds—or augmented seconds (C–E♭, F–A♭, B♭–D♭)—are slightly better (one *schisma* flatter or sharper respectively) than their Pythagorean equivalents, hence corresponding to the ratios 512:405 and 1215:1024 respectively.

From a practical point of view, Bonaventura's modification of the traditional system is almost insignificant, since the deviation is very slight; but its importance in the field of musical and acoustic theory is considerable. In fact, it leads to the acknowledgment of intervals ignored by the Pythagorean system but accepted in the next century as an integrating part of the new system codified by Zarlino. It is the same acknowledgment made some years before by Ramos de Pareia. The only differences between Ramos' and Bonaventura's systems lie in the starting point of the series of the eleven fifths and in the position chosen for the one-*schisma* narrow fifth: Ramos begins from D and tempers by one *schisma* the fifth C♯–G♯, while Bonaventura starts from the traditional *Fis* (considered as a real F♯) and takes the *schisma* from the fifth E♭–B♭ (D♯–A♯). Nevertheless, if in Bonaventura's system the "wolf fifth" remains, according to fifteenth-century usage, between B and F♯ and can therefore be easily avoided by the player, Ramos' "wolf fifth" is placed between G and D, making the practical application of his whole system very problematic, a drawback which his detractors, especially Hothby,[18] did not overlook. Hence one might suppose that Ramos' system could have been intended as a merely theoretical starting point, rather than a practical tuning system.[19] At any rate, both Ramos and Bonaventura made the important attempt to draw theory and practice together, "reducing"—as Spataro asserted, defending his teacher, Ramos—the Pythagorean intervals to the ones used by the musicians.[20]

It seems to be clear that the "new style" in the "gradation of sounds" in conformity with the "form and manner of modern times and new conso-

18. Johannes Octobi, *Excitatio quaedam musicae artis per refutationem*, ms. in Florence, Biblioteca Nazionale (Pal. 472), edited by A. Seay (see note 10 above), pp. 17–57 (especially pp. 20–21).

19. According to Mark Lindley's interpretation (see note 13 above) the practical system intended by Ramos would already have been meantone temperament.

20. Giovanni Spataro, *Errori di Franchino Gaffurio da Lodi*, (Bologna: B. di Ettore, 1521), fol. 21ᵛ ff.

nances," to which the organ building contract of 1468 quoted above refers, was characterized above all by the intervals called in the same document "perfect thirds." The traditional Pythagorean system, which allowed the presence of only four almost-perfect major thirds (really perfect in the modified form suggested by Bonaventura da Brescia) in a normal keyboard instrument, was increasingly unable to satisfy the demands of musicians. Hence the number of "consonant" major thirds was augmented, with the addition of supplementary notes through split keys (as the Cesena and Lucca contracts of 1468 and 1480 stipulated); but the real solution to this problem had to be found in the temperament (usually called *participation* by ancient writers). This practice seems to be reflected, though not clearly, in the treatise of Ramos de Pareia,[21] but the first explicit hint of it is given at the end of the century by Franchino Gaffurio. In his *Practica musicae*, published in 1496, Gaffurio mentions the organ tuners' practice of letting the fifth undergo a small diminution (qualified as "latent and uncertain") called *participata*.[22]

It is hard to specify when the use of the temperament—in its variants proposed in the first decades of the sixteenth century by Schlick,[23] Aron,[24] and Lanfranco[25]—became general and supplanted the Pythagorean tuning system. In the last decades of the fifteenth century conservative tendencies and innovative experiments seem to have coexisted.[26]

Very interesting evidence of the persistence of the Pythagorean tuning as late as 1480 is to be found in an exceptional iconographic document: the clavichord represented with "photographic" precision in one of the famous tarsias (datable 1479–82) of Federico da Montefeltro's study (the so-called *studiolo*) in the ducal palace of Urbino.[27] This instrument already shows the remarkable

21. See note 19 above.

22. Franchino Gaffurio, *Practica musicae* (Milan: P. Lomazzo, 1496), Liber II, chapter 3.

23. Arnolt Schlick, *Spiegel der Orgelmacher und Organisten* (Speyer: P. Drach, 1511; reprint, Mainz: Rheingold-Verlag, 1959), chapter 8. See M. Lindley, "Early Sixteenth-Century Temperaments" in *Musica Disciplina* XXVIII (1974), pp. 129–51.

24. Pietro Aron, *Thoscanello de la musica* (Venice: B. & M. de Vitali, 1523; reprint of the later edition, *Toscanello in musica*, Venice: M. Sessa, 1532; Kassel: Bärenreiter, 1970), Lib. II, chapter XLI.

25. Giovan Maria Lanfranco, *Scintille di musica* (Brescia: Lodovico Britannico, 1533; reprint, Bologna: Forni, 1970), pp. 132–36.

26. Marco Tiella's hypothesis—in his essays on the positive built by Lorenzo Gusnasco in 1494—that one of the two stops of this organ would have been tuned according to the Pythagorean system and the other in meantone temperament, is attractive, but seems to us not to be supported by sufficient proof. See M. Tiella, "The Positive of Lorenzo da Pavia (1494)" in *The Organ Yearbook* VII (1976), pp. 4–15, and "Das Positiv von Lorenzo da Pavia (1494)" in *Acta organologica* 10 (1976), pp. 82–104.

27. From the point of view of organology, this iconographic document has been investigated by

compass of four octaves (F–f'''', without F$^\sharp$ and G$^\sharp$, i.e., forty-seven keys), a compass destined to remain customary in Italy until about the middle of the following century, yet it has only seventeen pairs of strings (which are reproduced with startling realism by means of real brass wires incorporated in the tarsia). Each of the first five notes (from F to B) corresponds to a single string pair, while the following forty-two are alternately ranged in groups of three and four on twelve pairs of strings. The exactness of the image is so astonishing that it is possible to survey and calculate, on the basis of the positions of the tangents, the intervals of tone and semitone which each string pair would produce.[28] Most importantly, one can deduce that the diatonic semitones (particularly the ones which were surely intended to be diatonic, as E/F and B/C) are not the large ones of the *just intonation* (ratio 16:15, i.e., about 112 cents, an interval codified at that time by Ramos de Pareia and Bonaventura da Brescia) or of the *meantone* temperament (about 117 cents), but the small ones *(limmata)* of the Pythagorean system (ratio 256:243, i.e., about 90 cents). The twelve semitones of the octave C–C are distributed in the succession s–l–(s)–l–s–s–l–s–l–s–l–s (s = small, l = large).[29] Thus, the tuning system shown by the Urbino clavichord is still the traditional one, based on the cycle of eleven pure fifths, from G$^\flat$ to B.[30] Yet it must be pointed out that the need for "perfect thirds" certainly was less peremptory in the clavichord than in the organ. We have already mentioned the organ at San Petronio in Bologna, a unique relic dating back to the seventh decade of the fifteenth century. We have pointed out that the scaling of its praestants (Principal 24' and Octave 12', both embracing fifty-one pipes) seems to have been calculated according to the old, traditional system, yet it is not certain that the adopted tuning system was strictly Pythagorean; on the contrary, the arrangement of the pipes according to intervals of major thirds (excepting the first seventeen pipes, ordered by tones) could suggest that the organ builder wanted to follow the *stylus novi temporis* and to favor the *modernae concordantiae*, i.e., the "perfect" major thirds. At any rate, when this instrument was restored and modified in 1532 by Giovanni Battista Facchetti, who equipped it with three pairs of split keys for the notes G$^\sharp$/A$^\flat$, it was certainly tuned according to the *meantone* temperament.

Edward M. Ripin, "The Early Clavichord" in *The Musical Quarterly* LIII (1967), pp. 518–38 (see especially pp. 531 ff.).

28. We were able to examine the tarsia in Bologna about ten years ago, when the *studiolo* was in Prof. Otello Caprara's restoration laboratory. We sincerely thank Prof. Caprara.

29. Some perplexity could persist regarding the semitones dividing the tones D–E and A–B: in the octave c–c'—where the intervals can be better surveyed because of the greater string length—the semitones D–E$^\flat$ and A–B$^\flat$ are divided between two different strings and therefore cannot be calculated, while the semitones E$^\flat$–E and B$^\flat$–B are decidedly large. In the octave c'–c'', on the other hand, the intervals mentioned show a value halfway between the large and the small semitone. This could be attributed to a slight imprecision of the reproduction, but could also be

explained as intentional raising of the notes B^b and E^b, in order to favor the major thirds B^b–D and E^b–G.

30. Michael Thomas also analysed the Urbino tarsia, obtaining analogous results. See M. Thomas, "The Tuning and Pitch of Early Clavichords" in *The English Harpsichord Magazine*, I (1976), pp. 175–80.

CHAPTER THIRTEEN

A Chronicle of the Restoration of a Mexican Colonial Organ

SUSAN TATTERSHALL

In the late summer of 1984, Ted Blankenship and I spent seven weeks in Huamantla, Tlaxcala, restoring two organs. One had already had its constituent parts restored and needed assembly and tuning. This chronicle is the story of the other, which had to be restored entirely on-site. It attempts to reconstruct that experience not only with reference to the work of the restoration, but also to events happening around us in the town, and to thoughts on organ restoration in general, and that of Mexican organs in particular. Huamantla is an isolated town of about 45,000 souls, located some twenty-five kilometers due east of Apizaco, in the eastern portion of the state of Tlaxcala.

July 25, 1984: Ted Blankenship and I arrived in Huamantla last night, and went to don Enrique's shop early this morning to get the key to the church. We knew we'd need all day just to clean out the organ loft. The church is called La Iglesia del Señor del Despojo, but is known throughout town as El Santuario. It was built by Jesuit monks when they obtained permission from the already established Franciscans to live, worship, and teach in Huamantla in the early seventeenth century. The Jesuit order was expelled from Mexico in the 1770s and allowed to reenter some years later, but unfortunately no details pertinent to the life of this particular church have yet surfaced. However, the people who consider this church to be *their* neighborhood church told me that for about a hundred years now, it has endured alternating periods of energetic maintenance (spiritual and architectural) and total abandonment and decline. Presently, it is in another renaissance, begun three years ago. It is a compact, narrow, tall building that strikes the visitor as a miniaturization of a grand convent church.

The small organ is one of the few decorative elements in it. Turned ninety degrees to the width of the church and covered with thick dust, it is nearly imperceptible in the high, small loft. Only upon close inspection were the delicacy and intricacy of its case decoration apparent. It is miniaturized grandness, like the church! The Jesuit fathers seem to have spared no expense in making it—the case is mostly mahogany, not *ayacahuite* (a sort of fir) and *cedro rojo* as most Tlaxcalan organs are. But what spoiled splendor: the keyboard is covered with a thick layer of crusted black dirt; most of the center pipes are gone; the chest is covered with fuzz, string, feathers, nutshells, mouse droppings, corn kernels, sunflower seeds, peach pits, straw, and crushed pipes. A variety of organic materials is so wedged between roller board and keyboard, and trackers and roller board, that absolutely nothing moves.

We asked don Enrique to please place glass in the paneless windows; he promised to get don Filiberto to do it. He also sent his sons to canvass the neighborhood for a kitchen table for us to use as a workbench, took one of the old locks from an organ case door in order to find its key, and sent for two young men to install spotlights in the loft. Two women arrived to arrange to bring us our midday meals, a custom that dates back to preconquest times.

How different their readiness to help is from my other experiences in Tlaxcala State. In Magdalena, my existence was ignored until the sound of the organ being played at New Year's Eve Mass so astounded the assembly that they universally rose to their feet, turned around, and backed away as if before a hovering spacecraft. In Sta. Anita I was begrudgingly allowed to enter the organ loft each day to accomplish the restoration, but once finished, I have never been allowed back in to visit the organ! Both in San Taddeo and San Andreas, the council of village headmen, unsmiling and suspicious, assembled to watch my every move as I merely inspected their pipe organs. It often takes several visits to a village just to find out who has the key to the church; and convincing him to use it is another matter entirely. It's frustrating: but of course this suspicion of outsiders has often been the only force at work in the preservation of national patrimony.

July 31, 1984: The organ is now as dismantled as it can be. Its disposition is the following:

Huamantla

Left Hand		Right Hand	
Flautado Abierto	4′	Flautado Abierto	4′
(10 interior pipes		(16 en façade,	
15 en façade)		8 interior pipes)	
Bardon	4′	Quincena	1′ (now gone)
Octava Clara	2′	Bardon	4′ (now 8′)
Quincena	1⅓′	Flautado Nasardo	4′
Docena	1′	Octava Clara	2′
Bajoncillo	4′	Corneta	2⅔′, 2′, 1⅗′

Compass: C-c‴, 49 notes

There are lots of mysteries here. The *Quincena/Docena* confusion appears
to be a mistake made simply when the stop labels (handwritten on rectangular
slips of paper) were glued on. The left outer tower's pipes used to speak, but now
have no tubing; the center tower pipes were found, crushed and torn, each into
two or three pieces, on the floor of the organ; the little *Quincena* in the right
hand is composed of tiny pipes, playing indiscriminate pitches, and in an odd
rackboard; the *Corneta's* pipes follow no order whatsoever, earthly or divine,
but their lengths indicate that it produced a resultant pitch of 8', and there is
no 8' stop in the right hand; however, the right hand *Bardon* is swimming in
rackboard holes too big for it, and its uppermost pipes are of discordant
manufacture. Otherwise, all the pipes and tubing in the organ can be considered to have come from the same source. Presently, a sturdy plank behind the
façade supports the ten interior bass *Flautado* pipes and the stopped pipes of the
left hand *Bardon*. The pipes are rather poorly made; the soldering is careless,
and wall thicknesses are highly variable. The façade pipes are interior pipes that
have been polished on one side.

A reasonable conjecture is that the façade was originally arranged to contain
a 4' stop in the left hand, and an 8' stop in the right hand. A *Corneta* was
probably mounted behind the right façade, an interior structure may have
supported several bass pipes of the left hand *Flautado* rank (not as many as
presently), and possibly there was another 8' stop in the right hand. We
considered trying to change the organ "back"; to do so would mean changing
the interior carpentry entirely, extensively revising pipework, possibly making
an entirely new façade, and remaking all tubing. But the evidence is simply not
there to convince me that my conjecture is absolutely correct; nor do we have
any documents to help us determine an original disposition. Such extensive
revision of the organ would be costly, and would produce an instrument that
conformed to one person's hypothesis, at worst a mere figment of the imagination. We don't have a sufficient picture of the entity to be recreated—we
wouldn't be "restoring" anything at all.

So we chose a more cautious path. It was obvious that the *Corneta* could use
an 8' foundation, and it was also obvious that the right hand *Bardon* was much
too small for its holes. So we decided to let it become an 8' *Bardon*. The odd
group of *Quincena* pipes, when wedded to the *Corneta* pipes, filled out the
Corneta perfectly; they had been so crowded by the left hand's *Bardon* toeboard
behind them that they did not even stand vertically in their holes. We decided
to simply cover the toeboard, as there is no room for any stop there at all, and
pray for forgiveness, or, better yet, an archival document to unravel the mystery.

I sometimes think, when confronted by such frustrating circumstances, that
"restoration" could more properly be called "resolution," and that the "resolution" of colonial organs involves so many other considerations than the purely

musical. Government policy no longer permits exportation of organs for repair, and villagers generally take exception to organs being removed from their churches, and often suspicions are well founded. In Tlaxcalanzingo, two "organ builders" removed the rotted cuneiform bellows, made a parallel-rise bellows that they connected to a smithy's blower, and cleaned the interior of the organ. But somehow they bungled the valve arrangement and no air reaches the organ; they took their money and ran, leaving the Tlaxcalanzingans with a wheezy, moaning non-instrument. The same pair removed an organ for repair from a village close to Huamantla, and simply never returned it.

August 6, 1984: The case has come clean with hot water, mild soap, and a brush of yellow straw, obtained at the local store—it's the type women use for scrubbing their clay pots. The waxiness of the twigs actually polishes the wood, yet they are stiff enough to clean thoroughly around the curves of a florid design. The top half of the case lifts off the bottom half, at keyboard level. It has hinged panels with locks (don Enrique has searched the sacristy, and the key is not to be found—he will make one) and each panel is pierced with *mudejar*-like cut-outs. The wood is either first-class *cedro rojo*, or mahogany, and is a warm, brown-red color.

We shall leave it just so. Most organ cases here in Tlaxcala are unfinished, natural wood. Those that are not are painted rather than stained and varnished, and usually have gilded pipe shades and other elements of sophistication. San Luis here in Huamantla had the only varnished case I know, but drops on the keyboard (changed in 1903) indicate that it was not so originally; in restoring it, the case was restored to its natural wood finish. Magdalena, Sta. Anita, Metepec, and Apizaquito all have painted cases. Ocotlán, Tlaxcala Cathedral, Nativitas, Tzompantempec, Buen Vecino, San Andreas, Ixtacuixtla, and San Pablo all have natural wood cases.

The chest is clean now, too. Rubbing its blackened skin surfaces with flour, removing the sooty flour with a vacuum, repeating the operation, swirling the flour around with a soft brush, and then finishing the operation by rubbing with soft school chalk has brought the sheepskin back to life. Pallets, slider beds, and toeboard undersides all received such treatment. Sliders are cleaned with a bit of alcohol, and given a waxing. The chest was made using the common practice of those days of burning the holes of the assembled chest with a hot poker, before glueing on the sheepskin that closes the underside of the chest. This burning not only seals the holes, but in charring the skin and the hot glue that holds it to toeboard and chest table, a little raised ring is created at the hole's entryway. The slider coasts on these raised rings and—to the extent that warpage has not occurred—will make a tight seal with table and toeboard even if the skin between holes is worn thin. Warpage, luckily, is rarely a problem with these old organs on the Tlaxcalan altiplano.

The tubing and chest surface have been cleaned of the wax that cements them together, and the façade toeboards have been cleaned as well. This wax is known as *cera de Campeche* and has the distinguishing feature of becoming quite soft and pliable with the heat of the hand, yet hardening to an amber-like consistency when exposed to air for several months. It was even used in tuning as it clings to metal as well as to wood, and neither shrinks in drying nor expands with moisture. Façade pipes, if cut slightly too deeply in tuning, will have a little morsel of rockhard *campeche* wax stuck to the edge of the pipe wall, at the deepest part of the tuning cut-out, the organ builder's fingerprints still visible where he rolled the wax into a little ball and pushed it on. Only placing the pipe on a mandril and giving the wax a well-placed blow with a pipe-slapper will shatter the crystalline stuff, and even then, a thin coat will stick to the pipe unless removed with gasoline. At first, I was quite nervous about admitting such a seemingly crude material into organ restoration practice, and distressed to learn when using it for the first time that it adheres to the fingers as tenaciously as to wood and metal. After seeing it used so universally in eighteenth-century organs, and after discovering that a bit of vegetable oil on the hands at frequent intervals keeps it from sticking to the fingers but, used sparingly, does not impede it from adhering to wood or metal, I have become comfortable with using it for tubing, and have even used it occasionally in final façade tuning, where soldering such a tiny bit onto a pipe is too gross a process for the result.

August 15, 1984: Our Lady's Assumption. I don't think anything was ac-complished anywhere in the city these last days. Yesterday everyone prepared for the all-night procession, the biggest annual event in Huamantla. Five miles of streets were decorated with brightly colored designs, over which the image of the Holy Virgin travelled on a splendid cart with pillars and canopy, covered with aluminum foil. These street designs, called *tapetes*, are not only astound-ing for their beauty, but for the whole social mechanism that brings them into being. The off-cuts and shavings of local woodworkers are turned into small splinters, and then sold in large bags. Each block-long portion of the proces-sional route will have a different design, and families on both sides of the street contribute more or less equally to buy the bags of splinters, called *aserrín*, and the dye to color them. In enormous vats, the color is mixed with water and boiled, the *aserrín* added to it until all the liquid is absorbed—wealthier neighborhoods can afford green dye, others must be content with blue, red, and yellow. Some of the neighbors make two stencils. One is about half the width of the street square, the other is that long, but much narrower. At about five o'clock in the evening, wheelbarrows full of white sand (a sort of crushed stone) begin to move through the streets, and a white band as wide as the larger stencil is laid down the middle of the street. The stencil is positioned at the beginning of the band, and appropriate colors are sieved through it, forming, for example, a red rose with green leaves, a blue cross with yellow rays, or simply swirls of various colors. This done, the stencil is carefully taken up, and placed down again where its design is to be repeated. Sometimes two stencilled designs will alternate. As dye of any kind is expensive, poorer neighborhoods tend to have sparser designs, and wealthier ones, dense, brilliant ones. When the length of the block is about finished, other neighbors start with the smaller stencil, making a border along each edge of the band.

By this time, the whole neighborhood is out on the street. Wheelbarrows of *aserrín* are careening to and fro, women are bringing soft drinks and tacos to the men, children are being drafted into service. Colored plastic straws, foil cut-outs, and plastic stars are all strung by the women into long bands that are hung from house to house, over the street. Spiraling garlands are made by inserting pine needles between two long pieces of rope as these are being twisted together. Those holes we had noticed in the sidewalks' edges at regular intervals suddenly made sense: poles are placed in them now, and the pine or plastic garlands are strung between them. In wealthier neighborhoods, local smiths make beautiful wrought iron lamps for these sidewalk poles.

Light bulbs are strung from roof to roof, and amazingly all is finished in time for everyone to go to late Mass, at about 10:30. After the Mass, the Holy Mother is placed on her carriage, and the procession begins. The crowds are so dense that one can hardly move. She makes Her way slowly through the colorful streets, Her parade thoroughly destroying any shred of evidence that Her path had been so carefully and luxuriously decorated for Her. Only at daybreak, with copious rounds of firecrackers and lively band music, does the image return to the church. The streets are swept, the poles are taken away, light bulbs are whisked into houses, the garlands are discarded; only a brass band playing in the church courtyard remains to remind us that a Grand Event just occurred.

What it must have been like when processional organs accompanied the throng! The surprising number of processional organs that have survived here in Tlaxcala attests to their popularity in the past. San Taddeo, San Matias, San Miguelito, Sta. Anita—all those churches still have their processional organs, San Matias being especially noteworthy as the only organ (out of fifty) inspected so far in Tlaxcala that doesn't have divided stops, and that retains its original chair! Chair, yes, but pipework, no.

No, today a brass band serenades the Holy Mother for Her Assumption Day. Significantly, although electric bands played in the church patio each night for two weeks before the procession, the traditional brass band was called upon for that most important event. This band is one of the best in the state; the members are from Ixtenco, about fifteen miles away. They play Mozart (Symphony no. 29, first movement), Beethoven (or so the maestro told me), and several pieces by Rossini and Donizetti—at the moment, an enthusiastic rendering of the "Charge of the Light Brigade" is filling the air—as well as the standard late nineteenth-century military marches that form the body of their repertoire. Not only has this musical tradition survived for a hundred years in an area that, otherwise, has practically no contact with Western European opera nor current military band music, but it continues to grow and expand with the inclusion of such numbers as "Lara's Theme" and "More."

The questions that this phenomenon provoke relate to organ preservation as well. What is the relation of musician to music, when all he has is a score or an instrument? What does Mozart *mean* to a clarinet player from Ixtenco? Where along the continuum between art music and popular music does this repertoire lie in the minds of the players? What are we doing restoring organs for people who haven't the least contact with their history, repertoire, liturgical function? Why, with those two splendid instruments in Mexico Cathedral, do they play the Hammond there on Sunday? Will we look back several generations from now and conclude that the pipe organ was an instrument briefly transplanted into a culture that simply had no use for it when that culture's awareness of itself grew beyond colonial self-awareness? Or will the organs make a glorious comeback in the wake of a greater awareness of the richness of some aspects of the colonial past? Although the citizens of the immediate postcolonial period understandably rejected many European things, at present the colonial period is viewed with less rancor, and with intent to understand it as a decisive period in the long history of contemporary Mexico.

Unfortunately, little music for the organ survives in Mexican archives. Reports of keyboard music in the Gaspar Fernandez MS in Oaxaca have turned out to be unfounded (the pieces seem to be simply instrumental works). The Sanchez Garza collection contains some pieces, which are soon to be published. References to organs as continuo instruments abound, however: one piece in the Oaxaca Cathedral Archives specifically mentions the *"Clarines del Organo"* on the title page, and in the Puebla Cathedral Archives some of the manuscripts indicate the use of three organs in performance. Will the organ ever resume its place as *the* liturgical instrument of the Mexican Catholic Church? Could a revival of that treasure trove of music, the seventeenth-century polyphonic *villancico*, provide employ for the organ as continuo instrument, giving it the opportunity to show off its bird-calls, *tambors*, and *campanitas* stops? Will the few Mexican organ aficionados finally decide that being able to play "the" Toccata and Fugue by Bach on a pipe organ is not the final criterion of its worth?

August 21, 1984: We've reassembled the windchest and placed it back in the organ case. The pallet springs had been made of a very thin brass wire and were too light to be effective, so new ones were made with a thicker wire, tempered with the help of a borrowed *comal*, the iron plate on which tortillas are heated.

Some bone keycovers were missing and luckily I had brought several pieces from Texas; although the mayor had promised us bull's femurs from last Saturday's bullfight, they never materialized. With the bone all replaced, it was time to reinstall the key action, and then the stop action. The trackers are rounded rods of *ayacahuite*, pierced at each end so that a wire can simply be threaded through the hole and have its two ends brought up and twisted together, then doubled over, to function as a hook. The old wires are brittle brass and don't suffer unbending and bending; we replace those that break with steel wire. Clearances are problematic, and the wires must be bent right back parallel with the tracker or they interfere with one another. The flat iron roller arms have been bent right or left, in many cases, to avoid such interference. The roller arms were fashioned from iron rod (about five milimeters thick), heated and pounded at one end to a tear drop shape, and then cut to be about nine or ten centimeters long. The end cut off the length of the rod was then heated and pounded into a square conical spike. The round, flat end was pierced, and the spiked end fed through a hole in the roller and pounded back into it to secure it, leaving just the five centimeters of rod with the round, pierced end revealed at the front of the roller. Where tracker meets key, a loop of iron wire was fed through a hole in the key, its two ends pulled through the bottom of the key and bent back to secure the loop above.

Today the bellows arrived. They were releathered by our friend Ignacio, who has been a part-time organ builder since 1977, at his house in Atlixco, Puebla. I remembered two and a half years ago when he took me to a tanner, a certain don Armando, to ask him to make some alum-tawed skins for the organ at Magdalena. Don Armando assured us that he could, but he didn't really understand that this test was a real test: the curing of the skins he eventually brought us was acceptable, but what skins! He'd used hides that looked like they'd been removed with a dull obsidian tool, and subsequently dragged around his shop by the family dog. There were huge holes, paper-thin areas, strange discolorations. He had insisted on adding an excessive amount of chrome in processing the skins (as he claims that this gives longer life to the skin) so they had a blue-green tinge—but today's skins are lovely, even and large, with the barest green cast. He still adds some chrome, though less, and one has to clean the skins of the occasional pigeon dropping, but they are wonderful skins to work with. Our first skins cost a hundred pesos apiece (about four dollars, then). Now I pay a thousand pesos apiece, which represents a 900 percent rate of inflation over two and a half years; but the peso has so devalued that my thousand pesos equals only five U.S. dollars today.

The economic aspects of life here are worth a moment's consideration. The amount of time and money Huamantlans (and Mexican townsfolk in general) dedicate to ritual activity is impressive. During the first half of August, Huamantla's work routine comes to a standstill because large, complex flower pictures are confected in front of the church each night. It takes all night for several men, accompanied by loud electric music, to make each one, and many dozens of rounds of firecrackers are exploded each morning at 5 a.m. to signal the completion of the night's project. Each of the nineteen barrios of Huamantla makes one. Probably every adult male head of family loses two weeks' work during this period, and families spend several thousands of pesos in contributions to their barrio's design. Persons raised in Protestant traditions generally find the impoverished Mexican's ritual expenditures scandalous. Yet the greatest portion of this money is invested in the local economy: food for *parites*, materials for decorations, flowers, and *aserrín*, the thousands of firecrackers, all are locally bought. Religious festivals are an integral and very important part of local economics, without which many more people would suffer financially than would profit!

So when the organ played an indispensible part in ritual activity, its construction and maintenance were routine expenses—local people helped in installation, or in fetching an imported organ from Mexico City (an entry to that effect exists in the church records for Texupan, Oaxaca, for 1552: the organ cost 180 pesos, and some villagers were paid 10 pesos to go fetch it from Mexico City). From what I have seen of bellows repairs and internal wood repairs, local craftsmen—for better or worse—intervened when an instrument needed work. Money paid to an organ builder from outside, however, is money "lost," especially if the congregation no longer feels a religious, emotional, or cultural link to the organ.

There are important reasons for opting for on-site work: one is that things that are structurally sound ought not be taken apart for transportation's sake; this is wasted energy. Another is that any climate other than the dry climate here on the Mexican altiplano where the temperature remains very constant, and especially the climate at our Texas workshop, is going to wreak havoc with old wood. But maybe the most far-reaching reason for on-site work here in Tlaxcala is the fact that gaining some degree of integration into the community who will listen to the instrument once the builder departs is very necessary right now. It's not solely a question of getting the organs working; the real problem at hand is convincing the populace that such expenditure of energy is worthwhile.

Clearly, one very effective means is economic interaction—staying at a local hotel, eating locally, buying materials at local stores, contributing to local festivals. More effective yet is having the opportunity to involve local craftsmen, tanners, turners, cabinetmakers, smiths. Then there is the sort of exchange where one's patience and willingness to talk are the legal tender: explaining what we're doing when schoolchildren come up to the loft, chatting with the sacristan, playing the just-finished or partly finished instrument for weddings, first communions, and so forth. Work is going to be interrupted almost daily for such things in many churches, so why not take advantage of a potentially frustrating situation and listen to the instrument!

In a sense, this amounts to pure self-interest. The extent to which the organ builder can get the neighborhood involved and provoke its interest and affection for the restoration project is the extent to which that organ will survive, be protected, and treasured. Simply repairing the organ, delivering it to the church, and going home is meaningless if the organ isn't subsequently played and looked after. A restoration is not fully achieved until the instrument's place in the community is also restored, and for that three elements participate: the playable organ, the player, and the listeners. After all, *that* listener who keeps the keys to the loft, and who makes sure the building is free of mice and birds is often the one who holds the welfare of the organ in his hands. The perilous situation of the pipe organ in Latin America has less to do with natural causes that hasten the deteriorization of organic materials, than with a century-old gap in the inhabitants' relationship to the instrument. Until that gap is closed, repairs to pipe organs themselves can only be regarded as superficial forays into restoration.

August 28, 1984: Sounds! The façade stop is in and tuned, and all the pipework has been repaired. We rounded all the pipes, soldered up the numerous tears old pipes always have around the top, sorted out the *Corneta*, made the necessary twelve first pipes for the *Bardon* in the right hand, and replaced missing ears on the *Bardon* stop as a whole. Incredibly, every little component of the lefthand *Bajoncillo* was eventually found, except a few tuning wires. Although many of its reed tongues were badly folded and bent, all straightened out with a bit of hammering. The original bellows stones were still there, too, so we are excited about having an authentic wind supply.

In organs as complete and well preserved as most are here in Tlaxcala, laying a temperament is as big or little a problem as one wishes to make it. The old pipes usually give a fairly close picture of the original tuning, and one's knowledge of history and of other instruments in the region can fill in the details. I usually start with the assumption that, except in extraordinary cases, a precise description of the temperament is not to be had. Thus the question at hand is to follow as closely as possible the outline that the façade and stopped ranks yield. If that outline presents no coherence, one simply has to impose a system that will be coherent with the age of the instrument and the musical necessities of its community.

The only reference I know for the question of organ temperaments in Mexico is the article in the *Gazeta de Mexico* of December 1730, which states that the organs in the Metropolitan Cathedral are tuned according to Pedro

Cerone's system of division of the comma. As it turns out, not only did Cerone plagiarize Lanfranco and Zarlino in describing tuning systems in his enormous treatise *El Melopeo*, but he seems unaware that the two contradict each other; Lanfranco's idea was basically to flatten the fifths just a bit, and allow the thirds to be as sharp as could be suffered (how sharp that was to ears accustomed to pure thirds is another matter), and Cerone notes those ideas in the form of general guidelines to laying a temperament. When he then presents a note-by-note tempering system on the next page, however, he says specifically to flatten each fifth by 2/7 comma, a system first proposed by Zarlino. This, of course, produces *flat* major thirds. A second note-by-note system "for beginners and crude people" gives no specific division of the comma, except to say that notes should be checked with their major third below and minor third above; no indication of beats to count or pure intervals is given.

Thus, we have to turn to Spain for historical information. Most sources there, including Nasarre, Tafall, and an anonymous MS in Sr. Rogent's library that *Anuario Musical* published over ten years ago, describe mean-tone tuning. Tafall, in 1872, argues that it was perhaps time to change to the equal-tempered system in use in France and Germany, even though it was clear to him that the mean-tone system sounded better.

What I have found in Tlaxcalan organs, however, is neither equal nor mean-tone, yet is consistent enough from one instrument to another to convince me that there was a practice in effect among organ builders that owed nothing to the writings of theorists. I've never found an organ with a definite "wolf" interval. Rather, the thirds C–E, F–A, and G–B range from pure to nearly pure, with C–E being the purest of the three. The rest of the problem consists in laying the remaining fifths more or less equally—they are usually nearly pure. To the theorist, this description must appear maddeningly formless and imprecise, compared to neat graphs with cents and frequency tables. But the organ builder has a concrete guide—namely, the pipes in front of him. And I guess we're lucky here in Tlaxcala that those pipes have rarely been extensively tampered with during the life of the organ.

September 5, 1984: The *Bajoncillo* is in and tuned; it makes a crisp rattle at the upper end of its extension and a throaty rumble in the lower, and makes a wonderful counterweight, coupled with the *Flautado*, to the *Corneta* in the right hand. The thinness of its pipewalls made tuning said *Corneta* a tremendously delicate operation. We spent yesterday tuning the whole organ, *Blockwerk*-style; today we made a little concert for the neighborhood.

We had all sorts of last-minute tribulations last week. Only with persistent nagging from Enrique and myself did don Filiberto finally put the glass panes in the empty windows. A loss of current got us an electrician who created a spaghetti-like mass of wiring on one wall, which, when connected, blew out all our bulbs, the heating coil, and the Dustbuster, a genuine loss as getting hands on a vacuum device here is next to impossible. Don Enrique brought us a lovely forged ring and fastener needed for one of the bellows levers. Alejandro, an extremely talented cabinetmaker here in town, brought us the missing stop knobs for the *tambor* and *pajarito*, and an impeccable plank of cedar needed for an open rectangle in the case front, through which the bungs that seal the chest could be seen. And the long-awaited key for the case panels materialized.

The children of the neighborhood have been hanging out at the loft door, asking repeatedly if we REALLY are going to leave; they can't believe that we don't intend to be permanent fixtures, and regret that the work is over. To me, too, it seems impossible that only a week ago this tiny loft was a chaos of pipes, skins, soldering equipment, notebooks, organ case panels, and sundry organ parts. Now the tools are in the car, and all is swept. We know there is no one here in town to play the organ on Sundays, so we asked don Enrique to give the organ air each Sunday, pull out its stops, and play all the keys, to be sure that dust doesn't settle in the pipes, and to discourage any little animal that may like nesting in unused organs. We also suggested that an Official Church Cat be obtained and maintained to discourage mice from inhabiting the loft.

And so our little concert was great fun. As small as the organ is, it has a great variety of sounds. Its disposition lends itself wonderfully to *Tientos Partidos*, and its temperament gives drama to *Tientos de Falsas*. The availability of *Bajoncillo* in the left hand and *Corneta* in the right also give it enough variety for playing *Diferencias* and dance pieces. Clearly, the repertoire for single-manual instruments from any tradition—if it doesn't demand 8' sound—is well suited to this organ. The keyboard is light and responsive. The acoustics of the church are interesting because the building has been modified by the placement of inverted pottery vessels in the ceiling: small holes can be seen at the junctures of vault ribs and wall, one hole per juncture. These are the mouths of the vessels, whose amplitude extends on the other side of the ceiling—between ceiling and roof, in other words. They appear to dampen any pingpong effect, and perhaps amplify certain frequencies. I do not know precisely how they function, but the sound of the organ in this church is astonishingly equal in strength and clarity in all parts of the building.

All during our little musicmaking, people from this and other neighborhoods wandered into the church in order to see and hear the resurrected instrument, which we repositioned so that it faces right down the nave. Neither priest nor parishioners objected to this, since the old dictum against turning one's back to the alter is losing its force, and everyone involved felt that it was more important to reveal the organ's beauty than to worry about the organist having to play it back-to-altar. (The same was done in Magdalena, for the same reasons; no problems occur in voicing as a result, and so many people have remarked to us here that they had never realised how truly lovely the organ case is.) At concert's end, formal speeches of thanks were made, as is mandatory on such occasions in Tlaxcala. We were touched to see how visibly moved many of our acquaintances were in hearing the instrument for the first time, and by how sincerely they regretted our departure.

One high school student in particular had been our companion these last weeks, and had helped us often by serving as *entonador* (calcant) during voicing and tuning. He was eager to learn to play, and when I needed to turn to soldering a pipe-toe or repairing a seam, he used to give the organ air, run around the keyboard, and poke at individual keys with the right hand while playing a tonally unidentifiable rhythmic pattern with the left hand. Then he'd stop and sing a little, and start all over. After several tries, he told me he thought he was "getting it." He explained that it was a dance that his dad used to play on the accordion, and he thought it would sound great on a pipe organ.

Our incredulity quickly turned to serious consideration of the question: what did he see and hear when confronted with that organ? Obviously, neither Bach nor Pachelbel sprang to his mind (he had never heard of either). The whole cultural and historical apparatus that Ted and I bring to this task and to the problem as a whole is totally divergent from that of our friend. What we treasure, what excites us in the organ's past means nothing to those of this neighborhood. In a town as small as Huamantla, there are perhaps a dozen people who enjoy and understand, to an extent, music of the European baroque and classical epochs (I am not including the Ixtenco Band's rendition of Mozart's Symphony no. 29 as European music: it belongs to a repertoire that has distinct functions and is consumed by a distinct class of people). But so little music of the Spanish baroque has been disseminated that authors like Arauxo, Cabanilles, Bruna, or others whose music is sublimely suited for Tlaxcalan pipe organs are totally unknown. It is not the case here that the organ builder has a greater knowledge of a common cultural past than the average church-goer, as might be true in Germany or France; there is amazingly little in common in our respective cultural pasts. Nor is there an older generation that remembers a body of literature special to the instrument which can now be revived to satisfy some nostalgic longing for the special sound of that instrument.

There is currently a great interest in the Mexican pipe organ in the United States and Europe. Mexico seems to be the latest frontier for organ tourists, those pilgrims whose desire to worship objects of the sacred organistic past (as good as their intentions might be) can only bring them into superficial contact with a cultural object whose underlying substance, the life it represented, they will never grasp. Naturally, the agencies in Mexico interested in organ restoration are proud of their achievements, and welcome international interest in and recognition of their rich artistic traditions. But the organ aficionado's penchant for expanding his repertoire of experiences through participation in "cultural productions" will not nurture a steady growth of organ use and reintegration in Mexico.

But before pondering the future, it is worthwhile to think briefly about the past. During the two centuries between approximately 1600 and 1800, and likely well beyond, the *villancico* cycles sung as responsories in the Nocturns of feast days were grand theatrical productions, with dancing, scenery, costumes, and the like. *Villancico* texts contained comic imitations of the accents of gypsies, Tlaxcalan indians, Negroes, Moors, and Basques, and sometimes consisted of chains of hilarious puns. There were also texts of adoration, allegorical texts, and texts in Latin, some expressing deeply spiritual or philosophically complex feelings and ideas. However, wedged into many Christmas *villancico* cycles are amorous episodes among the shepherds and shepherdesses going to visit the Christ child, and texts for Corpus Christi almost invariably include food (in great quantities) as subject matter. They were written for several annual feasts, not merely for Christmas, as is commonly believed.

The point is that not only are these villancicos of utmost importance to understanding the sociology of religious life and the religiosity of social life in Mexico during these two centuries, they are also a key to understanding the organ's role and repertoire during that time. For one thing, I feel that this *villancico* tradition largely explains the long survival of "toy stops" in Mexico. Whatever comes to light now that serious research into the polyphonic *villancico* of that time has begun, we know that a very broad spectrum of activities transpired in churches in the seventeenth and eighteenth centuries, and the organ was an integral part, if not often the leading player, in them. Our historical view of the instrument has to change from seeing it solely as the solemn, grandeloquent king up in the loft, to understanding it as a party-goer too, even in its churchly context.

So our student friend wants to learn his accordion tune on the pipe organ— so be it. The appearance of a highly developed western European instrument in a given geographical area, in this case, does not mean the existence of a community in that area with a correspondingly developed western European aesthetic, material culture, or musical tradition. The future of these restored (and unrestored) organs will probably be the result of a fresh encounter between contemporary *mestizo* culture (which is no less highly developed) and the given instrument. And it will probably surprise us all!

The restoration of the Santuario organ, as well as those of San Luis, Huamantla, Buen Vecino, Tlaxcala, and Sta. Anita Huiloac, was effected under the generous patronage of the Instituto Tlaxcalteca de Cultura, Dr. Sabino Yano, director.

CHAPTER FOURTEEN

The Classical Organ Case:
Considerations in Design and Construction

GEORGE TAYLOR & JOHN BOODY

ACQUAINTANCE WITH AN ORGAN begins most often with an observation of its case. If the case and front pipes form a beautiful and well-executed design, they evoke those spontaneous reactions of surprise and pleasure which are so prized by an organ builder. Even dearer is the occasional response of speechless awe, rarer today than it once was, for so few things have the power to impress us. Yet, just as in meeting a striking person for the first time, so the visual impression of a fine organ still registers deeply, attracting attention, arousing curiosity, and shaping expectations of its sound. The eye is at once busy moving about, vertically, horizontally, and diagonally, measuring proportions and searching out harmonies and rhythms in form and light. These, it senses, are its own bridge to the music within. The search for synthesis between what is heard and what is seen comes naturally to us, as both sound and light travel in wave forms, with related systems of perception. It is hardly an exaggeration to say that an organ case more than anything else represents the marriage of music and architecture in a single object. The potential of this relationship for artistic expression must have been known to the earliest organ builders, for while, strictly speaking, organs could exist without cases, all early organs known to us not only had cases, but remarkably beautiful ones at that. Indeed, the same care has traditionally been lavished on organ cases as was accorded to altars and pulpits, thereby placing the significance of the organ's music on a plane equal to that of the sacraments and the word.[1]

The building of organ cases over the centuries represents a considerable investment of human effort, documented by many surviving examples. Although there has been some valuable scholarly study of the field, there is room for much more, particularly of a practical nature. Today's young organ builders typically receive little if any instruction in the fundamentals and history of case design. When faced with the challenge of drawing an organ, they find themselves at sea. Those with talent sense intuitively that they must

1. Walter Haacke, *Orgeln in aller Welt* (Königstein im Taunus: Karl Robert Langewiesche, 1965), p. 3.

imitate the work of others before establishing their own style. Most, however, learn haphazardly, without clear ideas as to where to begin or how to proceed. If the primary focus of a builder's work is where it should be—that is, on producing an instrument which above all makes music—then the subsidiary calling to master the case's architecture can easily confound. The present lack of an artistic style with clear boundaries does not simplify the problem, but there is no way around it. Knowing how to design an appropriate case is part of being an organ builder.

It is our intention merely to touch on matters of concern to the designer, to raise a few questions and perhaps provoke constructive controversy. Anyone who expects to find here a formula for the design of a classical organ case will be disappointed. Such a formula is neither within our ability nor the scope of this paper. To develop one will require one's own research. There is no substitute for examining the work of others, both past and present, whose designs one admires. Through observation and study of the work of former masters, one can become conversant in what they did. By imitating their work, one can hope to learn how they went about it. Eventually it is possible to approach an understanding of why the work was done as it was. By systematically tracing this development from its beginning to the present, the student of case design can arrive at a secure foundation for building a valid personal style. To look for shortcuts may produce work of momentary fashion but little more.

Like so many artifacts of civilization which have evolved with increasing complexity, the organ case was first invented to meet a few simple needs. The most basic purpose of the case has always been to protect the pipes and mechanism. The working parts of an organ are subject to damage by people and animals, by falling debris, and at times by the elements. Without cases organs could never have earned their universal reputation for durability. The organ case can also provide the necessary frame for support of the organ's parts. At times builders have included independent support frames separate from the case. However, the goal of simplicity in design is best met when the frame for support of case, action, and windchests is integrated. Important, though less obvious, musical ends are also served by the organ case. The sound of the pipes is blended within the case and focused in the direction of the audience. Likewise, the case offers the builder the organ's largest soundboard, which can be made to reflect, absorb, or resonate with the energy of the music. There is a need for much investigation into the effect of the case on the sound if builders are to make informed choices in design.

Recently we have come to respect historic organ cases for a new reason. Being—by nature—of sturdy construction, the cases tend to outlast the working parts. Often an old organ's case stands as the last proud reminder of the music it once contained, long after chests, action, and pipes have fallen into disrepair—or, worse yet, been removed to make way for a newer organ. The Spanish, by contrast, must be credited with consistently preserving organs. When an old Spanish organ became unusable, the people neither discarded it nor changed it, but replaced it with a newer instrument elsewhere in the church. In other countries, surviving cases frequently provide our only information about the organs they were built to house. Thus the natural longevity of organ cases, combined with people's inclination to preserve them for their value as furnishings, has elevated them to the rank of major guardian of the organ's heritage.

The history of case design is rich with confusing variety. So long as the rudimentary requirements of enclosure and support were met, organ builders appear to have enjoyed limitless freedom for expression in visual design. Close examination, however, shows that the earliest builders actually settled on a narrow set of conventions which have persisted throughout the history of organ design to the present. The sum of these conventions may be gathered under the term *classical*. With this term we refer to those recurring properties or features of organ design which through their continued application have formed the very definition of the case. By contrast, elements peculiar to any one period can be designated elements of style. It has never been easy to disentangle these persistent classical features from the fabric of style to which each period clings for its identity. What designer would not be pleased to consider his stylistic elements as indispensable to the definition of the norm? It is nevertheless important to make a distinction between that which has temporal appeal and that which has been shown to have lasting value. If we fail to recognize this distinction, we risk overlooking the salient features in our designs today. Only by including them can we be assured that our work will find acceptance beyond our own generation. These timeless elements make the historic organs as valid today as they were centuries ago.

A classical organ case is composed of a handful of basic components (see figure 14–1). The lower case houses keyboards, action, and sometimes a division of short pipes. A strong horizontal frame, called the impost, rests on the lower case and supports the upper case, the majority of the front pipes, and the main windchests of the organ. The upper case is rarely more than three feet in depth and comprises what is above the impost, including the stiles (columns separating the fields of pipes), the side panels, transoms, cornice boxes, and usually back panels and roof boards. Very large organs may have a second impost beam, to bear another windchest and its façade pipes higher in the organ. If the impost is wider than the lower case, there are spandrels between the impost and the lower case. Additional components include the pipe shades and other carvings, and the moldings. Although Rückpositiv and pedal towers do not sit on a lower case, they are in other respects composed of similar

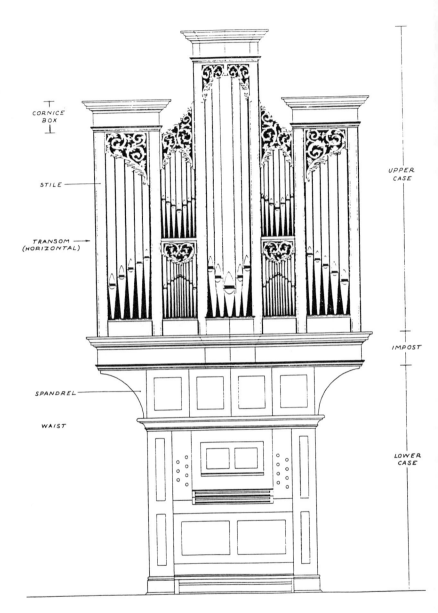

14–1. Drawing of an organ case with front pipes showing the names for the various parts of an organ case.

CREDIT: Case design by Bruce Shull after the organ in Brouwershaven, Zeeland.

components, such as the impost, upper case, carvings, and so forth. The first cases usually had shutters mounted on the side panels, which could be closed to keep birds and bats from getting into the organ. When opened, the shutters added a beautiful visual dimension to the organ and helped to focus its sound, but they were employed with decreasing frequency over the centuries and cannot be considered an essential part of the classical case.

People are surprised to learn that organ cases are engineered on an elementary level. The most common form of construction is that of the post and lintel, derived from primitive architecture. Children use similar principles when they stack blocks. This must not be obvious, since the most common question asked by visitors to an organ shop is, "How do you get it out of here?," betraying their perception of the organ as a monolithic unit. The most daring means of support which organ builders have regularly used is the cantilever. Imposts project over lower cases, towers project forward of the impost, and Rückpositiv cases are expected to extend beyond the balcony railing. Relatively little sophistication is required to determine the strength of timbers. While this can be computed it is simpler for an organ builder to test the strength of a member by the practical approach of placing weights on it and measuring the deflection.

A solid background in joinery is prerequisite for the casemaker. In the past, glues did not have the elasticity and strength of those used today. The joinery itself needed to be of the highest quality, so that the pieces of wood interlocked structurally, with well-fitted dovetails and mortise-and-tenon joints. Our forefathers could not depend on glue to fill the cracks. Poor craftsmanship can have disastrous results, as is recorded in the history of the Jakobi Church in Hamburg. In 1576–77 Dirk Hoyer added a *Rückpositiv* and pedal towers to the existing organ. "Although the completed work had been approved by the organists from St. Jakobi, St. Petri and St. Nikolai, it was not of lasting quality. Runs soon appeared everywhere. And after a few years, as front pipes of the *Rückpositiv* threatened to come loose, a large basket had to be mounted under the *Rückpositiv* for the safety of the churchgoers."[2]

The traditional material for the construction of the classical case is solid wood. Oak was the wood of choice for most organ building because of its great strength. Its coarse grain structure is appropriate to the size of organs. Above all, oak was used because it was readily available to our forebears. The appearance must have been of secondary importance to the early builders, who frequently painted their cases.

The preparation of wood for use in cabinetmaking formerly involved techniques which have been largely forgotten. The value of lumber then was much greater than we can imagine, not because of the scarcity of trees, but because of the intense labor required to prepare it. Every effort was made to

2. Gustav Fock, *Arp Schnitger und seine Schule* (Kassel: Bärenreiter, 1974), p. 53.

render wood as easily workable as possible. Air drying was standard procedure. In addition, wherever feasible, freshly cut logs were floated in running water to wash away the saps and acids which make our kiln-dried wood so difficult to cut. This process, called leaching, was ideally done in estuarial streams, which received both fresh and salt water depending on the flow of the tides. Once the logs became saturated (waterlogged) they sank and were removed for sawing into timber. Leached timber was known to dry more quickly than unleached. It also suffered less distortion from warping and checking. The resulting wood was free of tensions and a delight to work, for it was lightweight and soft and caused less wear to the cutting edges of tools.

Cabinetmakers also placed a high value on the way lumber was cut from the tree. Wood has an internal structure of annual rings, grain, and fibers which determines its characteristics of stability, strength, resonance, flexibility, and so forth. Lumber which was sawn radially from the center of the tree after the log had been cut into quarters was most highly prized. Quartersawn boards show their annual rings standing when the board is laid flat (see figure 14–2). In the

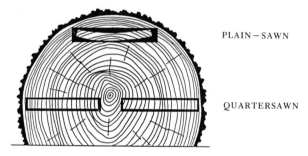

14–2. Cross section of a log showing the difference between quartersawing and plain–sawing.

twentieth century, quartersawing has fallen into disfavor. Logs are sawn from the outside inward for purposes of higher yield. Each board therefore runs perpendicular to the radius, its annual rings lying flat across the width (see figure 14–2). Such lumber, which we refer to as plain-sawn, is prone to warp. Plain-sawn oak expands and contracts with humidity changes twice as much as its quartersawn counterpart. This is vitally important to the designer concerned with dimensional stability.

In the past, lumber was carefully chosen for its intended use. The finest wood was selected for the most critical work. Arp Schnitger specified in his contracts that the woodpipes were to be made of *Wagenschoss* or wainscot, the best grade of oak, soft-textured and fine-grained. Lumber of comparable quality cannot be found on the market today. Trees which have matured slowly in virgin forests are rare. When they are found, they regularly become grist for a lumber industry oblivious to the quality of individual trees, or are sold as veneer logs on the international market. In order to have wood of this caliber for organ building one must find, saw, and dry it oneself. This entails an additional investment of labor, but the results make the effort worthwhile.

We easily forget the extent to which our perceptions of the historical case have been molded by the European organ revival. Next to mechanical action, the revival insisted on the free-standing case as essential to the construction of a proper organ. Before this was pointed out, there was no clear concept in our time of the traditional case. It is interesting to note just how far these twentieth-century pioneers were willing to go in turning back the clock. In an age bent on progress, their return to antiquity for ideas was very daring and full of pitfalls. The popular appreciation of old things and the concept of artistic preservation were still in the future. Contemporary art and architecture offered no solace, for both insisted on uniqueness and self-expression. Had the organ revival builders merely emulated the antiques they would have been ridiculed. The compromise between the old and the new which they settled upon was shrewd. They chose to present their fledgling ideas about cases under the banner of functionalism, the rallying standard of modern design. Organ revival cases reflect the uncomplicated principles of the earliest organs and have been invaluable in focusing our view of these fundamentals. The cases are shallow, often show sensitivity to good form and proportion, and are logically complete as enclosures. But each generation is selective in what it takes from history. The Germanic inclination toward orderliness led these builders to subdivide their cases into isolated compartments, which had been unknown before. The free flow of sound within the case was impeded by these partitions. Modern builders also rejected out-of-hand elements of classical case design for which they could find no functional justification. Their cases were stark and simple, intentionally devoid of moldings or any other ornamental details suggestive of the antiques. As in the story of the Emperor's new clothes, nudity was introduced as a novel disguise. Wherever possible, modern materials like plywood and steel proudly replaced solid wood, making the break with former models yet more obvious. Little would have been so distasteful to these builders as to label their work replicas.

The organ revival builders knew that interest in the case could be most easily sustained wherever the union between appearance and function was obvious. The significance of this bond had been so completely ignored in the meaning-less façades of the post-Romantic organs that any element of visual design which did not reflect musical honesty became suspect. For example, the use of false lengths and dummy (non-speaking) pipes was considered particularly reprehensible (although I know of no early school which did not rely on dummies once in a while to solve architectural problems). It is hardly surprising, then, that those historical traditions which most obviously reflected functional ideals, namely those of northern Germany and the Netherlands, became the focus of attention. Not only do cases from these traditions display the most important principals in the façade, the arrangement of the pipes indicated quite clearly how the remaining pipes stand inside and provides important clues as to where the divisions are located. In contrast, the imposing façade of classical French and Spanish organs are less easily comprehended, for their interior layouts follow the simple logic of their actions rather than the grand designs displayed in their architecture.

Clearly the art of case design is most faithfully served when it is prompted by the need for visual honesty. What better way is there to strengthen the synthesis between music and architecture? The successful case designer should make it difficult to imagine either a shape without music or music without a shape. Little wonder that architects have left a poor record as case designers. Architects who have not been trained to understand the inner workings of the organ produce designs that come across as unconvincing and weak. Even the best historical examples of cases designed by architects, of which the Nieuwe Kerk organ in Amsterdam has perhaps the most famous example, seem contrived to the eye of an organ builder.

The formula of the modern case has been wildly successful. It has appealed directly to current artistic impulses, and the cases have been uncomplicated to design and build using modern machinery. Not only were the venerable skills of carving and complex joinery no longer needed—they were ideologically spurned. Also, from an economic point of view, what could have been more convenient than this chaste style which required a minimum of laborious handwork? The point was not lost either on postwar European builders struggling against harsh financial realities, or later on American builders who had to compete with those who charged equivalent prices for organs with no case at all. At its roots, however, the organ revival was a reactionary movement, susceptible in the end to a narrowness equal to the decadence it chose to combat. In time a wider view was needed.

In America, a broader perspective on case design was first advanced through the work of Joseph Blanton. His handsome book, *The Organ in Church Design*, published in 1957, traces the history of case building with insights which are still fresh.[3] Blanton shows remarkable freedom of thought from the accepted norms of the period in which he wrote. The book stands as a major reference work for architects and organ builders alike. No one has since undertaken a survey of comparable breadth.

In 1965, Blanton published another book, entitled *The Revival of the Organ*

3. Joseph Edwin Blanton, *The Organ in Church Design* (Albany, Texas: Venture Press, 1957).

Case, in which he catalogued photographs of contemporary cases representative of work in the intervening decade.[4] Only three or four of the one hundred and twelve organs illustrated in this book make unabashed statements in an historical style. All the rest are strictly modern, and Blanton heartily approves. "It is my firm opinion that in both architecture and case design we should work within the modes of expression of our own time."[5] Having said this, he pauses to discuss with obvious admiration the lovely case which Charles Fisk and Leo Constantineau built for Mount Calvary Church in Baltimore. Blanton shows an uncommon understanding of this important American break with the modern style. "While I do not advocate making an *archaeo* out of designing a modern organ case, I can appreciate one well done, and I think no one versed in case design could justly say the Mount Calvary case was not well done. It is both beautiful in concept and execution."[6]

His comment raises many questions. Why did the Mount Calvary case warrant such special attention? True, it resembled the old Gothic cases at Amiens and Sion in form, but it was not a copy. Other modern cases had followed historical *forms* as closely without creating a stir. Could it be that through the simple addition of a few moldings and gilded carvings that builders had somehow called into question the assumptions of the *status quo?* Apparently so, for the stunning photograph of the case on the dedication brochure spoke to many of values which were lacking in other designs. The eye recognized that elsewhere it had been shortchanged. Perhaps the antiques could be perceived as being as beautiful to the modern eye as they ever were. Could it be that the skills required for case embellishment were only dormant and might be revived with practice? And what about the other aspects of the organ—the sound, the wind, the action; had we been cheated there as well? With the posing of such questions there was no longer any solid defense for the neo-Baroque arguments which had placed arbitrary limits on builders. A tide of experimentation has flowed through this breach, placing a new emphasis on the organ's appearance and the return to all the fundamentals of the classical case.

The heart of organ design lies in the arrangement of the front pipes. To begin anywhere else is to miss the point. The front pipes should always be the center of visual attention, just as they are the foundation of the principal chorus. The case with its ornamentation should serve only to amplify their beauty, never to distract from it. The elements of a picture frame are not to be examined individually, but to be sensed marginally. The frame focuses attention on the picture. So it is with the organ case, which is of peripheral importance to the

4. Joseph Edwin Blanton, *The Revival of the Organ Case* (Albany, Texas: Venture Press, 1965).

5. Blanton, *Revival*, p. 110.

6. Blanton, *Revival*, p. 111.

pipes at the center of the composition.[7]

While it is theoretically possible to arrange front pipes in countless ways, the desire for order has always imposed limits on the whimsey of designers. By combining structural and musical requirements into visually attractive configurations, our ancestors established a few basic forms, so simple and sound that they have persisted as the core of good design.

The first organs were small enough to have their pipes standing in chromatic order above the keys. With the invention of more sizeable instruments, the chromatic order proved impractical, for it did not distribute the weight of the bass pipes evenly across the width of the impost. Balance was created by alternating the pipes up the scale on either side of the center, as in the Gothic organs of Sion and Halberstadt, where the basses stood in towers to the outside and the trebles were placed in one wide center flat. With this arrangement, visual symmetry entered organ design and with few exceptions has remained as a norm for classical case design ever since. The desire for symmetry springs directly from the need for structural balance. We require symmetry only in the horizontal plane, not from top to bottom. The practical chromatic chest which does not require a rollerboard has survived in the German *Brustwerk*, the classical French *Positif de dos* and *Récit*, and in many parts of Spanish organs. Its lack of symmetry, however, has limited it to internal layouts not a part of the formal façade.

Acoustical phenomena have also played a major role in the development of standard case designs. Organ pipes, especially the smaller ones, which stand next to their neighbors in the musical scale often suffer from interference. This is true of pipes not only a half-step but also those a whole step apart. The whole-tone arrangement is not ideal. If whole-tone scales are subdivided into alternate halves, the interference problem disappears. In fact, this results in the harmonious major-third placement, which has been the focus of so much of the recent inquiry into temperaments. Such a pipe layout also renders an efficient use of space on a windchest. Both chromatic and whole-tone chests are crowded, by comparison, in the bass and wasteful of space in the treble. A little experience shows that treble pipes can be difficult to tune if they stand too close to reflective walls at the side or rear of the case. This could offer some explanation for the predominance of the five-field case, in which the treble flats were bracketed by tenor and bass towers to the side and center. The tendency to place a prominent group of large pipes in the center has both visual appeal and makes good structural sense, for it reduces the demands on the cantilevered sides of the impost. The lack of any central pipe field is disturbing. An example can be found in the old Gothic case in Rysum (Ostfriesland), which would

7. For a discussion of this see E. H. Gombrich, *The Sense of Order* (Ithaca: Cornell University Press, 1979), pp. 155–57.

appear to fall into two halves if the central field of dummy pipes had not been restored to its place above the treble flats.

The form or silhouette of the case develops directly from the choice of pipe arrangements. To be pleasing, this form should contain simple proportions among its elements. It must be easily perceived, and not obscured by secondary features of the design, a real temptation today with the rediscovery of the worth of ornamentation. Speaking of the art of printing type design, Warren Chappell has observed that designers "least certain of the basic symbol have been the most profligate with dressmaker details."[8]

There is no substitute for a good eye in choosing what is beautiful. An intuitive sense of fine proportion is of priceless value to the case designer. Such talent is latent in most people and can be developed with training. It is a rare artist who cannot learn from the work of his predecessors. With the rich history of organ cases which has survived for our study there is little excuse for anyone to make an ugly design.

Architectural design according to proportion is foreign to the contemporary mind. We like to excuse our ignorance by classifying the study of proportion along with the arcane sciences, or even alchemy, as toys of a murky past. The claims of our ancestors to mastery of underlying relationships of the cosmos seem both presumptuous and frightening. Such things now belong to the realm of science, while visual design takes its place among the arts. From our perspective it is unsettling to think that artists and craftsmen were the keepers of such truths of nature as proportion. Consequently, people today find it best to avoid the subject. Organ builders cannot dismiss the matter so easily. They constantly depend on proportions when making the organ's pipes. To use proportions to shape part of the instrument without letting them inform the entire design is arbitrary and foolish.

It is no accident that the traditional symbol of the organ builder is a pair of proportional dividers. This simple tool can be adjusted to measure or generate one dimension in a specific proportion to another. The dividers also double as a compass, making them important in the layout of pipes. Armed with a pair of proportional dividers, the student can begin a search for rational relationships in historic case designs. An introductory analysis of this subject was made by Daniel Brunzema in his little volume *Die Gestaltung des Orgelprospektes* . . . .[9] As Brunzema showed, the recurrent proportions in classical design are those of ratios between whole numbers, such as 1:2, 2:3, 3:4, 3:5, etc. These ratios should appear familiar to the organ builder, because they are also the simple

---

8. Warren Chappell, *The Living Alphabet* (Charlottesville: University Press of Virginia, 1975), p. 45.

9. Daniel Brunzema, *Die Gestaltung des Orgelprospektes* (Aurich: Verlag Ostfriesische Landschaft, 1958), pp. 49ff.

proportions used in the scaling of pipes. Proportions generate pipe lengths and diameters, mouth widths and cut-up heights. Musicians and organ builders alike will recognize the whole-number proportions as the relationships between pairs of notes in our musical scale. Pythagoras demonstrated that by using the proportion 2:3 he could generate all the notes in his scale. This order, discovered by the theoretician and employed by the designer, is perceived as coherence by the listener. If indeed the same thinking can be adapted to assure pleasing case dimensions for visual perception, and if the ratios are truly simple, why is this not the accepted mode of approaching case design? The answer is that beautifully proportioned, simple, and well-integrated designs demand a lot of hard work. One needs time to play with the elements of the design, to discover which proportions are appropriate to each problem, and to interrelate the aural and visual details in a harmonious way. One can only hope to master the subject after years of research and experience.

14–3. The golden section or divine proportion.

The most famous and intriguing of all ratios is the *golden section* or *divine proportion*. The ratio is deceptively simple, relating part a to part b, as part b is related to the sum of a plus b (see figure 14–3). The divine proportion is inherent to the structures of organic growth, from the lowliest organism to the most developed. Its perception creates resonances throughout our being, and produces feelings of harmony which we call beauty. The divine proportion has been used extensively in organ case design, at times forming the basis of an entire composition. An outstanding example is found in the case of the old organ from Scheemda which is presently in the Rijksmuseum in Amsterdam. In figures 14–1 and 14–4, the divine proportion has been used to fix the height of the transoms which separate the upper and lower fields of treble pipes. The dimensions a through d are arranged in a series according to these proportions. Dimensions e through m show how other ratios fit together in the design.

The work of the case designer would be complicated enough if organs could be planned without thought as to where they should stand. But organs, by virtue of their sheer weight and size, not to mention sound, are tied to specific locations. The wise designer has always taken this into account, first so that the product will fit into the intended space (which, with alarming frequency, it may not) and, second, so that the case will complement its surroundings. The form and proportions of the space present their own problems to the designer. The

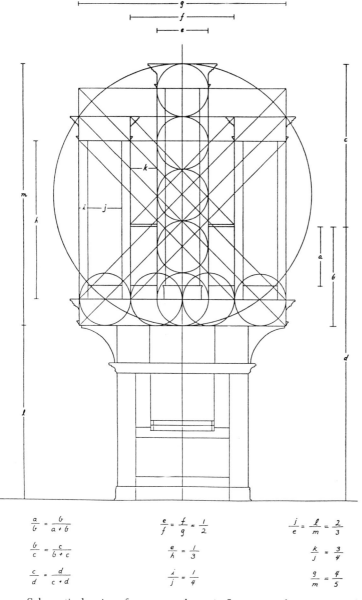

$$\frac{a}{b} = \frac{b}{a+b}$$

$$\frac{b}{c} = \frac{c}{b+c}$$

$$\frac{c}{d} = \frac{d}{c+d}$$

$$\frac{e}{f} = \frac{f}{g} = \frac{1}{2}$$

$$\frac{e}{h} = \frac{1}{3}$$

$$\frac{i}{j} = \frac{1}{4}$$

$$\frac{j}{e} = \frac{\ell}{m} = \frac{2}{3}$$

$$\frac{k}{j} = \frac{3}{4}$$

$$\frac{g}{m} = \frac{4}{5}$$

14–4. Schematic drawing of organ case shown in figure 14–1 demonstrating the various proportions used in its design.

CREDIT: Case design by Bruce Shull after the organ in Brouwershaven, Zeeland.

internal requirements of the organ and the external influences of the room's architecture converge in the organ's case. A successful case will appear inseparable from its surroundings. In scale it will, like Goldilocks's bed, seem neither too large nor too small, but just right. The effect on the observer should be grand but not overwhelming, delicate but never weak. It will hold one's attention longest if it appears to oscillate between these two extremes.

The size and proportions of the human body have profound bearing on objects of architectural scale, including the organ. When the elements of a composition are related to the dimensions of the body, the composition becomes approachable. Conversely, if one can find no point of reference to the scale of the body—as, for example, in a monolithic glass skyscraper—the effect is one of alienation. Parts of the body have long been used as units of measure— the foot, the hand, the thumb, and so on. This ancient habit of using the body as a standard is part of a timeless architectural vocabulary which provides a tangible link between people and the objects they create. Linear measurement based on these human standards has survived to our time in the English system, which is still used in many American organ shops.

The alternative metric system is based on an inorganic standard, related to the speed of light and the circumference of the earth. This child of the French Revolution has been welcomed by the scientific community; its decimal subdivisions are compatible with the numerical system. Long accepted throughout continental Europe, the metric system arrived in American organ shops under the influence of the organ revival. The advantages over the English system are obvious. An organ builder can be taught to think clearly in metric dimensions within an hour. Since there are no awkward fractions to be manipulated, errors are avoided. To anyone who recalls difficulties with arithmetic, the metric system appears as a godsend.

Old ways are rarely surrendered, however, without sacrifice. A change of standard has deeper implications than we like to think. The simple relationships of feet and inches, with their inherent hierarchies, are easily lost in a flood of millimeters. Furthermore, the ratios expressed by those fractions we consider awkward represent the proportions which naturally bind the system of measurement to our bodily rhythms. How quickly important ratios, like 1:2 or 2:3, become hidden behind a decimal point. Charles Fisk recognized this and doggedly refused to give up the use of the English system in designing his organs. He felt that only with this organic tool would important proportions be obvious to the designer.

Would that we, like Arp Schnitger, could use the Hamburg foot. That unit was divided two ways, into twelve *Zoll* and ten *Daumen*, with the benefits of both the duodecimal system, which can be divided by three and four, and the decimal system, which can be divided by five. With the help of the Hamburg

foot one can discover valuable relationships in Schnitger's work. These are lost
to us in research which records the dimensions in metric equivalents, the worst
of both worlds.

Organ cases are especially engaging when they can be made to resemble the
form and proportions of the human body. This is apparent in many historic
cases where front pipes lend themselves readily to arrangements within rectangular towers, taller than they are wide. One can often imagine that the organ
has a head, arms, and torso. The lower case also plays an important role in
reinforcing this metaphor. Less glamorous than the upper case, it must support
the weight of the great mass above it and requires most careful joinery. Because
the mechanism housed in the lower case does not take up much width, the
lower case can be made narrower than the windchests above it. The eye
appreciates the effect created by a slender lower case, which makes the organ
appear light on its feet. Narrow-waistedness is universally common to medieval
organs. The gradual widening of the lower case in relation to the impost over
the centuries, in the interest of ease of support, can be viewed as a loss of grace
and delicacy and thus represents a decadence in form.

In traditional cases, the spandrels below the impost hide the extremities of
the rollerboards from view. The spandrels do not actually support the cantilevered impost. It is nonetheless important that they appear to. Architects have
often included elements in design which were not required from a structural
standpoint, yet were worthwhile for reassuring the structural expectations of the
eye. Brunelleschi's treatment of columns on the Florence Cathedral is a case
in point. These traditional elements in the façade do not actually carry the load
we presume. The real work is done by Brunelleschi's inventive hidden means
of support. The columns must have been included for aesthetic reasons, lest
the design appear incomplete to the observer. If examples are any indication,
beautiful spandrel design is not easy. Old organs are rife with mediocre, clumsy,
or even outrageous models. But the spandrel was dependably there. Some
builders today are not so considerate as Brunelleschi. On occasion, they omit
the spandrel altogether, and in other ways seem to enjoy straining our sense of
visual credibility. Disguising modern materials with traditional ones makes this
possible. For example, by cloaking robust steel members in a veneer of wood,
case designers ask us to accept what seem to be impossible constructions.
Postmodern architects like to play similar tricks when they allow apparently
unsupported brickwork to jut out above the heads of pedestrians. The shock
effect is undeniable. Still we must ask whether such visual puns can hold our
attention long, or ever be integrated with a healthy aesthetic.

The natural shape of an impost beam encourages the designer to keep the
front of the case flat. Narrow scales of bass pipes in Gothic organs permitted
their façade pipes to stand in straight rows at the front of the chest, at times even

directly over their slider holes. With the development of wider bass scales in the Renaissance, organ builders found it increasingly necessary to build protruding towers to house the bass and even tenor pipes. Standing the same pipes in a straight row would have risked making the composition ungainly in its width and robbing the towers of their slender beauty. Articulations applied to the fronts of imposts and the cornices above them have taken many forms—triangular points, semicircles, or sections of a polygon. They have evolved into significant aesthetic features of the classical case by creating an exciting third dimension with a minimum of structural complication. Organ cases with projecting towers benefit from standing in galleries above the heads of the observers so that the effect of the projecting tower can be appreciated. Arp Schnitger's proposal drawings show how important this aspect of perspective was. The façades are drawn in two dimensions, as if viewed from straight on, except for the towers, which are depicted as if they were seen from below. By its location, a Rückpositiv case offers the boldest opportunity for exploring three dimensional aspects of design. The Dutch Renaissance builders showed the greatest creativity here, for they placed the façade pipes around the sides of the Rugwerk. In the organs of Jutphaas and Monnikendam, the entire instrument is located on the gallery rail within a circular plan which represents these trends in their most extravagant expression.

Organ builders who wish to imitate the beautiful proportions of antique cases are burdened with a problem unknown until the latter part of the seventeenth century. Before that time, the limited nature of keyboard tonality encouraged the building of short-octave basses. This meant that four of the largest pipes of every stop were omitted from the outset. Moreover, the compasses of the old keyboards were rarely wider than four octaves. These limitations made the windchests narrower in those days than those we can build with contemporary compasses. With clever engineering, today's builder can manage to shoehorn entire bass octaves or a wide compass into an old case form. The price for this compromise is paid in the music. Cramped pipes cannot speak to their fullest advantage. Old organs were not crowded on the inside as so many are today. There was not only adequate space between the pipes, but room to spare between chests and case as well. Solutions to this dilemma are not easy to find. One might suppose that the problem could be solved by merely increasing overall dimensions of the case. Yet, the length of the pipes which determine the height of the case has not changed; only the width of the chests is greater. Another approach would be to shorten the compass again by eliminating a few treble keys and perhaps even bass C$^{\sharp}$, since the great majority of organ literature can be performed without them. The sheer cost in time and energy of building organs makes questionable the inclusion of pipes which are almost never used. This suggestion however incurs strong criticism from organists, who interpret the omission as a rejection of the few pieces which require these keys, rather than on the strength of the merits in space and money saved and the increased effectiveness of an uncluttered case. Both builders and purchasers alike need to keep this unsolved problem in mind when planning new instruments along classical lines.

Until the recent past no organ would have been thought visually complete unless its case was adorned with molding and carvings. Because the design of these decorative elements has been the most obvious identifying mark of any given period, it has been easy to dismiss these adornments as no more than expressions of style. The weight of tradition, however, dictates that while their shape and treatment was open to interpretation, their presence was not a matter of choice.

Moldings are composed of highly stylized geometric shapes, originally derived from natural forms. Their development is tied directly to the most creative moments in architectural history, from which we have inherited them as archetypes. Traditional moldings have become such a predictable element of visual ornamentation that we rarely question how they acquired their peculiar shapes, or what qualities have made them so enduring. One answer lies in the study of moldings as compositions in themselves. A delicate balance is discovered between the flat or static elements, on which the eye comes to rest, and the curved portions, which invite it to move. Examination also shows that, here too, strict proportional relationships govern the most beautiful designs. Each molding presents the eye with a microcosm of rhythmic entertainment. Although the shapes of which moldings are made up have been inherited as archetypal forms, there is room for interpretation in how and where they are assembled. The place in which a molding is used largely determines the arrangement of its components. The most prominent moldings on organs are horizontal, a visual balance to the verticality of pipes and stiles. Moldings can be used to create a variety of effects. When a molding lends a sense of strength and muscular support to the objects it joins it is known as a bed molding. On the other hand, some compositions offer a light and graceful termination to the restless scanning activity of the eye. These are referred to as crown molding, for like the leaves or branches of a tree they seem to defy gravity and relieve the sense of heaviness. Confusion of the two in case design leads to disturbing results.

Organ builders have customarily relied on the architectural idiom of their own day for ornamentation of their cases, especially in the design of moldings. As we might expect, cabinetmakers in the Gothic period imitated in wood what their colleagues were building in stone. Those wonderful moldings so unlike anything from antiquity, the slender stiles supporting airy, perforated cornices, and the refined geometric patterns of the pipe shades all find their origins in the stonework of that era. The style was current and acceptable.

With the approach of the Renaissance, the ground shifted radically in stylistic detail. The new style, based on models from ancient Greece and Rome, did not arrive as a package, but had to be absorbed piecemeal. Cases built in this first major stylistic transition from Gothic to Renaissance are particularly intriguing. They show the organ builders groping with new ideas which they did not fully comprehend. The strict classical orders had not yet been delineated. Much was open to interpretation. There are examples of organs as late as the mid-seventeenth century which were built with Gothic-style lower cases and upper cases designed in Renaissance modes (e.g. Westerhusen, Ostfriesland, 1643). The lovely moldings on cases built for Hendrik Niehoff in the sixteenth century also show unique adaptations of classical motifs, unlike anything in antiquity.

The old builders took what they chose from their contemporaries, without feeling academically obliged to follow a strict style. This sense of freedom has characterized the best case design all along. Whenever designs become too rigorously tied to the rubrics of architecture, the results are sterile. After all, an organ case is not a building and need not pretend to be one.

Tooling has an influence on the design of moldings as well. The intricate shapes of moldings require that a cabinetmaker acquire complex planes or cutters. Once such an investment has been made, a builder will be inclined to use the same molding-cutters repeatedly, rather than obtaining more just to stay abreast of the fashion. The value of molding planes is reflected in the custom of handing them down from one generation to the next. Thus, tooling encourages a conservation of style.

The last major component of the classical organ case deserving mention is its freeform embellishment, the carvings. Many frankly object to the irregular space left between the tops of the front pipes and the horizontal cornice boxes above them. These openings have customarily been filled with perforated screens or shades, which in the simplest examples are no more than open fretwork. The majority, however, have been the basis of that splendid tradition of woodcarving which is so closely identified with organ cases. While the Gothic shades were very open, later carvers broke away from the geometric patterns and turned to plantlike forms, which they filled out with stylized foliage, fruit, and figures. These denser designs in time came to serve an important musical function. They acted as a check on the unimpeded egress of raw sound and assured a proper blend to the tone of the pipes before it entered the room.

Beautiful shade design depends upon the mastery of skeletal forms. An understanding of the interrelationships between circles and curves is the cornerstone of this art. Confidence in the ability to draw free forms without the help of drafting machinery is prerequisite. A little experimentation with a pen will show that we are very particular about which forms we find attractive. Straight lines or obvious vertical or horizontal stretches are unacceptable. Rather, we prefer that the carvings be composed of forms distinctly different from the rest of the case, to offset the predominance of its rectilinear construction. The natural world presents us with few harsh lines and a constantly changing variety of complex forms for our diversion. Our eyes course back and forth over this panorama, alternating between relaxation and interest. The activity is soothing. The carvings help to bring this natural dimension to the design of an organ case.

Carvings were traditionally placed in front of façade pipes, so that their bottom edge obscured the pipe tops. The practice has been difficult for modern builders to assimilate, since it offends their concept of visual honesty. After all, if the pipes are really the center of the picture, why should they not be completely in view? The first reason is practical. Predicting the exact length of pipes is difficult if they are to be cut to final pitch during voicing. Without knowing these lengths in advance, one can only guess at the shape of the space to be filled by the shade. Design and construction of the carvings is therefore expedited by allowing them to overlap the pipes. But it can be argued that this is not the only reason. Here again the decision centers around visual preference. The prominent verticality of the pipes draws our attention upward. On reaching the top, our eyes relish the gentle distraction encountered in a carving rather than the abrupt end of a pipe cylinder. The history of window design provides a wealth of examples based on similar inclinations. There, the tendency has been to minimize the awkwardness of horizontal lintels at the top. Of course, windows with pointed or round-arched frames avoid the problem altogether. Where it is not avoidable, we find that people have hastened to decorate the tops of the openings with lacy curtains or tasseled valances. Another example is found in Flemish and Italian paintings of the Renaissance. Again and again, we see that the upper mullions and the cames between the panes of windows were laid out in increasingly elaborate designs as they approached the lintel.

Sometimes carvings are also found around the feet of the front pipes. They fill in the voids and complete the effective framing of the pipes, as mentioned earlier. Many builders have not been content to limit their decoration to the boundaries of the case enclosure. Through the addition of external carvings, they have sought further to soften the case's outer form where the organ impinges on the building's architecture. As might be expected, such embellishment is most often to be found at the top. It is also common to find carvings gracing the sides of a case which has no shutters, or forming a beautiful ornamental pendant below the Rückpositiv. Sixteenth-century builders were fond of exaggerating the height of their cases by stacking kiosks atop the towers. Later generations turned to statuary for similar effects. All of these examples indicate a passion for the proper terminations of visual forms. They serve little other function, yet this alone has so often prompted their inclusion that they cannot be ignored in a discussion of the classical case.

By their nature, carvings require a disproportionate amount of effort in both design and execution. They represent the most intricate visible handwork in the organ, and are the product of skills developed through long practice. Carvings reflect both the pride of the builder and the opulence of the purchaser. The combination of the two has led to their excessive use in many places. This was a matter of concern for our ancestors, just as it is for us today. In his discussion of case design, Adlung warned against the proliferation of *Grips Graps*, or meaningless carvings, strewn indiscriminately over the case.[10] Unless the designer is guided by a sense of restraint, this free dimension will too easily degenerate into what an architect friend likes to dismiss as spinach. Another threat to good design lies in the absence of experience with similar ornamentation on the part of the contemporary observer. People are too easily impressed by the fact that ornamentation exists at all. A basis for constructive criticism is beyond most, and flattery is of limited value.

The desire for decoration found further expression in the custom of painting cases. Early furniture building reflects the same tendency. With the use of a variety of colors, it was possible to accentuate many details of moldings and carvings which are otherwise lost. Painted cases afford a colorful point of interest in churches with plain walls and clear windows. Interestingly enough, they never gained prominence in those countries which used stained glass. Historic cases were either completely painted or not painted at all. The modern penchant for applying a little color here and there is of our own invention. Gold leaf, on the other hand, has been appropriate to both painted and unpainted cases. It is most effective when applied to irregular surfaces, such as the curved parts of moldings or carvings. When also used to decorate the front pipes, gold can provide a visual link between pipes and case.

Without an inherent sense of appropriate scale, an organ builder will not fare well. Nowhere is this more obvious than in the timid attempts to dress up new cases with puny moldings and fussy ornamentation. Carving designs are too often busy with detail at the expense of that larger sense of the total form which governs all good compositions. How difficult it is to give up the myopic view and remember that an organ is intended to be seen from a distance. Designs which are most effective at a distance appear crude when seen close at hand. Actors have always understood the necessity of exaggerating their features

10. Jakob Adlung, *Musica Mechanica Organoedi* (Berlin, 1768; facsimile edition, Kassel: Bärenreiter, 1961), p. 18.

on stage, but the impulse does not come easily to contemporary craftsmen. The notion of machined perfection has interfered drastically with our natural perceptions of this truth. So deeply does the practice of necessary crudeness offend our modern sensibilities that those who attempt to revive it are vilified.

A sincere commitment to building better organs is bound to challenge the *status quo*. There will be unforeseen consequences included in the bargain. As noted in regard to case building, the modern style has systematically discouraged some of the finest skills in the history of the art. If we seriously wish to recover them, we cannot be surprised when the search goes against the grain of our comfortable assumptions.

This search helps us realize how contemporary attitudes toward craftsmanship often run at odds to the way the antique cases were built. There is a practical, roughhewn forthrightness about the construction of the antiques which is lacking in our polished imitations. The marks of the makers' tools are seen on the wood. Handwrought nails attach the moldings and carvings. Mortise-and-tenon joinery is rough and strong, appropriate to barn or mill building. Interiors of the cases are scrubplaned, and evidence of sawmilling and hewing is seen on the panels and timbers. By comparison, today's efforts come across as belabored and self-conscious. Even though our ideas have expanded to encompass an enormous body of dimensions and factual information from former times, our attitudes and methods for approaching handwork are shaped by the perfection in woodworking imposed on us by the machines we use.

There is the everpresent danger that, because we are building organs in an elaborate style by today's standards, we may elevate the execution and finishing of the cases to an unnecessarily high point of perfection. In all ages but our own, craftsmen embellished in some way whatever they made, be it organ case or wagon body. The decorative details found on these varied objects were more similar in both style and execution than we might expect. There were standard motifs of decoration which any good craftsman was prepared to execute forthrightly to embellish any object. We must dispense with the idea that organ cases were in any way deserving of unique decoration. Many a case was not even built by the organ builder. Because of the difficulty in transporting an organ, the case construction was, as a rule, left to the local cabinetmaker, who at best received only a sketchy idea from the organ builder as to how the whole instrument was to fit together. Without direct control over the details of case construction, the organ builder had to allow room in the design for inaccuracies.

To say that antique cases were made in a straightforward manner is not to imply that those we revere as monuments were cheap to build. Quite the opposite is true. The high value of skilled labor and the much greater relative value of materials in the past often made the cost of historic cases greater than the cost of the musical parts housed within. This is a discouraging thought, since nowadays the cost of the casework is expected to be included in the price of an organ, when the competition may propose an organ with a case of negligible value. One wonders at times whether it is worth building elaborate cases at all. The best casemaking does not ensure the musical success of an organ. Even the most handsome case cannot camouflage poor musical qualities for long, and we know that a very fine instrument can be built within a modest case.

In the end, an organ case must be judged on its own terms. The history of the instrument would be greatly impoverished and its survival jeopardized had not our ancestors been willing to invest their talents in this seemingly unimportant aspect of the organ. No art fares well under scrutiny of its practical or functional worth. The visual beauty of an organ is sufficient justification for its existence. So long as the priorities of the builder are clear there is little danger that the case will detract from the more important parts of the instrument. Good craftsmen know, above all, where to place their efforts. If an organ builder is secure in the aim to build an instrument which is at once musical, durable, and lovely to behold, then the methods for reaching these goals will become apparent with experience. Little is so exasperating to a craftsman as to witness someone wasting time on unimportant details at the expense of matters of real significance. The tenacity of these positive traits in craftsmen is the surest promise that superior workmanship is possible today and that the present generation can make a fresh contribution to the history of the classical case.

Some fear that interest in the history of the organ will lead to meaningless copies. In the process of learning, copying is a necessary stage which should not be avoided. Ultimately the creative craftsman will not be satisfied with imitation. Development will follow naturally if it is well informed by the heritage of the craft. As organ builders respond to the artistic needs of their own age, each will bring to the work a distinct and individual talent which can never be fully understood by another. A sense of mystery always remains about real works of art. This is what makes them so fascinating. The inquiry finds no end, even after years of study. As Charles Fisk said, upon looking up at the old organ case built in 1802 by David Tannenberg for Hebron Lutheran Church in Madison, Virginia, "Now tell me, George, what is it that makes this organ so beautiful?"

CHAPTER FIFTEEN

Tuning and Temperament
in the North German School of the
Seventeenth and Eighteenth Centuries

HARALD VOGEL

> . . . denn Theoria und praxis müssen/
> die Warheit zu ergründen/ beysammen seyn.
>
> ANDREAS WERCKMEISTER
> (Introduction to *Musicalische Temperatur*, 1691)
>
> *. . . for Theory and practice must come
> together in order to discover the truth.*

THE DEVELOPMENT of both the North German organ repertoire and North German organ building in the seventeenth and eighteenth centuries, which reached their zeniths respectively in the works of Dietrich Buxtehude and Arp Schnitger, is documented in few theoretical treatises. Fortunately the sources dealing with tuning and temperament are sufficient to provide an overview of the subject. And the richest source of information is not archival evidence and the writings of the theorists but is, rather, the original pipework from surviving antique instruments.

The opinions expressed by Michael Praetorius in his *Organographia* (1619) concerning tuning and temperament are of great importance.[1] He gives a practical explanation of tuning based, as was customary with organ builders, on the phenomenon of beats:

> Das wort Schweben aber ist ein Orgelmacherischer *Terminus*, und wird von inen gebraucht/wenn eine *Concordantz* nit reine stehet. . . . Dann schweben sol so viel heissen/wie unrein/das ist/entweder zu hoch oder zu niedrig gestimet . . . so schwebt der Resonantz und klang in den Pfeiffen/ und schlägt gleich eim *Tremulant* etliche Schläge.[2]

---

1. Michael Praetorius, *Syntagma musicum II: De Organographia*, (Wolfenbüttel: 1619; facsimile Kassel: Bärenreiter, 1958), pp. 148-58.

2. Praetorius, p. 151.

The word "beats," however, is a common term among organbuilders, and is used by them when an interval is not pure . . . for to beat means to be unpure, that is, to be tuned too high or tuned too low . . . so that the resulting beats of the pipes give the effect of a tremulant.

The tuning system which Praetorius referred to as a "standard" tuning[3] is known today as quarter-comma meantone. It is characterized by eight pure major thirds (above e♭, b♭, f, c, g, d, a, and e), and eleven tempered fifths (above e♭, b♭, f, c, g, d, a, e, b, f♯, and c♯) which are tuned flat by a quarter of a syntonic comma. (The syntonic comma—21.5 cents—is the difference between a pure major third [e.g., C-E] and the [pythagorean] third resulting from tuning four consecutive pure fifths [e.g., C-G-D-A-E].) This system results in four "wolf thirds" (above b, f♯, c♯, and g♯) and a wolf fifth (g♯-e♭), which render it impossible to play B, F♯, C♯, and G♯ major, as well as g♯, e♭, b♭, and f minor, chords (figure 15-2).

Along with pure meantone tuning, which was in use throughout Europe around 1600, Praetorius describes modifications to this system which aim to soften the "wolf" interval.

Die Quinten cs gs und fs cs/müssen nicht so gar falsch/und nicht so gar reine seyn/sondern nur etzlicher massen/doch dass sie nicht so sehr wie andere Quinten schweben/damit es/wann aus frembden *Clavibus*, und durch die *Semitonia* etwas geschlagen wird/nicht gar zu sehr dissonire. Wiewol etliche meynen die Quinta cs gs müsse gar rein seyn. . . .[4]

The fifths c♯-g♯ and f♯-c♯ should be neither quite so false nor quite so pure; rather, they should be tuned in such a way that they do not beat as much as other fifths so that when strange keys and many semitones are played, too much dissonance does not result. Some think that c♯-g♯ must be tuned pure. . . .

The most important interval requiring improvement, according to Praetorius, was the minor third f-g♯,[5] an interval which occurs constantly when transposing the second mode down a whole tone (from g to f). The cost of improving this minor third is a widening of the major third e-g♯:

3. Praetorius, p. 150.

4. Praetorius, p. 155.

5. Praetorius consistently names the semitones according to the terminology of organ builders and organists: c', d', f', g', and b♭. This terminology is based on the Pythagorean tuning system (with the wolf between b and f'), a system widely in use in the fifteenth century. In the Pythagorean system there are nearly pure major thirds (slightly narrow) above d, a, e, and b (see figure 15-2). See Mark Lindley, "Pythagorean Intonation and the Rise of the Triad," *R.M.A. Research Chronicle* no. 16, 1980, p. 4f. The terminology remained alive in the form of German organ tablature well into the eighteenth century. Indeed, German organ builders still use this system.

. . . und die *Tertiam Majorem* e gs nicht gar zu reine/sondern etwas weiter von einander gezogen/damit das gs ein wenig in die höhe dem a näher/ dem f aber weiter kommen/ und also fast/wiewohl nicht gar pro *Tertia Minore* zur Noth könne gebraucht werden.[6]

. . . and the Major Third e-g$^{\sharp}$ should not be too pure but rather widened so that g$^{\sharp}$ is raised towards a but away from f and thus, if necessary, can be used (although not well) as a Minor Third.

A modified meantone temperament of this sort (figure 15-5) was used at my suggestion in the 1975 restoration of the organ in Langwarden (c. 1650). The antique pipes—most of which retain their original lengths—served as a point of departure; they indicated that pure fifths had originally been tuned above b$^{\flat}$ and e$^{\flat}$, resulting in a softened wolf third b-d$^{\sharp}$. A similarly modified mean-tone—also deduced from the lengths of old pipework—is to be found in the organ in Uttum (c. 1650, with older pipe materials) in Ostfriesland.[7] The modifications to meantone temperament described by Michael Praetorius result in a compromise which renders the wolf intervals milder, but still not pleasant.

Another solution was experimented with in situations involving "professional" players. This involved the use of sub-semitones, built as split sharps, allowing the player to choose between d$^{\sharp}$ and e$^{\flat}$, or a$^{\flat}$ and g$^{\sharp}$, for example. The use of two sub-semitones per octave (d$^{\sharp}$/e$^{\flat}$ and g$^{\sharp}$/a$^{\flat}$), which provides fourteen notes per octave, was described by Praetorius for, among others, the relatively large Compenius organ in Bückeburg and the Fritzsche organ in the Dresden court chapel, where Heinrich Schütz held forth.[8] Michael Praetorius himself had Gottfried Fritzsche build a large organ in 1621 for the main church in Wolfenbüttel which utilized sixteen notes per octave, with four sub-semitones: c$^{\sharp}$/d$^{\flat}$, d$^{\sharp}$/e$^{\flat}$, g$^{\sharp}$/a$^{\flat}$, and a$^{\sharp}$/b$^{\flat}$.[9]

It was only by the construction of a new organ that sub-semitones could be included in all divisions; when renovating or enlarging an instrument, their inclusion was limited—principally for lack of space—to one of the smaller divisions (the *Brustwerk* or *Rückpositiv*). Thus Gottfried Fritzsche prepared a new spring chest with two sub-semitones per octave in 1635 for the *Rückpositiv* of the organ in the Hamburg Jakobikirche.[10]

6. Praetorius, p. 155.

7. The restoration of Uttum was carried out in 1957 by Jürgen Ahrend and Gerhard Brunzema. The restoration in Langwarden, still in progress, was begun in 1975 by Fritz Schild (Orgelbau Führer, Wilhelmshaven).

8. Praetorius, pp. 185–88.

9. Selmar Müller, *Geschichte der alten Orgel in der Hauptkirche B.M.V. in Wolfenbüttel* (Braunschweig: 1877), p. 6, and Uwe Pape, *Die Orgeln der Stadt Wolfenbüttel* (Berlin: 1973), p. 6.

10. Gustav Fock, *Arp Schnitger und seine Schule* (Kassel: 1974), p. 55f.

Compositions which exploit the presence of sub-semitones are rare in the North German repertoire of this period. To this small group belong the second and third verses of Jacob Praetorius' chorale variations on "Vater unser im Himmelreich."[11] In measure 21 of verse 3 a "chromatic concentration" (similar to those in the Toccatas "per il cimbalo cromatico" [1609] of Asconio Mayone) [12] calls for both d♯ and e♭ , as well as g♯ and a♭ ; measure 21 of verse 2 calls for both d♯ and e♭ . Both passages can be played on one manual and thus require sub-semitones on only one keyboard.

In Samuel Scheidt's *Tabulatura Nova* (1624), the semitone d♯ appears several times; however, it occurs together with e♭ only in the famous fantasy *Io son ferito ahi lasso*. In the last variation on "Da Jesus an dem Kreuze stund," d♯, which appears throughout the chromatic voice leading, can be realized by the re–tuning of one (or more) of the short–length reeds; in the other variations, the limits of regular meantone temperament are not overstepped.

At the beginning of the seventeenth century in North Germany, then, quarter-comma meantone temperament was by far the most common tuning. The keyboard repertoire of the time exploits the keys between E major and E♭ major only in exceptional cases. If the tonal boundaries of meantone temperament *were* overstepped, there were three possibilities at hand:

1. *The use of sub-semitones.* Instruments with sub-semitones were not very widespread and were available only where music was in the hands of "professional" players. Sub-semitones served first and foremost in continuo performance, since the chromatic style first appeared in the vocal-instrumental repertoire of the late Renaissance. The large organs of North Germany possessed sub-semitones only in exceptional cases.

2. *The re-tuning of individual semitones.* This was possible both on stringed keyboard instruments and on organs (using the short-length reeds such as the regal). Using this method, the tonality is not truly enlarged, but merely shifted, so that, for example, both d♯ and e♭ cannot be used in the same composition. (A detailed description of a re–tuning which makes it possible to play music based on all twelve notes of the chromatic scale is given by Giovanni Paolo Cima, *Partito de Ricercari alla Francese*, Milan, 1606.)

3. *The modification of fifths around the wolf fifth g♯ -e♭ in order to soften the dissonant thirds f-g♯ and b-d♯* . This compromise temperament is described by Praetorius (see above) and evidence for it can be deduced from the pipe work of several seventeenth-century organs.

Quarter-comma meantone temperament remained the dominant tuning system for keyboard instruments in North Germany throughout the seventeenth century. Andreas Werckmeister, in the preface to his *Musicalische*

11. Edition by Werner Breig (Kassel: 1974), p. 22f.

12. Ascanio Mayone, *Secondo Libro di Diversi Capricci Per Sonare* (Naples: 1609).

Temperatur (1691) called it "the so-called general temperament, in which one takes from every fifth a quarter of one comma. . . ." In chapter twenty-eight, Werckmeister describes meantone tuning—which he often refers to as "incorrect"—in the following manner:

> In der alten allgemeinen Temperatur kan man die quinten and quarten gis und dis, it. [em] die Tertien und Sexten H und dis nicht gebrauchen/wie in den meisten Orgeln solches die Erfahrung bezeugnet. . . .[13]

> In the old general temperament one cannot use the fifths and fourths g#-d#, or the thirds and sixths b-d#, as experience with most organs confirms. . . .

In many organ contracts and written discussions about tuning and temperament, meantone tuning in both its pure and modified forms is termed *praetorianisch*. This is due, of course, to the wide dissemination of Michael Praetorius' *Organographia* and his pragmatic presentation of tuning and temperament "in the manner of organ builders and organists, so that it is easily understandable."[14]

In the 1630s the North German repertoire began to include elaborately laid out works which require several manuals and which depart from the tonalities circumscribed by meantone temperament. D#, and to a lesser extent a♭, were called for more frequently. The *Magnificat* on the seventh mode of Heinrich Scheidemann, the organ *Te deum (Herr Gott wir loben dich)* of Franz Tunder, and various works of Mathias Weckmann (*Magnificat Secundi Toni*, first verse; *Komm, heiliger Geist, Herr Gott*, third verse; *O Lux Beata Trinitas*, sixth verse; *Nun freut euch, lieben Christen g'mein*, third verse) are examples of this type of composition.

In spite of the increased use of d# and a♭, no known documents substantiate increased activity in the addition of sub-semitones to North German organs during this period. On the contrary, sub-semitones, which at the beginning of the seventeenth century had appeared even in large instruments with more than one manual, were no longer included even in new organs.

Of the three possibilities for expanding meantone temperament, it appears that modifying the interval structure around the wolf fifth to soften the dissonant thirds was most common. We are fortunate to have a source which describes one such tempering procedure—a report dating from 1641 written by Jacob Praetorius and Heinrich Scheidemann concerning the organ built by Johann

13. Andreas Werckmeister, *Musicalische Temperatur* (Quedlinburg: 1691), p. 76.
14. Praetorius, p. 155.

and Jost Sieburg for Bremen's Liebfrauenkirche.[15] In addition to many other defects found in the instrument, its meantone temperament was criticized and the following changes were recommended:

> Joh. Siborch will versuchen so viehl immer müghligen dieselbe Quinta zwischen a und d rein zu stimmen und die tertien zu schärffen und die schwebende Quinta an andere Oerter zu bringen.

> Joh. Siborch [Sieburg] shall try as much as possible to tune the fifth between a and d pure and sharpen the thirds and distribute the beating fifth in other places.

The authority of Jacob Praetorius and Heinrich Scheidemann, who were North Germany's most respected organists in the period around 1640, gives this source great importance. In contrast to the recommendation of Michael Praetorius, the temperament here proceeds from "sharpened" thirds. Taken together with the pure fifth d-a (which is especially felicitous for continuo accompaniment of stringed instruments), these thirds could be interpreted as thirds tuned a quarter-comma too wide. The tuning procedure is quite easy: from d and a, which are tuned as a pure fifth, tune two pure thirds (d-b♭ and a-c♯); the fifths contained within these intervals are tuned a quarter of a syntonic comma narrow; lastly, b♭ and c♯ are corrected so that the fifths f-b♭ and f♯-c♯ are pure. With this model one achieves a uniform structure with sharp major thirds (all major thirds between b♭ and c♯ are ¼–comma wide) and a perfect fifth d-a. The second recommendation—"to bring the beating fifth to other places"—refers to the wolf fifth g♯-e♭. Scheidemann's increased use of the semitone d♯ leads to the conclusion that the third b-d♯ was not larger than a Pythagorean third, since this third (obtained by the tuning of four consecutive pure fifths and equaling 407.8 cents) can be understood as a sharp third, and not as a strong dissonance. Figure 15-4 shows my reconstruction of the Scheidemann/J. Praetorius temperament, with a (mild) wolf fifth between g♯ and e♭, and acceptable thirds b-d♯ and f-g♯ to permit the use of the B major and f minor chords.

It is very interesting to compare this temperament with the few precise descriptions we have concerning temperaments of Schnitger's organs. The Schnitger organ (1698) in the Bremen Dom was tested by Vincent Lübeck. He praised the instrument in every regard and said that it was "voiced and tuned better than we had heard in any other place."[16] In 1755, when the organ was to be re–tuned, then-organist Grave remarked:

15. Fritz Piersig, "Die Orgeln der bremischen Stadtkirchen im 17. und 18. Jahrhundert," *Bremisches Jahrbuch*, 1935, p. 401.

16. Fock, p. 88.

Eine reine stimmung ist höchstnothwendig, und zwar nach der alten Praetorianischen Temperatur, so wie diese Orgel gestanden; die neue Temperatur ist wohl besser, allein solches kann man von dem orgelbauer nicht praetendiren, denn es würde ihm gar zu viele Mühe geben zudem müsste das Pfeiffwerck abgeschnitten werden, wodurch unsere Orgel ihre Krafft verlieren und wohl gäntzlich verdorben würde. Die neue Temperatur ist wohl in der Music besser, weil aber die Music vor unsere Orgel nur ein nebenwerck ist, und sie hauptsächlich zum Choral bey der Gemeine dienen muss, so ist die Praetorianische Temperatur gut, obgleich ein starker Wolff im gis und dis sich hören lässt, welches er nicht vermögend ist, herauszubringen.[17]

A pure tuning is most necessary, namely, the old Praetorian temperament as in this organ. The new temperament is probably better, but this cannot be demanded of the organbuilder, because it would be too much trouble; moreover, all the pipes would have to be cut shorter, whereby our organ would lose its force and would be completely ruined. The new temperament is probably better for literature, but because the playing of literature is only a secondary matter as far as our organ is concerned, since it has to serve mainly for playing the chorales with the congregation; therefore the Praetorian temperament is good, in spite of the strong wolf which can be heard between g#-d#, which is not possible to eliminate.

These comments are remarkable for their conservative view of tuning and temperament. The presence of a wolf fifth between g# and d# (e♭) indicates that this was not a well-tempered tuning, or even close to well-tempered. And yet this was the tuning which Vincent Lübeck so highly praised in 1698.

A second and even more precise report can be gleaned from the three organists Evert Haverkamp (Amsterdam), Nicolaas Woordhouder (Rotterdam), and Ae. E. Veldcamps (Den Haag), in their evaluation of the large Schnitger organ in Zwolle in 1721:

Aangaande het Accoort van't Gantsche Orgel vinden wey, dat wel passieren kan, dogh is niet gestelt op die manier, als men gewoont is in Holland de Orgels te stellen, om dat de Terz van g en h en die van g en e wat groote sijn gemaakt, om de terzen h en ds eenigszins passabel te maken.[18]

In respect to the tuning of the whole organ, it may pass, despite the fact that it is not done in the manner in which we are used to tuning organs in Holland, in that the thirds between g and b, and between g and e, are wider in order to make the third between b and d# acceptable.

17. Fock, p. 89.

18. J.W. Enschede, "G. Havingha en het Orgel in de Sint Laurenskerk te Alkmaar," *Tijdschrift der Vereeniging voor Noord-Nederlandse Muziekgeschedenis*, 1908.

These reports, which refer to sharpened (major and minor) thirds in the area of the most used keys, and a just-usable third from b to d$^\sharp$, stand in full agreement with my reconstruction of the Scheidemann/J. Praetorius tuning.

The available sources indicate that North German organs were tuned in meantone or modified meantone well into the eighteenth century. Even in Magdeburg—a city near where Andreas Werckmeister worked—Schnitger did not tune his organ in a well-tempered system. Indeed, the organist Christian David Graff remarked in 1742, in describing the organ in Magdeburg's St. Ulrichskirche (built by Schnitger in 1698-1700):

> Die Temperatur oder Stimmung ist so eingerichtet, dass man aus allen Tonarten ohne Disharmonie spielen kann, welches ehedem nicht gewesen, sondern erstl. 1721 mit grosser Mühe ohne Kosten der Kirche geändert und bisher erhalten worden.[19]

> The temperament or tuning is arranged so that one can play in all keys without disharmony, which was not the case before, but only since 1721 when [the temperament] was changed with great effort, but without cost to the church, and has been maintained until the present.

Over the course of the seventeenth century, the use of remote tonalities gradually grew and the meantone temperament described by Praetorius was slowly modified. It is likely, however, that quarter-comma meantone was retained in small towns. Even in the treatises of Werckmeister and Neidhart, which advocated well-tempered systems and equal temperament, the use of meantone was considered acceptable for instruments in small towns. Therefore the presence as late as 1739 of an only slightly modified meantone temperament (figure 15-12), as was found during Fritz Schild's restoration of the organ in Jade (Oldenburg), is not surprising.

What *is* surprising is the retention of meantone or modified meantone tuning in the circle of the great North German organ composers such as Vincent Lübeck. Indeed, the restraint displayed by these composers in the use of remote tonalities (F$^\sharp$ major, C$^\sharp$ major, A$^\flat$ major) is quite remarkable. A thorough discussion both of this matter and of the hypothesis that some works of North German masters have been transmitted in transposed keys has already been published.[20] A summary must suffice here.

Important research by Kerala Snyder shows that in October of 1683 Dietrich Buxtehude had the organ builder Briegel re-tune the two organs in the Lübeck Marienkirche. Many arguments support the view that Buxtehude, who was in

19. Fock, p. 196.

20. Harald Vogel, "North German Organ Building of the Late Seventeenth Century: Registration and Tuning," in *J.S. Bach as Organist* (Bloomington: Indiana University Press, 1986), p. 38-40.

close contact with Werckmeister and had composed a dedicatory poem in 1702 for Werckmeister's *Harmonologia Musica*, was very interested in having his organs tuned in a well-tempered system.[21] That this tuning took only thirty-six days to complete seems to suggest that the purported temperament change could not have been radical. The tuning of a well-tempered system in the style of Andreas Werckmeister from an unmodified or slightly modified quarter-comma meantone temperament would not have been possible, especially since almost all of the stopped ranks of both instruments were soldered. A comparison between quarter-comma meantone and Werckmeister III (figures 15-2 and 15-6) shows that the greatest difference encountered is 19.6 cents. A comparison between modified meantone tuning in the style of Scheidemann/J. Praetorius and Werckmeister III (figures 15-4 and 15-6), however, shows a maximum differentiation of only 8.8 cents. Such a minor re-tuning could have been achieved in thirty-six days, even under the difficult working conditions of the seventeenth century. The evidence, then, suggests that the organs in the Marienkirche in 1683 were already tuned in a modified meantone temperament, perhaps in the style of Scheidemann/J. Praetorius.

It is very important, and quite surprising, to note that Werckmeister's tuning was not revolutionary: comparing among pure quarter-comma meantone (or only slightly modified), the modified meantone of Scheidemann/J. Praetorius, and Werckmeister III reveals that Werckmeister's temperament was just another step along the road of a gradual modification to meantone temperament. In fact, the difference between pure quarter-comma meantone and the Scheidemann/J. Praetorius temperament (a maximum deviation of 10.8 cents) is *larger* than between the Scheidemann/J. Praetorius temperament and Werckmeister's well–tempered system (a maximum deviation of 8.8 cents).

Although Werckmeister's temperament was not revolutionary from the point of view of temperament, it was revolutionary from a musical point of view. It introduced a qualitatively new musical dimension—the possibility of playing in all keys, and it is no wonder that a progressive composer like Buxtehude was eager to exploit its possibilities.

From the available sources, one can assume the presence of the well-tempered system in North Germany only in the Marienkirche instruments (after 1683). (From the repertoire of this period, one may assume that the well-tempered system was also in use in Braunschweig, an area geographically close to Andreas Werckmeister.[22]) With this in mind, one can divide the North German repertoire into six parts:

21. Kerala Snyder, "Buxtehude's Organs / Helsingør, Helsingborg, Lübeck - 2: The Lübeck Organs," *The Musical Times* cxxvi (1985), 427-34.

22. The E Major Praeambulum of Jacob Bölsche, who worked from 1669-84 in Braunschweig, has the year 1683 marked in the manuscript (MS LM 5056, Yale University). See Klaus Beckmann,

1. *Meantone—pure or slightly modified (M. Praetorius).*
Compositions which do not exceed the meantone boundaries (eight major thirds from e♭ to e and nine minor thirds from c to g♯).

2. *Expanded meantone—using sub-semitones.*
Compositions which make use of sub-semitones (usually d♯ and a♭ , only rarely a♯ and d♭).

3. *Expanded meantone—modified (Scheidemann/J. Praetorius).*
Compositions which exceed the meantone boundaries by using the major third b-d♯ and the minor third f-a♭ .

4. *Expanded meantone—transposition.*
Compositions which do not exceed the meantone boundaries of seventeen thirds (eight major and nine minor), but move about in the circle of fifths; that is, pieces which, if transposed, could be played in the normal meantone framework.

5. *Expanded meantone—using strong dissonances.*
Compositions which exceed the boundaries of meantone temperament only to exploit the "shock value" of some dissonances (b-d♯, f♯-a♯, a♭ -c, d♭ -f, or f-a♭).

6. *Well-tempered.*
Compositions whose modulations regularly exceed the boundaries of meantone temperament, and, by making regular use of complicated seventh chords, require a well-tempered tuning.

The following elaborations on each point may help to clarify them:
1. Most North German organ compositions belong to this group; only the semitones c♯, e♭ , f♯, g♯, and b♭ are called for. The voluminous sources of North German music in the first half of the seventeenth century—including the Celle tablature of 1601, the Visby tablature, the *Tabulatura Nova* of Samuel Scheidt, the Zellerfelder tablatures, and the Lüneburg tablatures—demonstrate only insignificant departures from the boundaries of quarter-comma meantone temperament. Compositions which employ only the above-mentioned five semitones form an important part of the repertoire of the last decades of the seventeenth century as well.
2. A few isolated examples belong to this group, such as the two variations cited above on "Vater unser in Himmelreich" by Jacob Praetorius. These are compositions for instruments with sub-semitones. This group takes on much larger proportions if one includes continuo parts of vocal and instrumental works.

"Jacob Bölsche (d. 1684)—Praeambulum in E-dur," *Ars Organi* XXXII, 4 (1984). The E♭ Major Praeludium of Bölsche's successor, Georg Dietrich Leiding (1664-1710), also requires a well-tempered tuning.

3. The third group includes works written for instruments in a modified meantone tuning (Scheidemann/J. Praetorius, 1641). The semitones d$^\sharp$ and a$^\flat$ appear with some regularity—especially in works in transposed church modes (the aforementioned *Magnificat VII* by Heinrich Scheidemann, for example)—or in isolation at places of sudden modulation or tonal deviation (e.g., the *Praeludium in C*, BuxWV 137, of Buxtehude; the chorale fantasia *An Wasserflüssen Babylon* of Johann Adam Reincken; the *Praeludium in C* of Georg Böhm; and the *Praeludium in G* and *Praeludium in g*, as well as the chorale fantasia *Nun komm, der Heiden Heiland* of Nicolaus Bruhns). Fully a third of the chorale preludes of Buxtehude overstep the boundaries of meantone by occasionally employing d$^\sharp$ or a$^\flat$; in another seven chorale-based settings these semitones appear, but only once. However, more than half of the chorale-based settings by Buxtehude use only the five semitones of the pure quarter-comma meantone system.

4. The fourth group includes several of the free works of Buxtehude (*Praeludium in E*, the "small" *Praeludium in e*, *Praeludium in A*), both of the e-minor *Praeludia* of Bruhns, and the Lübeck *Praeludium in E*. Transpositions of this sort are encountered in other contexts, for example, the *Toccata in C/E* (BWV 566) of Johann Sebastian Bach. A few chorale-based compositions also belong to this group, such as the large chorale fantasia *Ich ruf zu dir, Herr Jesu Christ* of Vincent Lübeck.

5. The fifth group contains only a few compositions, such as the *Praeludium in F* (BuxWV 145, mm. 20-21) and the *Toccata in F* (BuxWV 156, mm. 83-88) of Buxtehude.

6. The sixth group—well-tempered compositions—is very small. The most important example is the *Praeludium in f$^\sharp$* of Buxtehude. Several other free works, such as the *Praeludium in e* (BuxWV 142) of Buxtehude, which can only be performed in well-tempered tuning—even when transposed to a meantone key—are possibly later reworkings of compositions which originally did not exceed the boundaries of meantone's seventeen triads.[23]

During the seventeenth century and in the beginning of the eighteenth century, one can observe a slow but continual development from quarter-comma meantone to well-tempered tuning. It is important to note that by 1640 a modified meantone tuning was already in use which had considerably evolved from pure quarter-comma meantone and which made use of sharpened thirds. This is especially emphasized by Werckmeister himself, who, writing in his *Kurtzer Unterricht, wie man ein Clavier stimen und wohl temperiren könne*, said:

23. A detailed discussion of the relation between intervals and tuning systems, with particular attention to the organ works of Buxtehude, will be undertaken in a future article.

248   HARALD VOGEL

Ich kan mich genung verwundern wen man die alte hypothesin behaup-
ten will, das alle Quinten ein viertel eines Commatis in gantzen Clavier
herunter, and alle Tertien rein seyn müssen, da ich doch in ihren Orgel-
Wercken gefunden, dass die meisten Tertiae majores zu gross, und über
sich schweben. . . . Es findet sich auch in den alten Wercken nicht, dass
die Quinten 1/4 Comat. wie sie vorgeben schweben solten, es würde sonst
wunderlich heraus komen, die letzte Quinta wolte den Hunden und
Raben zu Theile werden.[24]

I cannot help but be surprised when one attaches credence to the old
hypothesis that every fifth be narrowed by a quarter of a comma, and that
all thirds must be pure, since I have found that in their organs most thirds
are too wide, and beat. . . . It also cannot be found in the old organs that
the fifths beat at quarter-comma, as they should, otherwise the result
would be very peculiar, with a last fifth not even fit for a dog.

Such a temperament—a modified meantone with beating fifths, but no wolf
fifth (figure 15-8)—was employed by Jürgen Ahrend in the 1985 restoration of
the large Schnitger organ in the Ludgerikirche in Norden (Ostfriesland). In this
temperament, the fifths between f and f# are narrowed by one-fifth of a
Pythagorean comma. The temperament I developed for the Fisk organ in
Stanford also uses one-fifth comma tempering (figure 15-14) and works splen-
didly for the performance of the North German repertoire. A similar tuning
(figure 15-9) was discovered by Fritz Schild in the 1973 restoration of the
1694-99 organ by Joachim Kayser (a Schnitger contemporary) in Hohenkirchen (Oldenburg). The difference between this and the Norden tuning lies in
the use of quarter-comma temperament between c and b, producing two pure
major thirds (c-e and g-b) in Hohenkirchen. A similar modified meantone
tuning was employed in 1975 on my recommendation when Jürgen Ahrend
restored the Schnitger organ in St. Cosmae in Stade (figure 15-7).

In comparison to these modified meantone tunings, which indicate the
framework within which possible departures may exist, the Vater organs in
Bockhorn (1722) and Wiefelstede (1731), with tuning systems preserved in the
original soldered stopped ranks, represent a step toward well-tempered tuning
(figures 15-10 and 15-11). Since their recent restorations by Fritz Schild, both
organs are once again in their original tunings—tunings which exceed the
limits of the Pythagorean third only slightly (in Bockhorn the thirds above f#,
c#, and g#; in Wiefelstede, the third above g#).

The late changeover to well-tempered tuning in the North accounts for the
small amount of well-tempered literature in the North German organ reper-

24. Contained in "Die nothwendigsten Anmerckungen und Regeln, wie der Bassus continuus oder
General-Bass wol Könne tractiret werden" (Aschersleben: 1698), preserved in manuscript copy in
the Yale University Library, supplement to MS MA 21 Y // A 35.

toire. A completely different situation existed in the eastern foothills of the Harz mountains, in the area of Andreas Werckmeister, and in Thuringia, where in the late seventeenth century Werckmeister's well-tempered tuning had found foothold. Thus J.S. Bach was born into a musical environment in which the possibilities of the well-tempered system for organ composition were wide open. This was in complete contrast to the traditional center of organ activity, North Germany, where apparently Buxtehude's introduction of the well-tempered system constituted an island in a sea of meantone. Werckmeister appears to have had strong influence only in the northern foothills of the Harz around Hildesheim, and also in Braunschweig. In his *Organographia Hildesiensis Specialis*, published in 1738, Johann Hermann Biermann describes in anecdotal fashion various attempts to re-tune organs "from the Praetorian to the other, newly-discovered" tuning (that is, from modified meantone to well-tempered).[25] All the attempts failed, and the organs were re–tuned in "Praetorian" tuning. The Johann Conrad Müller organ of 1761, in Liebenburg, is an example from this area of a well-tempered tuning reconstructed from original pipework (figure 15-13). Since Fritz Schild's restoration, this two-manual instrument once again sounds in its original tuning—an interesting variant of Werckmeister's tuning concept.

It was not until 1740 that well-tempered tuning found general acceptance throughout North Germany (interestingly enough, often against the wishes of the organist, as, for example, in the above-mentioned discussion of the re-tuning of the organ in the Bremen Cathedral, or the 1742 re-tuning of the famous instruments in Hamburg's Katherinenkirche, which Telemann had to defend to then-organist Uthmöller).[26] At this point the eminent North German tradition of organ composition—which in the 1680s had begun to exploit the possibilities of the well-tempered system—came to an end. The North German repertoire was disseminated further in central Germany by Bach and Walther,

25. Johann Hermann Biermann, *Organographia Hildesiensis Specialis* (Hildesheim: 1738), p. 24: "Man hatte sich vor einigen nicht gar langen Jahren von einem frembden Orgelmacher dahin bereden lassen dieses Werck aus der Praetorianischen in eine andere neu–erfundene ['Temperatur] zu setzen / wo nemlich die Quinten und Quarten rein / hergegen die Tertiau majores desto härter lauten / wobey es dann ein oder ander Sache halber sein Verbleiben gehabt / allein weilen bey der Music keine blasende Instrumenta damit harmonieren wolten noch konten / so muste dann alles wieder ergäntzet / was zuvor abgeschnitten und benommen war / wiederum angesetzet / und also in die vorige Temperatur hergestellet worden." ("Not many years ago, a foreign organ builder talked us into retuning this organ from the Praetorian temperament into a newly discovered [tuning]/in which the fifths are pure, but the major thirds, as a result, are harsher/and for one reason or another he had his way/except that for [concerted] music, the wind-instruments did not want to, and could not, play in tune with [the new temperament]/and so everything that had been cut [from the pipes]/ had to be replaced/ and the old temperament was restored.")

26. *Hamburg-St. Katharinen, Memorialbuch der Juraten*, (September 1742), p. 417, in the Hamburg Staatsarchiv: "Ferner brachte unser Organist Uthmöller an, das er mit der Temperatur . . . gar nicht friedlich, sondern nach der alten Temperatur wie sie gewesen haben wolle, wie nun hernach unser vorbenandte Organisten nebst Orgel Bauer [Johann Dietrich Busch] in die Sacristei

but not in North Germany. We are therefore in the lamentable situation of possessing almost no Northern German sources for the great North German repertoire of the late seventeenth century.

The study of the organs of this epoch and the questions which arise during their restoration have brought us a greater understanding of North German organ music in recent years, one which could not have been gleaned from the musical sources alone. We are beginning to understand that the steps from meantone to well-tempered tuning are reflected in many facets of the North German organ repertoire, without—with the exception of a few works of Buxtehude—the last step being fully taken. The critical step of embracing the potentials of the well-tempered system was taken by Johann Sebastian Bach who thereby founded an aesthetic of organ composition, registration, and technique which was totally new.

The musical experiences with both antique and new instruments in various tuning systems have made it possible for us to judge correctly for the first time the mutual effect of interval relationships and compositional structures. We thereby gain a dimension of musical understanding impossible to find by theoretical reflection alone.

Charles Fisk, especially in the later years of his life, turned more and more toward the North German style. This led to an intensive collaboration and friendship between us which benefited my understanding of music as much as had my contact with original instruments. The Wellesley organ, with two sub-semitones per octave on three-manuals and pedal, brought with it an unawaited, intensive reincarnation of the musical ideas of Friedrich Stellwagen and Gottfried Fritzsche; the works of the seventeenth century, from Scheidt to Buxtehude, are today heard considerably more clearly here than in the places of their composition. At this point a new instrument offers a more authentic performance of a part of the old organ literature than is possible on original instruments. With the Stanford organ project, Charles went even further: the presence of both meantone and well-tempered tunings, combined with the tonal qualities of the instrument and the acoustical qualities of the room, makes it possible to trace the musical development which led to the individualistic style of J.S. Bach. In this organ the move from eclecticism to universality—to which we all so passionately strive—was accomplished.

gefordert und letzterer declariret, wie itzo die temperatur gesetzt . . . also es auch sein verbleiben dabey hätte, besonders da der Cantor Thelemann so auch dabey fordern lassen, der . . . aussagte, dass diese temperatur besser als [die] vorige wäre." ("Furthermore our organist Uthmöller charged that he was not happy with the new temperament, but wanted the organ in the old temperament, and so our above-named organist and the organ builder [Johann Dietrich Busch] were summoned into the Sacristy, and the latter explained how the temperament is now set . . . and he had his way, especially since the cantor Telemann was also summoned, who . . . said, that this temperament was better than the last.")

PYTHAGOREAN TUNING

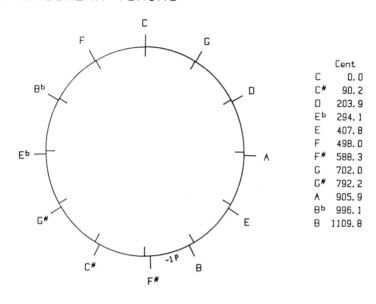

	Cent
C	0.0
C#	90.2
D	203.9
Eb	294.1
E	407.8
F	498.0
F#	588.3
G	702.0
G#	792.2
A	905.9
Bb	996.1
B	1109.8

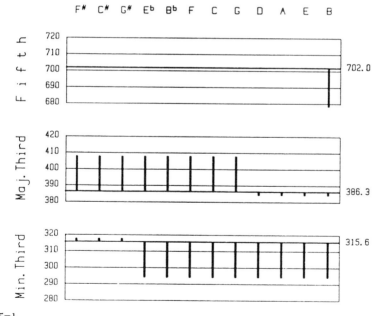

15—1.

P=Pythagorean comma; S=syntonic comma; the absence
of any mark indicates a pure interval.

(C) G. Schnell 1984

MEANTONE TEMPERAMENT (1/4 comma)

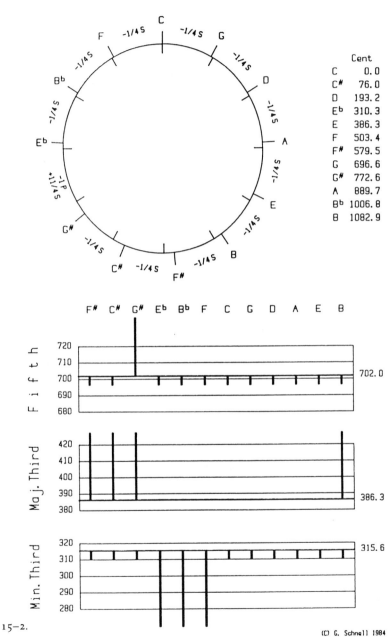

Cent
C   0.0
C#   76.0
D   193.2
Eb   310.3
E   386.3
F   503.4
F#   579.5
G   696.6
G#   772.6
A   889.7
Bb   1006.8
B   1082.9

15—2.

(C) G. Schnell 1984

EQUAL TEMPERAMENT

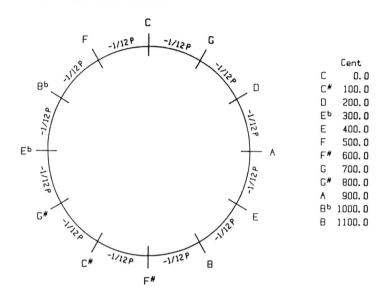

	Cent
C	0.0
C#	100.0
D	200.0
Eb	300.0
E	400.0
F	500.0
F#	600.0
G	700.0
G#	800.0
A	900.0
Bb	1000.0
B	1100.0

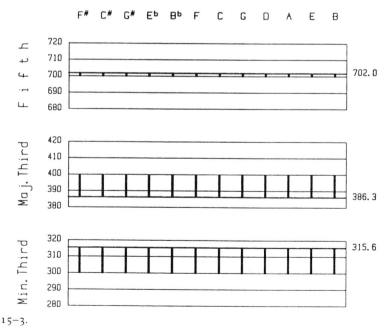

15-3.

BREMEN - Liebfrauenkirche 1641   (Scheidemann/J.Praetorius)

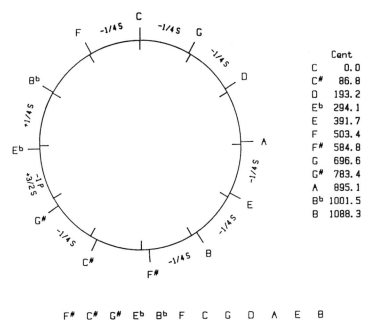

	Cent
C	0.0
C♯	86.8
D	193.2
E♭	294.1
E	391.7
F	503.4
F♯	584.8
G	696.6
G♯	783.4
A	895.1
B♭	1001.5
B	1088.3

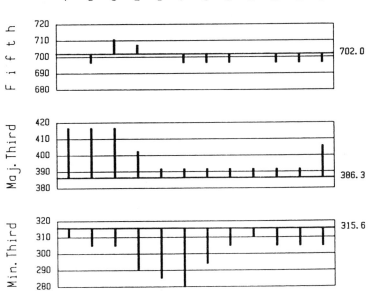

15-4.   (C) G. Schnell 1984

LANGWARDEN   1650 H. Kröger

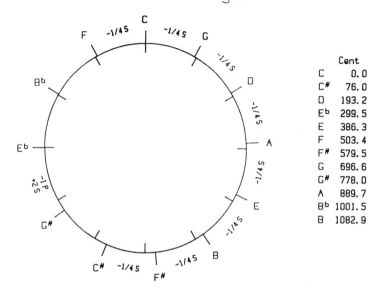

	Cent
C	0.0
C#	76.0
D	193.2
Eb	299.5
E	386.3
F	503.4
F#	579.5
G	696.6
G#	778.0
A	889.7
Bb	1001.5
B	1082.9

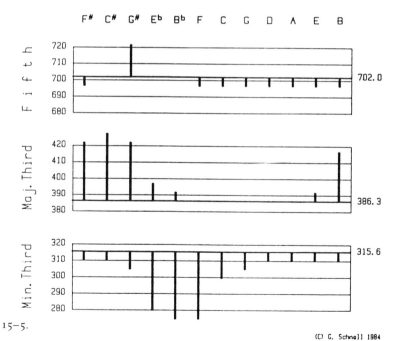

15-5.

WERCKMEISTER III

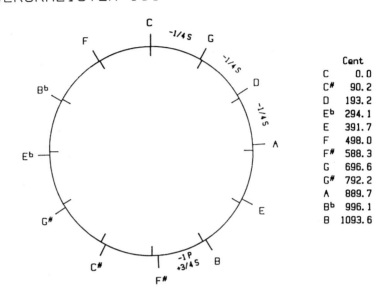

	Cent
C	0.0
C♯	90.2
D	193.2
E♭	294.1
E	391.7
F	498.0
F♯	588.3
G	696.6
G♯	792.2
A	889.7
B♭	996.1
B	1093.6

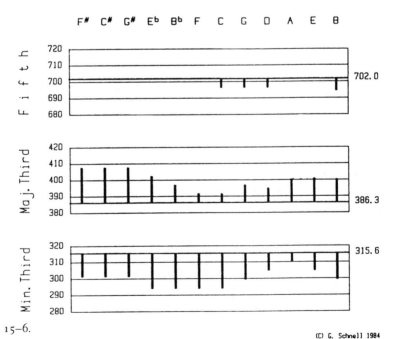

15–6.

STADE - St. Cosmae 1675 Arp Schnitger (Restoration 1975)

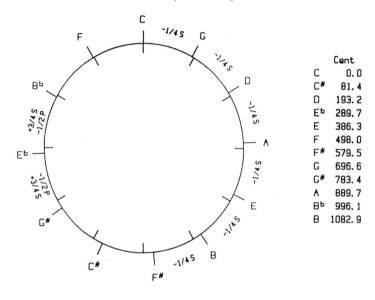

Cent	
C	0.0
C♯	81.4
D	193.2
E♭	289.7
E	386.3
F	498.0
F♯	579.5
G	696.6
G♯	783.4
A	889.7
B♭	996.1
B	1082.9

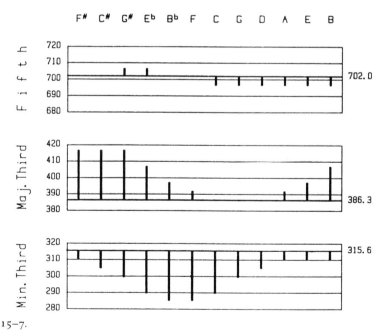

15-7.

NORDEN - St.Ludgeri 1688 Arp Schnitger (Restoration 1985)

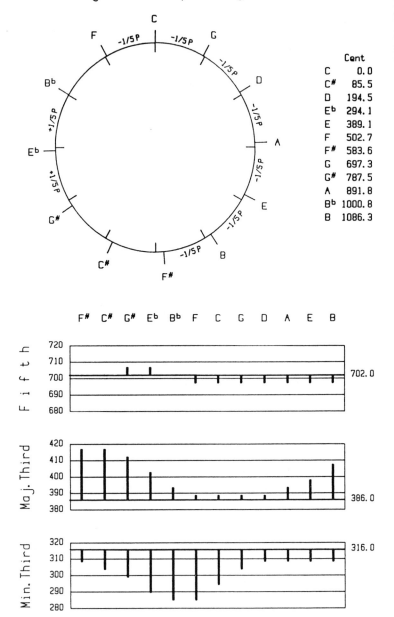

	Cent
C	0.0
C#	85.5
D	194.5
Eb	294.1
E	389.1
F	502.7
F#	583.6
G	697.3
G#	787.5
A	891.8
Bb	1000.8
B	1086.3

15–8.

HOHENKIRCHEN 1694-99 Joachim Kayser

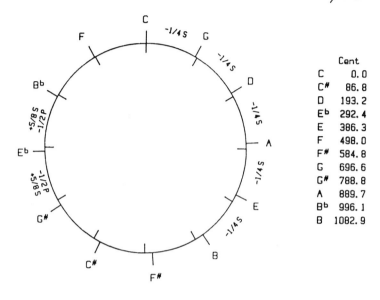

	Cent
C	0.0
C#	86.8
D	193.2
Eb	292.4
E	386.3
F	498.0
F#	584.8
G	696.6
G#	788.8
A	889.7
Bb	996.1
B	1082.9

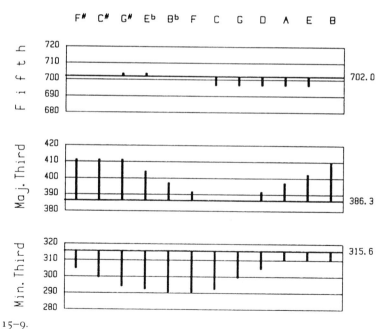

15-9.

BOCKHORN   1722 Christian Vater

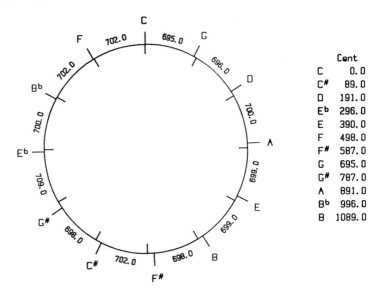

	Cent
C	0.0
C#	89.0
D	191.0
Eb	296.0
E	390.0
F	498.0
F#	587.0
G	695.0
G#	787.0
A	891.0
Bb	996.0
B	1089.0

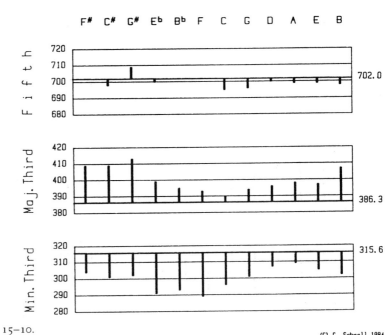

15—10.

WIEFELSTEDE   1731 Christian Vater

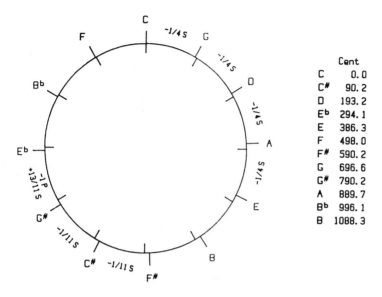

	Cent
C	0.0
C#	90.2
D	193.2
Eb	294.1
E	386.3
F	498.0
F#	590.2
G	696.6
G#	790.2
A	889.7
Bb	996.1
B	1088.3

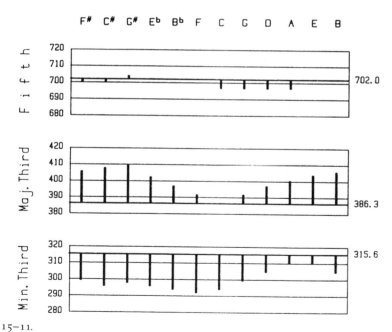

15—11.

JADE   1739 J. Dietrich Busch

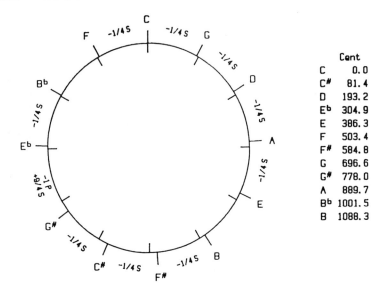

Cent	
C	0.0
C#	81.4
D	193.2
Eb	304.9
E	386.3
F	503.4
F#	584.8
G	696.6
G#	778.0
A	889.7
Bb	1001.5
B	1088.3

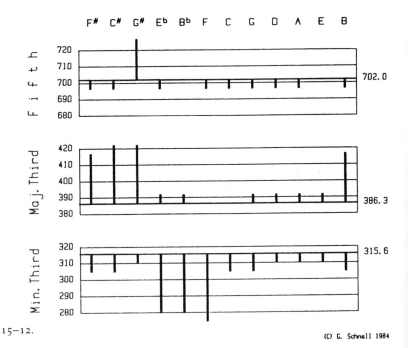

15—12.

LIEBENBURG   1761   J. Conrad Müller

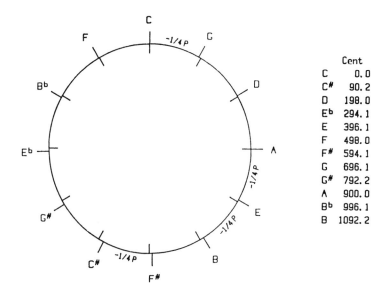

	Cent
C	0.0
C#	90.2
D	198.0
Eb	294.1
E	396.1
F	498.0
F#	594.1
G	696.1
G#	792.2
A	900.0
Bb	996.1
B	1092.2

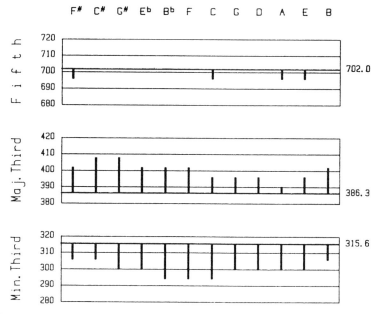

15—13.

STANFORD VOGEL 5/M (meantone)

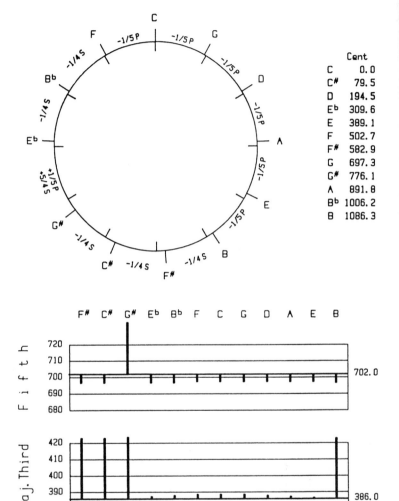

	Cent
C	0.0
C#	79.5
D	194.5
Eb	309.6
E	389.1
F	502.7
F#	582.9
G	697.3
G#	776.1
A	891.8
Bb	1006.2
B	1086.3

15-14.

STANFORD VOGEL 5/W (elltempered)

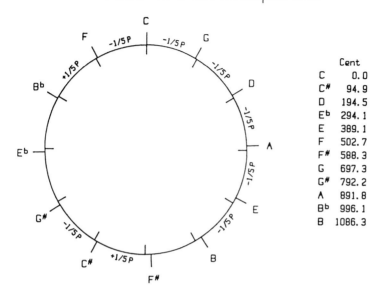

	Cent
C	0.0
C#	94.9
D	194.5
Eb	294.1
E	389.1
F	502.7
F#	588.3
G	697.3
G#	792.2
A	891.8
Bb	996.1
B	1086.3

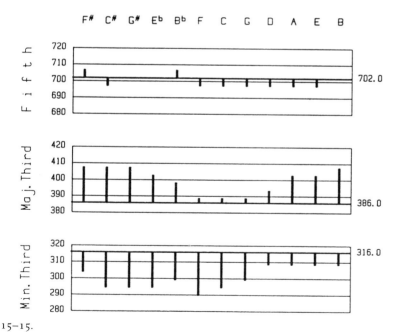

15—15.

(C) G. Schnell 1984

CHAPTER SIXTEEN

The Acquisitive Minds of Handel & Bach: Some Reflections on the Nature of "Influences"

PETER WILLIAMS

Today we tend to talk very grandly in terms of "influences." It is something to which many of us constantly have resort; both players and scholars often find it useful for one reason or another not only to hear resemblances between such-and-such composers but to conjecture that the resemblances come from one "influencing" the other; most teachers have seen students speculating on "influences" and coming to conclusions that might have been different had they a wider knowledge. Of course, a great composer, like any other extraordinary person, will have some hold on the way those in contact with him will think or act after that contact has been made, even if for local reasons he has not come into contact with many people. Some huge questions in music history, as in every other avenue of human development (particularly in western culture?) hang on the perception we have of "extraordinary persons": do they govern development or merely typify it? Did diatonicism develop as a consequence of the way certain very particular composers thought and provoked others to think, or was it inevitable, a stage in the unfolding tale of music, a plateau on the rising slope of musical achievement, always located there (so to speak) and only waiting for an explorer to find it?

Such questions are not often the concern of musicians, but it is also the case that we often underrate the problems of small-scale influence too: what *is* the nature of Vivaldi's influence on Bach? Is it really demonstrable? In what way? At what point does our conjecture take over from fact? If Bach really had to know Vivaldi's concertos before he could achieve sophisticated ritornello form, how does it come about that he found it himself already in the early D major Fugue for Organ, BWV 532? As a salute to the memory of a man fascinated by the power of certain personalities to influence others, and how those influences can be accurately defined, I would like to take some examples from the keyboard works of two particular composers, composers known as charismatic organists, both of them veritable St. Augustines "into and from whom all things flow."

Some details in Handel's Harpsichord Music

While Handel's fondness for repeating himself (re-using his own material) has received some attention over the years, it is doubtful if the impact of other music on him particularly before 1715 or so (that is, before he took themes from Telemann, etc.) has always been understood. The following remarks, concerned chiefly with a group of Allemandes, redress the balance only to a certain point; but they are not merely an attempt to show Handel taking other people's ideas and making them his own. The relationship is more complicated. Quite apart from difficult questions of chronology—who came first—it is so that with a whirlwind talent such as his, more the point is how it would absorb and reshape and how its aims differed from those of his contemporaries. That the subtlest of the possible areas of influence shown—the absorption of a single harmonic progression and the testing of its potential—is the only one published in the authorized 1720 Collection of Suites may well not be coincidence.

Firstly, while the D minor Allemande HWV449 seems to be an early work, shows the character of an "archetypal allemande," and is the work of a composer capable of invention, its resemblance to the opening of an unpublished sonata in the same key by B. Marcello (1686–1739) is striking: see figure 16–1. What are we to suppose from this? That Handel knew the sonata or Marcello the suite? That either unconsciously quoted from the other and thus Marcello thinned out the texture and/or Handel thickened it, specifying more clearly a *sostenuto* touch? Handel's suite-movement has a distinctive Italian flavor in its second half (not given here), while Marcello's proceeds to expand much further on the succession of thin harpsichord *formulae* characteristic of Italian sonatas. Or does Handel's version suggest that "thin" *formulae* were "thickened" in performance?

In figure 16–2, the priority seems clearer: the G minor Allemande of Mattheson was published in 1714 (London), while Handel's is presumed to date from c. 1739 when he set out two model suites for the young Princess Louisa, daughter of the king. Both composers moreover use the motif elsewhere in the movement, one no doubt with a better melodic sense and notion of texture than the other. The question remains whether the resemblance suggests chance memory on Handel's part or whether he re-used an earlier movement originally written in answer to its "model." The former is more likely—and is suggested by the sources—since it is so much more consistently composed than Mattheson's and its returning to the theme (bars 5, 10, 12, 26) seems reminiscent of Mattheson's.

The consistency of texture in Handel's suite-movements, whether Italianate or Frenchified, comes largely from an inventive use of conventional motifs he could have found not only in German sets of variations (aria-doubles, chorale-

16-3. Rameau, Premier Livre (ornaments omitted)

Handel, Suite HWV 438

16-4. Couperin, Allemande à deux clavecins

Handel, Suite HWV 426

partitas, etc.) of an earlier generation but from up-to-date suite-publications by Parisian composers. Thus while the motif called *figura suspirans* (see figure 16–3) was known to older composers, it is its use in e.g. Rameau's Allemandes (*Premier Livre de Pièces de Clavecin*, 1706 etc.) that produced the allemande texture *par excellence*. Rameau's A minor Allemande also contains other motifs much worked by Handel. In such examples, it is not so much a matter of themes being alike as motif-cells having family likenesses: Handel's repertory of *figurae* is specifically Rameauesque, so much so as to suggest that he assumed e.g. the articulation of Rameau's b. 10 above in his various treatments of that particular motif (e.g. in the first Variation in the well-known Suite in E major, 1720 Collection). In what may be supposed to be Handel's earliest attempts at suite-movements, such as the C major Suite HWV443, the style is more melodious, more Froberger-like, less *figura*-riven. It could well be that Rameau's influence on German keyboard music has not yet been properly understood, an influence so strong that even in the 1750s, a good deal of material in J. S. Bach's *Obituary* should be seen as attempts by its authors to show its subject to have had an impact as great as Rameau's.[1]

The fourth example (see figure 16–4) is the subtlest and accordingly more speculative. In the Courante of Handel's A major Suite, 1720 Collection No. 1, a very striking $\frac{9}{7}$ chord occurs no less than five times (bb. 7, 17, 32, 36, 46); it is not the least striking feature in a remarkably pretty movement. However, in 1717 Couperin had published his own A major Suite in the *Second Livre* in which is an *Allemande à deux clavecins* with the same chord. (Other similarities too can be found between it and the Allemande in Handel's A major Suite.) Now of course, a $\frac{9}{7}$ chord was within the vocabulary of any good composer; but there does seem some relationship between the examples here, if only as a further indication of the unconscious workings of a mind absorbing whatever it came into contact with. It does not seem very farfetched to imagine Handel very taken with the beauty of this chord—which he will have heard in Italian recitative but not, I think, in suite-dances before—and making thematic use of it.

No doubt there are many more parallels of this kind to be made. For example, comparison between Handel's and Mattheson's suites suggests the following:

—fast triplet arpeggios, as in some of Handel's free preludes, may have been particularly liked by the Hamburgers, who alternated the left and right hands, slurred fast scales and spread simple chords marked *arpeggiato* (Mattheson, Suite No. 2 in A major).

—a 3/4 or 3/8 Allegro with continuous quavers or semiquavers can be a kind

1. This is particularly so in the case of advances in keyboard-playing (versatile fingering, etc.) which the authors attribute to J. S. Bach.

of Courante even if there is no upbeat—another favorite of the Hamburgers?
—sarabandes with melodies on the top, particularly when there is no pattern
(see figure 16–5), are called *Air;* they appear (a) to be played more slowly, (b)
to require no filling in and (c) to expect a *petite reprise* from time to time
(Mattheson, Suite No. 10 in E minor).
—doubles follow certain conventions, e.g. those with semiquaver alto lines
serve as exercises in *legato* for the right hand fingers 1, 2, 3.
Handel too must have been familiar with the Hamburg organ-arts, as he was
with more widely familiar Italian violin music. Thus the little Prelude in D
minor HWV 564, attributed to Handel in its one source, has two distinctive
sections, each adapting and then together amalgamating very derivative
themes:

> 1. the opening praeludium-like passagio, very reminiscent of Buxtehude and
> other north Germans (see figure 16–6a)
> 2. the imitative section built (at the same pitch) on a passage from the Finale
> of Vivaldi's Concerto Op. III No. 11 (Amsterdam c. 1711) (see figure 16–6b).

The Prelude HWV 564 makes great use of neither theme; perhaps somebody
compiled it from drafts? J.S. Bach, too, knew the second theme (BWV 596,
Finale).

Broader Influences

When J. S. Bach published a set of harpsichord partitas in 1725–31, he had so
arranged the six works that not only did they have a recognizable key-sequence[2]

2. B♭ C A D G E—the next would be F, key of the harpsichord work he next published, the *Italian
Concerto.*

but each begins with a distinct kind of prelude: six genres with six different names *Praeludium, Sinfonia, Fantasia, Ouverture, Praeambulum, Toccata)* at least three of which *(Praeludium, Sinfonia,* and especially *Praeambulum)* are surprising terms. There are other systematic differences, carefully planned distinctions, between the *partitas,* such as the array of *Allemandes,* each presenting a distinct character of theme and texture though each undeniably an allemande. Now any competent composer presents variety in his work, particularly in a set of given pieces (concertos, quartets, sonatas, etc.); Handel's Op. VI *concerti grossi* are a good example of a constantly surprising collection of pieces, as if the composer left his listener in doubt as to what was to come next. But the systematic variety in the set of *partitas* is of a different order. Was it an invention of J. S. Bach, or where could he have learnt it?

The answer is, probably, that he invented it. But some systems, in all kinds of sources, must have influenced him—for example the idea in the first place of compiling a set of *six* partitas, cello suites, chamber concertos, etc. From many non-musical sources it is clear he understood symmetry and certain kinds of number-reference[3] from even a superficial examination it is clear that he sought out interesting or to him evocative terms ("Sinfonia," "Invention," "Capriccio," "Pièce d'Orgue," etc.) where others might not have done; and it is evident he had the kind of mind that takes pleasure in finding six different words for the prelude to a suite, although he did not do so in his earlier set of *English Suites* (where the non-autograph calls them all "Prélude"). But perhaps he was prompted by an earlier publication: Mattheson's *Pièces de Clavecin* (London, 1714), in which twelve suites are prefaced by different kinds of prelude. The old habit of compiling or publishing a set of very similarly constructed pieces (Froberger, Krieger) had been giving way to more varied presentations, as one can see by comparing the second part of Kuhnau's *Neue Clavierübung* with the first; perhaps Mattheson saw the point of taking the variety further. Some of Mattheson's titles correspond to Bach's *(Ouverture, Symphonie, Prelude, Fantasie, Toccatine),* and if Bach knew them,[4] it would help to explain how he came to call the prelude to Partita No. 3 in A minor (a two-part Invention) "Fantasia," a term by no means obvious[5] (see figure 16–7). The incomparable musical achievement does not affect the question of influence, of course. In Mattheson's set one sees too an example of an otherwise puzzling movement in another of Bach's Suites, the *Loure* (see figure 16–8). There can be no doubt

3. This is not to justify the arcane numerological fancies of some of today's Bach-admirers, only to evoke the 27 of *Clavierübung III* or the 24 of the *WTC,* etc.

4. That Mattheson (no. 11), Handel (1720 Collection no. 4) and Bach (English Suite no. 5) all began certain suites with a prelude-less fugue may be coincidence.

5. Two-part *Fantasien* are also known outside keyboard music (e.g. chamber fantasias of Telemann), but Bach had already given his Inventions yet another name: *Praeambula* (in the *Clavierbüchlein W. F. Bach).*

16-7.

16-8.

that Mattheson's suites were known to Handel; one sees similarities even in movements that might be thought typically Handelian, namely the improvised preludes in which evidently the Hamburgers liked lots of triplets. In a case of this kind, it is not that a colossus like Handel needed a pedant like Mattheson to "influence" his improvisations, but that similarities make it look very likely that Handel learnt to improvise in the same Hamburg context as his sparring partner Mattheson.

Mention of Mattheson raises another point about "influences." Though Mattheson is today much quoted and respected, he is not a composer with whom musicians would necessarily find themselves often occupied. On the contrary. But such minor composers cannot be ignored in our search for influences: if we are to understand the minds of the great we have to see them as jackdaws picking up anything from anybody. In the case of J. S. Bach, it has long been considered that Buxtehude was a key figure in the moulding of his style, particularly (but why particularly?) of organ-music; to a lesser extent, Pachelbel too. But the direct influence of these two masters must have been much less than it seems to us. We tend to dwell on Parnassus and do not seek lowlier groves, so a good composer like Buxtehude is assumed to have been more important to J. S. Bach than the Buttstedts, Kuhnaus, Zachaus, Matthesons, and J. G. Walthers; but these minor lights must often have shone brightly in their period.[6]

It is not simply a question of similarities that happen to strike us. For example, although the following example (see figure 16–9) cannot be coincidence, the relationship is by no means clear. Who took from whom? Since the chronology is not known, it would be over-rash to suppose that J. S. Bach's patent superiority meant that Walther wrote his piece first and therefore "influenced" Bach. Either way, such thematic similarities are not as important as what lies behind them—the fact that both Bach and Walther were playing with canonic solutions for particular hymns, that there was a Thuringian tradition for this (hence their presence in that masterwork of Thuringian music, the *Orgelbüchlein*) and that their note-patterns *(figurae)* were alike. Even had there been no surface similarity of the kind shown in figure 16–9, one would be missing a major—perhaps *the* major—element in J. S. Bach's constant process of self-education and vigilant absorption at a key moment in his life, namely the common interest he had with his cousin Walther in certain specifiable kinds of musical composition. (One can imagine them discussing it, stimulating each other perhaps, even vying with each other in their Weimar positions.) In this way we might suppose Walther to have been quite as big an influence on

6. For example, Mattheson's suites might bear on Handel's in concrete ways. Thus one of his sarabandes (no. 10) is like some of Handel's (a characteristic rhythm, the three simple parts, a melody in the top); but it also has a *petite reprise*. Does this support the idea that although (to my knowledge) Handel does not give *petite reprise* rubrics, they were nevertheless part of the idiom?

J. S. Bach as Buxtehude or any other exceptionally good composer of the past.

And yet the questions are far from simple. There is, for example, the particular sense of common-property themes. If Bach or Handel use in their preludes, as they do, motifs found in J. K. F. Fischer's preludes (see in particular Handel's E major Suite and the Prelude in C major *WTC* Bk. 2), there need be no question of direct influence; there might be, but we will never know for certain. Obviously, the familiar *ostinato* basses are another case: not least in their common key, the following examples suggest a tradition for variations of one kind or another (see figure 16–10). As has long been recognized, one can easily find other outcroppings of a theme that rooted away under the baroque soil in apparently unlikely places (see figure 16–11). Also, other variation-themes are strikingly like it (see figure 16–12). But there is a more particular question raised by the Handel, Muffat and Bach themes in figure 16–10: they all make a very conscious attempt to create above this common-property bass a graceful, imaginative melody full of *colorature* or *fiorature:* two examples in figure 16–13. That most of us would agree to finding the *Goldberg* the most expressive and touching is not material: Muffat did his best. It is this kind of common cause—the popular attempt to follow a fashion and create with it something new—that prompted (and still prompts) composers to creative acts. Identifying such common causes—themes, *figurae*, formal conventions—is more instructive than finding mere thematic resemblances between composers.

16–14.   Handel, HWV 426 (Allemande)

Bach, BWV 806 (Courante)

16–15.   HWV 426 (Gigue)

HWV 433 (Gigue)

Circumspection in understanding "Influences"

It is an unfortunate irony for the keyboard-player in particular that just when the situation becomes most complex, around 1700—myriad styles, prolific composers, voluminous publications—he has to search alone, without the help of books summarizing the history of keyboard music.[7] Therefore, it is easy to miss what might have been backgrounds or contexts for Handel and Bach.

7. The books on the history of keyboard music tend to stop at 1700 and in any case emphasize formal considerations above stylistic or those other intimate details of music so crucial to the performer and the informed listener.

For example, Handel's Suite in A major has some details that can be easily paralleled elsewhere, some that cannot; his own individuality colors both, so one cannot assume that the recognizable details are "unoriginal" and the unrecognizable "original." Like Mattheson's Suite in A, Handel's begins with arpeggiated prelude (otherwise rather unusual) and has no sarabande (ditto). He would not need to have Mattheson's permission, so to speak, to do this, but no doubt precedent helps. But then, in addition to the Couperinesque ninth chord already referred to (figure 16–4), the Allemande of Handel's suite has a very Frenchified cadence, just as the Courante from J. S. Bach's A major Suite does (figure 16–14). Perhaps for these German composers A major was allusive to or in some way evoked French idioms. None of these parallels implies any degree of actual "influence": one has to think more broadly than this.

But so one does about Handel's A major suite as a whole, for it has a more complex pedigree than Bach's. Considered as a whole, Handel's suite gives the impression not of a French suite at all (even at best, a rather loosely arbitrarily organized art-form) but of the determined progression of movements much more characteristic of the Italian sonata. An Italian flavor, even Scarlattian in detail, occasionally surfaces, as in the Gigue to this Suite (and No. 8 in the same Collection): figure 16–15. More important, however, is the overall Italian shape. It is clear from Handel's next suite in the 1720 Collection (No. 2 in F major) that whatever "*Suite de pièces*" means to dictionaries today, for Handel it could also mean a well-balanced Italian sonata (slow-fast-slow-fast), one movement of which was a finely wrought, fully fledged fugue.[8]

Now it would be easy for the keyboardist to miss this factor in Handel's understanding and to assume merely that he had allowed himself license in the makeup of his suites, or even that he did not think it out carefully and allowed his engraver to lump together whatever was at hand. But on the contrary, the F major Suite is as systematically organized as anything of J. S. Bach, though Handel had a lighter, less Germanic touch than Bach, his "system" less didactic and underscored. He may well not have wished to make much of the fact that in his set of suites, the D minor and G minor have a prelude-and-fugue very different from each other (free prelude with sombre "keyboard" fugue in D minor, French ouverture and dotted "string" fugue in G minor); in the case of Bach's six partitas, the preludes-with-fugues are much more explicitly differentiated. Even the fact that the numbers alternate and the tonality rises (No. 2 in C minor, No. 4 in D major, No. 6 in E minor) is probably no coincidence.

Unlike the young Bach who, if indeed the composer of the "early" Sonata in D major BWV963, followed Kuhnau very closely in planning Italian movements around a homophonic ritornello theme, Handel kept as his chief sonata

8. Its first movement, a celebrated *coloratura* melody, even has a specifically Italianate modulation plan (beginning in F and ending in A minor) known in another Italianate work: the first movement of the Pastorale in F, attributed to J. S. Bach (BWV590.1).

movement the fugue, in which he might well have been following Corelli. Indeed, Corelli's influence on virtually every early eighteenth-century composer (not always excluding French) has probably still not been fully grasped. In general, one may suppose Italian influences to be often difficult to see, since they are so basic: "Italian music" is a kind of tautology, so much a norm was it. Only a musical equivalent of the process of elimination allows one to see that in such passages as the following, behind the jerky rhythmic motif is a sustained harmonic progression of the kind called *durezza* by earlier Italian organists (see figure 16–16). The ease with which both Bach and Handel can pour out *durezza* passages (often transformed into a lively *alla breve* style) can itself help us to miss the lineage of such techniques. Perhaps that is true of all "influences" on the great composers.

As we consider what it means precisely for a composer to be "influenced" by the music he happens to know, we might also bear in mind the much broader issues involved in his background. It seems to me very important for musicians today—particularly in the USA, perhaps, which is (relatively to Europe) so unconscious of the machinations both of class and of nationalism—to grasp just how provincial and culturally dependent on others were the many principalities and kingdoms we now call "Germany," and just how impossible it was in 1700 (even in 1750?) to guess that those areas would soon dominate music for two hundred years. As we know, J. S. Bach remained in "Germany"; and Handel's personal experience of other cultures, gained no doubt only through much trouble and the expenditure of much energy, must have acted as a kind of reproach to the authors of Bach's *Obituary*. Indeed, many points made in the *Obituary* can only be understood fully if one assumes that the authors had Handel's cosmopolitanism, fame, and wealth in mind, seeing the last two as a consequence of the first. It was vital for the *Obituary* authors to show that Bach had no need to leave Thuringia (he could learn by observation and hard work), that he did travel to hear *(behorchen)* the then most famous German master (Buxtehude in Lübeck), that the mantle of authority was passed to him by the then senior German master (Reincken in Hamburg, who it seems thought the old German art of improvisation otherwise dead), that he was admired by the then most powerful monarch in the world (Frederick II in Potsdam), and that at least by default he had conquered the then most admired composer of France (Louis Marchand in Dresden).

In comparison, Handel's "obituary" author John Mainwaring was only too anxious to show *his* hero as having recognized the limitations of Germany:

> On his return to Hall[e], he began to feel himself more, to be conscious of his own superiority, to discover that spirit of emulation, and passion for fame, which urged him strongly to go into the world. . . . His acquaintance with the eminent masters [Italian opera composers] at Berlin had opened his mind to new ideas of excellence . . . he never could endure the thought of staying long at home, either as a pupil or substitute to his old master Zackaw.
>
> [*Memoirs of the Life of the late George Frederic Handel*, London, 1760, pp. 26–27]

That it was as the eventual successor (if not "substitute") to Zachow that Bach in some sense applied for the same job in Halle some ten or more years later only underlines the irony of musical history here: both young men assiduously learnt what they could and applied their gifts to being "influenced" by what they got to know, strikingly different though their way of going about it was. However much we may now be inclined to think that the greatest in any art comes from a kind of intense, concentrated provincialism (and not from broad, well-educated cosmopolitanism), we may suppose that this was not at all clear to the young Bach and Handel in 1700.

CHAPTER SEVENTEEN

Johann Sebastian Bach's Third Part of the *Clavier-Übung*

CHRISTOPH WOLFF

IT IS ESSENTIAL to our understanding of Part III of Bach's *Clavier-Übung* that it was conceived as an autonomous and clearly defined collection of organ music within the extended context of the magnificent series of exemplary keyboard works published under the title *Clavier-Übung*.[1] The idea of broadly compartmentalized material in a quasi-encyclopedic series arose from the spirit of the Baroque era, especially in the visual arts, the sciences, and literature. Bach displayed in this series what he understood to be *musicalische Wissenschafft*, musical scholarship in both the practical and the theoretical senses. The four parts of the *Clavier-Übung* are to be seen as a public statement and documentation of his unparalleled virtuosity in keyboard composition and performance.

Bach began the set of *Clavier-Übungen* in the mid-1720s with the publication of several individual suites—or, more precisely, six partitas—which, issued together in 1731, formed the first part of the *Clavier-Übung* and Bach's "Opus 1." That Bach showed special caution by first publishing the partitas separately, between 1726 and 1730, indicates that he needed to test the market. He acted as his own publisher, at his own financial risk, and could not have expected a great number of customers from the start, since the pieces were extremely difficult to perform and hardly any equivalent keyboard music was then available. Nevertheless, the sales must have finally been good enough for Bach to venture a second printing in the collected edition of 1731. It is important to realize, at the same time, that with his keyboard publications of the 1720s Bach apparently gave music publishing in Leipzig a major boost. Up to that point Leipzig had been the German capital of book printing and publishing. Music printing played virtually no role. However, by the 1750s— and clearly with Bach's help, primarily through his later connections with Breitkopf—Leipzig had also assumed a leading position in music printing and publishing.

By calling the collected edition of the partitas "Opus 1," implying that other

1. Facsimile edition of J. S. Bach, *Clavier-Übung, Parts I–IV*, with critical commentary, ed. C. Wolff (Leipzig: Peters, 1984).

numbers would follow, Bach exposed his intention to create a series. We cannot infer, however, how detailed his concept was at that time. Presumably, the total work, finished ten years later, took on its final form over the course of time, unhindered by the great flexibility of its title, *Clavier-Übung*. In both title and content, Bach obviously alluded to the *Clavier-Übung* in two parts of his predecessor Johann Kuhnau, which also consisted of suites (seven in each volume, published in 1689 and 1692). In contrast to Kuhnau, Bach did not include another set of suites in the second part of his *Clavier-Übung*, but instead gave his project a broader objective. Kuhnau was probably the first to use the term *Clavier-Übung* (keyboard exercise) for a publication of keyboard music. He did this evidently in imitation of the Italian use of *essercizi*, which dates back to the early seventeenth century and was still used by Domenico Scarlatti *(Essercizi per gravicembalo,* London, 1738) and Telemann *(Essercizii musici,* Hamburg, 1739–40). Johann Krieger published in 1699 a collection of organ compositions (ricercars, preludes, fugues, etc.) under the title *Anmuthige Clavier-Übung*. The title proved to be extraordinarily flexible because it could be used to refer to all the diverse keyboard instruments and to different compositional genres as well. Vincent Lübeck's *Clavier-Übung* of 1728, which includes a chorale setting of "Lobt Gott, ihr Christen, allzugleich" and free-form movements such as prelude, fugue, allemande, courante, etc., exemplified the usefulness of this title as a neutral name for a collection of heterogeneous works for keyboard instruments, and Bach was undoubtedly already aware of this advantage when he published his first partita in 1726.

We are obviously unable to determine whether and to what extent Bach had already planned the project as a multi-part *Clavier-Übung* at that time. Yet it appears that his scheme to offer *exempla classica* of his preferred métier, keyboard music, and this as an encyclopedic, or all-embracing challenge, originated no later than 1735 on the occasion of the publication of Part II. Bach was not alone in his time in planning a musical work with several sequels. Georg Philipp Telemann, for instance, had a similar intention, though in a completely different area, with a most ambitious series begun in 1728 and called

The True Music Master arranged for both singers and instrumentalists containing all types of musical pieces for different voices and nearly all commonly-used instruments with moral, operatic, and other arias as well as trios, duets, solos, etc., sonatas, overtures, etc., and also fugues, counterpoints, canons, etc., thus, the most current music according to Italian, French, English, and Polish tastes in serious, spirited, and light-hearted fashion . . . you could want to perform. . . .

In 1733, Telemann published a less comprehensive three-part collection of instrumental ensemble music entitled *Musique de Table*, which contained all types of settings. But in the realm of keyboard music there was no analogous, representative collection and so it remained for Bach to undertake such a task. His already undisputed reputation as a master of the organ and other keyboard instruments seemed to make him predestined for such a project. It was not only by chance that the review of Bach's organ recital in Dresden on September 14, 1731, which was "attended by all the court musicians and virtuosos," ended with a poem of praise:[2]

> Tis said, when Orpheus did his lyre string awake,
> All creatures in the forest answered to the sound;
> But sure, 'twere better that such praise of Bach we spake,
> Since he, whene'er he plays, doth each and all astound.

Bach was surely aware of his calling, and it cannot be a coincidence that his four-part *Clavier-Übung* originated in the period during which he devoted his professional skills particularly to instrumental virtuosity.

The *Clavier-Übung*, in which Bach exhibited an encyclopedic survey of his art in the field of keyboard music for "amateurs and especially for connoisseurs of such works to refresh their spirits," developed an overall plan that took several different factors into account. Above all, the most important keyboard instruments were considered: one-manual harpsichord (Part I), two-manual harpsichord (Parts II and IV), and large organ as well as organ without pedals (Part III). Then, all important styles of composition were represented: the leading national styles were contrasted in Part II, and stylistic breadth was explored in Parts III and IV (including a range of works from retrospective settings to the most fashionable mannerisms). Moreover, all decisive forms were considered: suite, concerto, prelude, fugue, chorale settings of all sorts, and variations. All fundamental compositional techniques were employed, from free-voiced improvisatory pieces to movements using various types of imitative polyphony through strict canon, from two-voice to an obbligato six-voice setting ("Aus tiefer Not," in Part III), all possible *cantus firmus* techniques, and finally, a broad spectrum of sizes and formats of movements, levels of difficulty, and an enormous variety of keys and modes (within the still prevailing system of unequal temperament, i.e., keys and modes containing no more than three sharps or flats). Indeed with these four parts of the *Clavier-Übung* Bach offered his contemporaries the largest and most demanding publication of keyboard music to date.

2. *The Bach Reader*, H. T. David and A. Mendel, ed. (New York: W. W. Norton, rev. ed. 1966), p. 226.

Clavier-Übung III cannot really be appreciated without this background. It follows the second part, which presented an Italian concerto and a French overture, a quasi-programmatic juxtaposition of the two then-prevalent national styles. It precedes the fourth part, which contained the Goldberg Variations, a monothematic cycle of unprecedented character. The third part, then—the only part dedicated to organ repertory—mediates between the two adjacent parts. The principle of stylistic contrast prevalent in the second was raised to a more multivalent level in the third part. By giving the chorales at least twofold and varied settings and by providing the whole collection with a framing device, Bach employed the principle of cyclic organization and thematic variation that signals ahead to the fourth part and, in general, to the large-scale monothematic works of the 1740s.

Part III appeared at the Michaelmas fair of 1739. On September 28, 1739, Johann Elias Bach, who at the time was acting as private secretary to the cantor of St. Thomas, informed Johann Wilhelm Koch of Ronneburg "that the copper-engraved work of my cousin is now finished and a copy may be had from him for three reichstaler."[3] Evidently, the work should have been published earlier, for in a previous message, dated 10 January of the same year, Elias Bach mentioned "that my honored cousin will bring out some pieces for keyboard instruments, which are principally intended for organists and are exceedingly well-composed. They will probably be ready in time for the coming Easter fair and make up some 80 pages."[4] The delay in publishing such an extensive work was most likely due to the fact that Bach, again his own publisher, changed engravers after more than half the plates had been completed. The work was not wholly engraved by Balthasar Schmid of Nuremberg—as was hitherto thought (for if that were the case it probably would have been published by him as well)—but only in part.[5] The engraving of the music was actually begun in Johann Gottfried Krügner's workshop in Leipzig by an engraver who had also worked on the *Schemelli Gesangbuch* for Breitkopf of Leipzig. It was the several pages of Krügner's engraving, which appeared so like Bach's own hand, that led to the assumption that Bach himself had been responsible for etching a portion of the work. But Krügner, who primarily reproduced pictures rather than music, was, unlike ordinary music engravers, intent upon reproducing the original—in this case Bach's manuscript—with meticulous accuracy, resulting in a facsimile-like image of Bach's autograph. The few extant copies of Part III of the *Clavier-Übung* contain Leipzig paper

3. *Bach-Dokumente*, vol. II [Dok II], W. Neumann and H.-J. Schulze, ed. (Kassel: Bärenreiter, 1969), no. 455.

4. Dok II, no. 434.

5. G. G. Butler, "Leipziger Stecher in Bachs Originaldrucken," *Bach-Jahrbuch*, 66 (1980), pp. 9–26.

for those pages engraved at Krügner's shop and Nuremberg paper for those pages engraved by Schmid. This suggests that for the first edition the sheets were pulled in different locations.

Krügner's workshop at the time was extremely busy, though not with music. It is possible that Bach's publication project befell a fate similar to Johann Gottfried Walther's variations on "Allein Gott in der Höh sei Ehr." On January 26, 1736, Walther wrote Heinrich Bokemeyer of Wolfenbüttel regarding certain problems in the printing of his variations:[6]

> Herr Krügner of Leipzig was introduced and recommended to me by the Capellmeister Bach, but he had to excuse himself because he already had too many projects at hand and would not be able to complete them for a long time. Moreover, it would have been too expensive.

The seventy-eight plates of Bach's entire project may also have overtasked Krügner's capacity. Whatever the causes for Krügner's not having completed the engraving for Bach, the problems must already have arisen in 1738. When Elias Bach in January 1739 reckoned that the work would appear at the Easter fair, Krügner (having completed, at most, forty-three plates) could no longer have been involved. Schmid, however, evidently could not meet the Easter deadline. These details concerning the prepublication history of Part III of the *Clavier-Übung*, though still unclear, are nonetheless of the highest relevance to our understanding the genesis of Bach's composition. They show that the work was most likely composed significantly earlier than is generally assumed, perhaps as early as 1737–38, if not 1736–37—certainly much closer in time to the 1735 publication date of Part II of the series.

Nothing is known about the genesis itself; there is no autograph and we lack any concrete clues that might reveal the occasion of its beginning. Yet a certain link may be recognized between the composition of at least a portion of the third part and the important organ recital Bach gave at the new Silbermann organ of the Dresden Frauenkirche on December 1, 1736, to celebrate his appointment as *Compositeur* of the Electoral-Saxon and Royal-Polish court.[7] Bach had applied for that position in 1733 with the dedication of a Mass (Kyrie and Gloria of the later B-minor Mass).[8] It is therefore possible that he offered his thanks for the honorary title with a Mass of another sort: Kyrie and Gloria arrangements constitute the beginning of the collection of the chorale settings. In addition, we know from a report by the early Bach biographer Johann

6. Dok II, no. 377.

7. *The Bach Reader*, p. 151.

8. Ibid., p. 128; cf. preface to the facsimile edition of J. S. Bach, *Missa h-Moll*, ed. H.-J. Schulze (Leipzig: Peters, 1983).

Nicolaus Forkel (1802), that Bach frequently liked to incorporate chorale settings in the middle of his often more than one-hour organ concerts and frame them with a prelude and fugue *pro organo pleno*.[9] In terms of approach the third part thereby displays something of the organization of a typically Bachian organ concert. However, it would be inappropriate to push hypothetical thought so far as to insist Bach had created a major cyclical composition with a specific program in mind. The publication presents a completely heterogeneous collection of exemplary pieces ranging from chorale settings to free compositions:

Praeludium (pro organo pleno)

Kyrie, Gott Vater (C.f. in Soprano)
Christe, aller Welt Trost (C.f. in Tenore)
Kyrie, Gott heiliger Geist (C.f. in Basso, con organo pleno)

Kyrie, Gott Vater (manualiter)
Christe, aller Welt Trost (manualiter)
Kyrie, Gott heiliger Geist (manualiter)

Allein Gott in der Höh (Trio F Major)
Allein Gott in der Höh (Trio G Major a 2 Clav. e Ped.)
Allein Gott in der Höh (Trio A Major; manualiter, Fughetta)

Dies sind die heilgen zehn Gebot (a 2 Clav. e Ped., C.f. in Canone)
Dies sind die heilgen zehn Gebot (manualiter)

Wir glauben all an einen Gott (in organo pleno)
Wir glauben all an einen Gott (manualiter)

Vater unser im Himmelreich (a 2 Clav. e Ped., C.f. in Canone)
Vater unser im Himmelreich (manualiter)

Christ, unser Herr, zum Jordan kam (a 2 Clav., C.f. in Ped.)
Christ, unser Herr, zum Jordan kam (manualiter)

Aus tiefer Not schrei ich zu dir (a 6, in organo pleno)
Aus tiefer Not schrei ich zu dir (manualiter)

Jesus Christus, unser Heiland (a 2 Clav., C.f. in Ped.)
Jesus Christus, unser Heiland (manualiter)

Duetto I (e minor)
Duetto II (F Major)
Duetto III (G Major)
Duetto IV (a minor)

Fuga (a 5 voci, pro organo pleno)

9. Cf. G. B. Stauffer, *The Organ Preludes of Johann Sebastian Bach* (Ann Arbor: UMI Press, 1980), 105f.

It seems out of the question that Bach would have viewed the small and large settings in the context of a program. Moreover, very pragmatic considerations might explain Bach's inclusion of pieces for manuals alone. After all, it is in this way that other keyboardists could derive some practical use from *Clavier-Übung III*. The small chorale settings are quite suited for the harpsichord and the appropriate pendant to the organ Prelude and Fugue in E-flat Major would then be the four duets. Probably primarily for marketing reasons Bach must have recognized that not only those who could master the great and technically very demanding organ pieces would purchase this printed work.

On the other hand, it cannot be overlooked that the entire work is governed by one structural plan. Elements of cyclical planning influence the assembly of smaller and larger groups of movements. This is already evident in the framing function of the prelude and fugue which mark the beginning and end of the collection like massive blocks. The symmetry thus emphasized also shows that the formal musical sections—unlike architectonic structures—are subject to time and are not static structural components. This is illustrated by the asymmetrical arrangement of the two corner pillars of the third part, whose organization might be schematically sketched as:

Prelude: A (axa)—B—A (axa)

[A = ritornello with overture-like frame sections and tutti/solo middle part: axa; B = fugal section]

Fugue: A—B (+ a)—C (+ a)

[A = development of the main theme; B (+ a) = development of a second theme that incorporates the main theme; C (+ a) = development of a third theme and combination with the main theme]

The chorale settings, too, present variously tiered relationships.[10] First of all it is noticeable that the Mass chorales and the Catechism chorales are delimited from one another as groups. The German Kyrie hymns arranged in a traditional polyphonic style (the *cantus firmus* is carried from the soprano through the tenor to the bass) are juxtaposed with the Gloria-hymns, which are presented in dense trio settings (in ascending keys: F-G-A). The Lutheran Catechism hymns are in turn divided into two groups of three pieces each. In each case an *organo-pleno* setting occupies the center: "Wir glauben all an einen Gott" (fugue with independent, ostinato theme in the pedal) and "Aus tiefer Not schrei ich zu dir" (a six-voice motet movement with double pedal, *cantus firmus* in the first bass: organist's right foot). Two chorales with canonic *cantus firmus* arrangements ("Dies sind die heilgen zehn Gebot" and "Vater unser im

10. Cf. C. Wolff, "Ordnungsprinzipien in den Originaldrucken Bachscher Werke," *Bach-Interpretationen*, ed. M. Geck (Göttingen: Vandenhoek & Ruprecht, 1969), pp. 144–67.

Himmelreich," in which the rhythmic finesse of the last setting hardly can be surpassed) surround the first *plenum* piece. The second group boasts a frame of two settings with the bass (= pedal) *cantus firmus* accompanied by virtuosic textures in the treble *(manualiter)* parts.

Clavier-Übung III marks the first of Bach's late works and unequivocally indicates the scope of Bach's genius of composition, since it ranges from the instrumental settings themselves all the way to the imitation of vocal motets. It comprises a strong theoretical and historical component introducing a new dimension in Bach's personal style.[11] This is evident in the juxtaposition of retrospective and modernistic styles and particularly in Bach's systematic approach to dealing with the old church modes (aiming at an enrichment of the standard major-minor tonality) and in the thoroughly contrapuntal design of every single setting. It does not surprise us that in the late 1730s Bach was surrounded by a number of very gifted students who later became important theorists: Lorenz Christoph Mizler, Johann Friedrich Agricola, and Johann Philipp Kirnberger.

The chorale settings and free compositions which seemingly reflect the entire spectrum of organ music and organ performance by means of a well-ordered integration of changing formats, setting techniques, and contemporary as well as historical models of style, are united in something comparable to an "iconological program." In this way Bach exceeds the genre of the French "Livre d'orgue" with which he was familiar through his own hand-copied score of Nicholas de Grigny's work (1700).[12] But Bach would hardly have wanted to offer an instruction manual for liturgical organ performance or—didactically speaking—a model book of compositional techniques useful in producing chorale settings. However, he clearly gives a summary view of his organistic art rather than presenting a utilitarian collection for service or recital playing. It is hardly a coincidence that *Clavier-Übung III* does not include any hymns for the church year—chorales that would then be related to only specific Sundays or feasts of the liturgical year. Bach also does not include any modern or even seventeenth-century hymns. He deliberately sticks to the classic sixteenth-century Lutheran repertory of hymns and, most importantly, selects them from two major categories: Mass and Catechism—hymns of general and year-round application.

Worship service and theological doctrine are fundamental to Christian life. *Soli Deo Gloria* and *musicalische Wissenschafft* are the basis for Bach's organistic art and his teaching of it. Perhaps Bach was even thinking of "catechism" in terms of a musical analogy to theological doctrine, teaching, and wisdom, in

11. Cf. C. Wolff, "Problems and New Perspectives of Bach Biography," *Proteus*, 2 (1985), p. 6.

12. M.-C. Alain, "Reflexions sur le Livre d'orgue de Nicholas de Grigny d'après la copie de J. S. Bach," *L'Orgue à notre époque*, ed. D. Mackey (Montreal: McGill University, 1982), pp. 91–106.

other words thinking of *Clavier-Übung III* serving as a catechism of organ music. At any rate, the work represented ultimately not only his greatest and most extensive collection of organ music, but the quintessence of his art of organ composition and performance. According to its title, Bach intended it "particularly for connoisseurs of such work" (*"besonders denen Kennern von dergleichen Arbeit"*). Lorenz Christoph Mizler's words are by no means exaggerating when he wrote in his review of Bach's *Clavier-Übung III* in 1740: "The author has here given proof that in his field of composition he is more practiced and more fortunate than many others. No one will surpass him in it and few will be able to imitate him."